INTENTIONAL LEADERSHIP FOR EFFECTIVE INCLUSION IN EARLY CHILDHOOD EDUCATION AND CARE

Intentional leadership can unite, motivate and empower all educators to work towards the common goal of creating a truly inclusive culture in which all children, with or without disabilities, are supported and enabled to fully participate in every aspect of daily life and learning.

This book recognises diverse manifestations of special educational needs, from communication difficulties and delays in learning, to social and physical disabilities, and considers the ways in which these needs might be embraced within inclusive mainstream settings. Key to this is robust and purposeful leadership that removes barriers to learning, changes existing attitudes and values, motivates staff and foregrounds holistic learning opportunities and experiences. Chapters draw on theoretical models, reflect on international and national policies, and consider topics including:

- the image of the child
- physical, aesthetic and temporal aspects of the learning environment
- relational pedagogy
- long-, medium- and short-term planning
- the role of assessment
- collaborative working with parents, families and other professionals.

In-depth descriptions of behaviours and leadership strategies, practice scenarios and activities support the reader's understanding. *Intentional Leadership for Effective Inclusion in Early Childhood Education and Care* is a comprehensive guide for students, teachers and practitioners involved in Early Childhood Education and Care, Social Care and Early Intervention programmes.

Dr Mary Moloney is a researcher, author and lecturer in Early Childhood Care and Education at Mary Immaculate College, Ireland. Mary previously worked as an early years educator, and has extensive experience of working with young children, and of leadership and management in the early childhood education and care field.

Eucharia McCarthy is senior lecturer and Director of the Curriculum Development Unit and lecturer in Special Education at Mary Immaculate College, Ireland. She is also a PhD student at the University of Northampton.

INTENTIONAL LEADERSHIP FOR EFFECTIVE INCLUSION IN EARLY CHILDHOOD EDUCATION AND CARE

Exploring Core Themes and Strategies

Mary Moloney with Eucharia McCarthy

Routledge
Taylor & Francis Group

LONDON AND NEW YORK

First published 2018
by Routledge
2 Park Square, Milton Park, Abingdon, Oxon OX14 4RN

and by Routledge
711 Third Avenue, New York, NY 10017

Routledge is an imprint of the Taylor & Francis Group, an informa business

© 2018 Mary Moloney with Eucharia McCarthy

British Library Cataloguing in Publication Data
A catalogue record for this book is available from the British Library

Library of Congress Cataloging in Publication Data
Names: Moloney, Mary, author. | McCarthy, Eucharia.
Title: Intentional leadership for effective inclusion in early childhood education and care/Mary Moloney with Eucharia McCarthy.
Description: Abingdon, Oxon; New York, NY: Routledge, 2018.
Identifiers: LCCN 2017059130 (print) | LCCN 2018011039 (ebook) |
ISBN 9781315107219 (eb) | ISBN 9781138092877 (hbk) |
ISBN 9781138092884 (pbk) | ISBN 9781315107219 (ebk)
Subjects: LCSH: Children with disabilities–Education (Early childhood) |
Inclusive education. | Early childhood education–Administration.
Classification: LCC LC4019.3 (ebook) | LCC LC4019.3 .M65 2018 (print) |
DDC 372.21–dc23
LC record available at https://lccn.loc.gov/2017059130

ISBN: 978-1-138-09287-7 (hbk)
ISBN: 978-1-138-09288-4 (pbk)
ISBN: 978-1-315-10721-9 (ebk)

Typeset in Bembo
by Out of House Publishing

Printed and bound in Great Britain by
TJ International Ltd, Padstow, Cornwall

CONTENTS

FIGURES

TABLES

ACKNOWLEDGEMENTS

The inspiration for this book began many years ago, when Eucharia and I were undertaking a national research study on the inclusion of children with special educational needs in early years settings in Ireland. While we were inspired by the tremendous commitment of ECEC providers and educators to inclusion, we were struck by their desire for information and, training with regards to effectively supporting children with SEN in their settings. We hope that this book will will motivate and encourage providers and educators to enhance the quality of children's experiences on a daily basis in ECEC settings. All young children, with and without special educational needs, see a world of wonder, ripe for exploration, a world without limitations. They are confident, competent, capable learners, full of potential. This book is dedicated to young children with special educational needs, their parents and carers everywhere, who, on a daily basis, teach us so much about life, love and living.

ABBREVIATIONS

AAC	Augmentative and Alternative Communication
ACECQA	Australian Children's Education and Care Quality Authority
ADD	attention deficit disorder
ADHD	attention deficit hyperactivity disorder
AIM	Access and Inclusion Model
ASD	autism spectrum disorder
CCEA	Council for Curriculum, Examinations and Assessment
CDC	Centre for Disease Control and Prevention
CECDE	Centre for Early Childhood Development and Education
CPD	continuing professional development
DEEWR	Department of Education, Employment and Workplace Relations
DEC	Division for Early Childhood
DES	Department for Education and Skills
DCYA	Department for Children and Youth Affairs
DfE	Department for Education
DHC	Department of Health and Children
EADSNE	European Agency for Development in Special Needs Education
ECEC	early childhood education and care
ELMS	Effective Leadership and Management Scheme
EPPE	Effective Provision of Pre-school Education
EYFS	Early Years Foundation Stage
FERPA	Family Educational Rights and Privacy Act
HIPAA	Health Insurance Portability and Accountability Act
IDEA	Individuals with Disabilities Education Act
IELS	International Early Learning Study
InCo	inclusion coordinator
IP	Inclusion Plan

LINC	Leadership for Inclusion
MoE	Ministry of Education
NAEYC	National Association for the Education of Young Children
NEPS	National Education Psychology Service
NCCA	National Council for Curriculum and Assessment
NICHCY	National Dissemination Centre for Children with Disabilities
NQS-PLP	National Quality Standard Professional Learning Programme
OECD	Organisation for Economic Co-operation and Development
OT	occupational therapist
PEAT	Physical, Emotional, Aesthetic and Temporal
PLE	Pedagogy, Learning and Education
PPCT	process, person, context and time
SEN	special educational needs
SENCO	special educational needs coordinator
SNAP	Scottish Network for Able Pupils
UN	United Nations
UNCRC	United Nations Convention on the Rights of the Child
UNCRPD	UN Convention on the Rights of Persons with Disabilities
UNESCO	United Nations Educational Scientific and Cultural Organisation
UNICEF	United Nations Children's Fund
VBL	value-based leadership
WHO	World Health Organization

1

INTRODUCTION

Flowers are red young man
Green leaves are green
There's no need to see flowers any other way
Than the way they always have been seen
But the little boy said
There are so many colours in the rainbow
So many colours in the morning sun
So many colours in the flower and I see every one
(Chapin, 1981)

Introduction

In this song, written by Harry Chapin, the little boy is full of wonder, he sees a world full of colour, and in his world, there are no limitations. He is a confident, competent and capable learner; he is full of potential. Of course, these lyrics can be interpreted in another way, the lyric 'there are so many colours in the rainbow' could just as easily refer to differences between children, the vastly different rates in their development and how their developmental and learning patterns can be episodic, uneven and rapid (Ackerman & Coley, 2012), as well as how they see, interpret, make sense of and, understand the world.

This book is concerned with the concept of intentional leadership for inclusion in early childhood education and care (ECEC) settings. Early childhood, the period from birth to six or eight years (depending on school starting age in individual countries) is a crucial period in a young child's learning and development. It presents a vital window of opportunity for supporting young children's learning and development, for preventing potential developmental delays and/or supporting children who present with special educational needs and disabilities. Working with young children, with and without special educational needs and/or disabilities, is an enormous privilege, it is also a tremendous responsibility.

It is important at the outset, to discuss the dichotomy between special educational needs and disability. Special educational needs are discussed in Chapter 2: 'Understanding special educational needs and disabilities', in terms of the following four areas:

1. **Communicating and interacting**, where children with speech, language and communication difficulties find it difficult to make sense of language or to understand how to communicate effectively and appropriately with others (children and adults);
2. **Cognition and learning**, where children learn at a slower pace than others of the same age. Children have difficulty with understanding aspects of the curriculum, have difficulties with organisation and memory skills, or have a specific difficulty affecting one particular part of their learning performance, such as in literacy or numeracy;
3. **Social, emotional and mental health difficulties**, where children have difficulty in managing their relationships with other people, are withdrawn, or behave in ways that may hinder their own and other children's learning, or that have an impact on their health and wellbeing;
4. **Sensory and/or physical needs** includes children with visual and/or hearing impairments, or a physical need that means they must have additional ongoing support and equipment.

As explained in Chapter 2, some children may have special educational needs (SEN) that cover more than one of these areas. Furthermore, children with SEN may also have a disability, i.e., 'long-term physical, mental, intellectual, or sensory impairments which in interaction with various barriers may hinder their full and effective participation in society on an equal basis with others' (UN Convention on the Rights of Persons with Disabilities (UNCRPD), 2006, Article 1). Because children may present with both a special educational need and a disability, the term SEND, which derives from the Children and Families Act 2014, in England, seems appropriate. Throughout this book, both terms: special educational needs and disabilities that are inclusive of exceptionally able and talented children, are used.

There is no doubt, that in the 21st century, children with special educational needs and disabilities, are increasingly visible in society. However, this was not always the case. In the past, these children were marginalised members of society. They were isolated from mainstream educational provision. Why? Historically, their needs were seen as a medical rather than an educational issue. The predominant focus was upon children's 'impairments rather than their potential' (Carpenter, Ashdown & Bovair, 1996, p.269), and there were limited expectations of children with special educational needs, either academically or socially.

Over time, isolation and segregation gave way to integration, where children with special educational needs were permitted physical access to mainstream classrooms. Overall, however, they were widely expected to adapt to the school, rather than the school adapting to accommodate a greater diversity of pupils. While integration resulted in children having a place in the school, they clearly did not belong. They had little or no interaction with the class teacher or the other children. They did not participate in the general curriculum, or in regular classroom activities, and they were unable to make friends. They were seen as, and treated as *different*, as *other*.

Various legislative enactments and policy initiatives, including the UN Convention on the Rights of the Child (UNCRC, 1989); the Salamanca Statement and Framework for Action on Special Education Needs (2004); the UNESCO Guidelines for Inclusion (2005, 2009) and the UN Convention of the Rights of Persons with Disabilities (UNCRPD, 2006), coupled with increasing awareness of the benefits of early intervention, means that children with SEN are now increasingly visible in society; in early childhood settings, schools, universities, employment and in the wider community.

Article 23 of the UNCRC stipulates that children with disabilities should have:

> effective access to and receive education, training, health care services, rehabilitation services, preparation for employment and recreation opportunities in a manner conducive to the child's achieving the fullest possible social integration and individual development, including his/her cultural and spiritual development

Inclusion and participation are therefore 'essential to human dignity and to the enjoyment and exercise of human rights' (UNESCO, 1994, p.11).

Initiatives including the UNCRC (1989), UNESCO (2009), and the UNCRPD (2006) clearly envisage inclusion as an ongoing process, concerned with respecting diversity and eliminating discrimination. Although inclusive education was historically associated solely with children with special educational needs, today, it has a broader focus, encompassing all children, including those from ethnic and linguistic minorities, children with HIV, nomadic children, children living in poverty, refugee children, rural populations, children with disabilities and any at-risk children (UNESCO, 2009). As observed by Devarakonda (2013, p.12) inclusive education 'is increasingly seen as an approach for all disadvantaged groups, as well as migrants and minorities and even pupils who are identified as gifted or talented'.

While mindful of the broader inclusion discourse, this book is concerned with inclusion as it relates to children with SEND, including exceptionally able and gifted children, in the context of early childhood education and care. Although it is beyond the scope of this book to address inclusion more broadly, it is important to note that when we establish and maintain an inclusive culture and remove barriers to learning within the ECEC setting, we enhance learning opportunities and experiences for all children.

Locating inclusion within a positive construct, UNESCO (2005, p.12) describe it as 'a dynamic approach of responding positively to pupil diversity and of seeing individual differences not as problems, but as opportunities for enriching learning'. Furthermore, the UNCRC (1989) and the UNCRPD (2006) together provide a framework for a rights-based approach for all children, ensuring the rights of children with special educational needs, in particular, are not marginalised or forgotten.

Inclusive education offers the best educational opportunities for children with disabilities (UNCRPD, 2006, Article 24). It is an overarching concept directed towards developing children's 'personality, talents and creativity, as well as their mental and physical abilities, to their fullest potential, [and] enabling [them] to participate effectively in a free society' (Article 24). This definition in particular, embraces the notion of holistic child development, affording equal importance to the child's personality, talents and creativity, physical and academic development. It challenges attitudes, values and beliefs, how we view children with special educational needs and disabilities and, critically, it contests our understanding of the purpose of education.

Crucially, the UNCRPD sees inclusion as a legal right for all children that requires:

> A change in an educational culture where, rather than focusing on individual support (usually based upon a medical diagnosis), the system provides support to schools to increase their capability to respond to learners' diverse needs without the need to categorise or label them.
>
> *(Meijer & Watkins, 2016, p.6)*

From a rights perspective, the fundamental principle of inclusion is that all children should learn together, regardless of differences or difficulties within mainstream settings.

A recurring theme throughout this book relates to how attitudes, values and beliefs are central to establishing an inclusive culture, which ultimately enables all children to feel respected and valued, and able to fully participate in all activities and routines within the ECEC setting. This is not as easy as it sounds. In fact, because inclusion is so firmly embedded in everyday parlance, it is at risk of being taken for granted, on the basis that everybody is mindful of, knowledgeable about and capable of establishing and maintaining inclusive practice. However, inclusion is a process that involves 'improving inputs, processes and environments to foster learning at the level of the learner in his/her learning environment as well as at the level of the system which supports the learning experience' (UNESCO, 2005, p.16). It is about overcoming a range of obstacles including:

- prevailing attitudes, values and beliefs;
- image of the child;
- understanding holistic development and learning;
- knowledge and skills;
- resources.

Responsibility for overcoming these various challenges is a joint endeavour involving government macro-level and setting micro level responses. The simple fact is that inclusion cannot be left to chance. Policy initiatives alone are not a guarantor of inclusion, neither is physical access to an early childhood setting. Consequently, this book is premised upon the need for intentional leadership for meaningful inclusion within early childhood education and care.

What is intentional leadership? To be intentional is to be deliberate and purposeful in everything you do. When applied to the concept of inclusion, being deliberate and purposeful is critical. It means that inclusion is not left to chance, that somebody – or a number of people within the setting (see Chapter 4) – takes responsibility for inclusion, ensuring that children are not just physically present, but that all children with and without disabilities, are supported and enabled to fully participate in every aspect of daily life within the setting.

Drawing upon Underwood and Frankel (2012) and Underwood (2013), inclusive early childhood settings are underpinned by six key components:

1. Accessible to all children and their families;
2. Designed, and implemented with consideration for the unique needs, and abilities of each child;
3. Include ongoing evaluation of programmes to ensure children's full participation;
4. Policies that promote inclusion;
5. Leadership that supports inclusion;
6. Staff who believe in inclusion.

Meaningful inclusion is therefore dependent upon two critical but interrelated factors: staff who understand, believe in and are committed to inclusion, and leadership that supports inclusion. In relation to the latter, this book reinforces the idea that leadership for inclusion is paramount. Accordingly, when it comes to inclusion, robust, intentional leadership is essential to progress from tokenistic to meaningful and effective inclusion. Intentional leadership is therefore the unifying thread throughout each chapter in this book.

Meet the children

Various practice scenarios are interspersed throughout the chapters of this book. They are used to support your understanding, and reflective practice as you read each chapter. These practice scenarios include children with a specific diagnosis, as well as children who do not have a diagnosis but whose behaviour and development gives rise to particular concerns. Throughout the book, therefore, you will meet the following children: four-year-old Antonio from Poland who has recently had corrective surgery for tongue tie, Arielle who has been diagnosed with autism, Jacob, a four-year-old wheelchair user, as well as four-year-old Rebecca who has retinitis pigmentosa feature in Chapter 2; while Amelia, a two-year-old, with Apert syndrome is introduced in Chapter 3, where you will also meet Anshul, a 3½-year-old boy with autism.

Chapter 5 introduces Jawad, who is three years old. Although his mother describes him as chatty, stating that he talks to her and his siblings at home all the time, he has not spoken to anybody in ECEC setting since he started attending six months ago. Five-year-old Naomi, who is now quadriplegic following an accident in a swimming pool, also features in Chapter 5.

Sahar and Adham (both five years old) make their debut in Chapter 6, where four-year-old Jack also makes an appearance. In Chapter 7, it is three-year-old Jordan who requires support, while in the same chapter, 3½-year-old Monika and 2½-year-old Ruby also present some developmental concerns.

In Chapter 8, the educator Shaun is concerned about four-year-old Erika, who reacts negatively to any change in routine, often having a complete meltdown that involves her repeatedly banging into the wall. Also in Chapter 8, 3½-year-old Florrie, along with her friends Tom, Precious, Lucy and Zac, as well as their educator Claudia feature in a learning story. Later in Chapter 8, parents Beth and Josh attend a parent meeting with their child Millie's educator. This chapter also includes a sample Inclusion Plan for Madu, who is two years and eight months old, and whose main areas of difficulty are in social communication and play.

Four-year-old Ben who features in Chapter 9, has a diagnosed expressive language delay and is becoming increasingly withdrawn and demonstrating aggressive behaviour.

Role of policy in this book

As indicated in the introduction, this book is underscored by international policy developments: UNCRC, UNCRPD, UNESCO, etc. However, national policy also plays a vital role in informing and shaping inclusion. Accordingly, the chapters in this book utilise various inclusion policies including the Access and Inclusion Model (AIM, 2016) in Ireland and the Special Educational Needs Code of Practice (2015) in England, both of which point to the need for a leadership role; inclusion coordinator (InCo) in the case of Ireland, and special educational needs coordinator (SENCO) in the case of England.

More broadly, the image of the child is very much influenced by educational policy, and in particular by early childhood curriculum in individual countries. For example, the opening line of the foreword to the revised version of *Te Whāriki: Early Childhood Curriculum* in New Zealand (2017) describes a child as 'a treasure, to be nurtured, to grow to flourish' – 'He taonga te mokopuna, kia whāngaia, kia tipu, kia rea' (Ministry of Education, New Zealand, 2017, p. 2). Congruent with *Te Whāriki*, early childhood curricula internationally recognise the intrinsic value of early childhood, the uniqueness of each child and promote an image of the child as a competent and confident learner. As a result, much of the discussion throughout this book is informed by curricular models/frameworks, for example, *Belonging, Being and Becoming* (Australia); *Aistear: The Early Childhood Curriculum Framework* (Ireland); the *Early Years Foundation Stage* (England); *Framework Plan for the Content and Tasks of Kindergartens* (Norway) and the *Curriculum for the Preschool Lpfö 98* (Sweden).

Chapter overview

A detailed account of special educational needs, and disabilities, and how these may impact upon a child, is provided in Chapter 2. The intention is to assist educators in recognising potential early indicators of SEN and enable him/her to differentiate activities and adapt the learning environment to meet individual needs. Building upon the UNESCO definition of inclusion vis-à-vis seeing individual differences not as problems but as opportunities for enriching learning, Chapter 2 advises you to think 'possibility instead of disability'. To help you in doing this, Chapter 2 provides a broad range of strategies to: support communication, language and inter-action in children; support children with physical and motor difficulties; support play and learning; support children with visual difficulties; support children with a hearing impairment; and much more.

Chapter 3: 'Attitudes, values and beliefs' is concerned with how these impact upon the image of the child, the concept of inclusion, and approaches to working with children in early childhood settings. Attitudes, values and beliefs come from within. They are deeply ingrained and develop in a myriad of ways and through a range of processes (Mulvihill, Shearer & Van-Horn, 2002) including a person's upbringing, education and life experiences. In turn, attitudes shape beliefs relating to the image of the child, which is at the very core of inclusion and cannot be isolated from beliefs about how children learn and develop. Whether consciously, or uncon-sciously, educators can either facilitate or create barriers to inclusion. Educators can reinforce negative attitudes and prejudice by the way they act towards children with a disability, by whether they draw attention to them or through their expectations of children. A shared value system that supports inclusive practices is founded upon the view that diversity in the early childhood period is beneficial for all children. A positive approach to meeting and supporting children's diverse needs within early childhood, is an essential aspect of the setting's culture and approach, to promoting and maintaining inclusive practices.

Building upon Chapter 3, Chapter 4: 'Leading and sustaining an inclusive cul-ture' examines the relationship between leadership and the establishment and main-tenance of an inclusive culture in ECEC. Drawing upon Schein (2004), this chapter asserts that establishing an inclusive culture begins with the manager of the setting, who not only decides the basic purpose and the environmental context in which the setting operates, s/he also selects the staff team and invariably imposes his/her assumptions, attitudes, values and beliefs on them. Accordingly, if the manager is not committed to the principles of inclusion, it is unlikely that a culture of inclu-sion will be fostered. As determined in Chapter 4, the setting's culture dictates the atmosphere within the setting and conveys what is and what is not valued. The culture determines the extent to which individual difference is embraced as an opportunity for learning, or perceived as a problem within the setting.

Although Chapter 4 locates leadership at the interface of relationships – shared vision, values, beliefs, planning, evaluation and reflection – it recognises the role of leadership theory that addresses the question of what makes certain people become leaders, determines leadership style and is linked to professional values and beliefs. It is thought that distributed leadership, which supports the notion that leadership practice extends beyond the roles and responsibilities style of leadership usually associated with the manager, has become the most pervasive model of leadership in ECEC. While Lindon and Lindon (2012) describe it as a 'deliberate process' of sharing leadership behaviour, so that team members other than the manager can take an active lead and accept responsibility for some areas of the work and developing best practice, Harris (2013, p.vii) sees it as 'primarily concerned with the interactions and dynamics of leadership practice rather than a pre-occupation with the formal roles and responsibilities traditionally associated with those who lead'. Distributed leadership is not about being 'the overall leader of the setting, but of practitioners adopting a leadership role' (Lindon & Lindon, 2012, p.119). Chapter 4 suggests that there are spheres of influence within the setting, with concomitant layers of leadership, and distributed leadership underpins the need to mobilise leadership expertise at all levels within the setting.

Given the many aspects of inclusion, there is a danger that a single leadership role (e.g., the manager) may be spread too thinly across too many areas, thus undermining inclusive practice. Consequently, this chapter indicates that other leadership roles such as pedagogical and advocacy leadership may be required. Distributed leadership can be used as an effective means of embedding intentional leadership practice within ECEC, of ensuring the development of an inclusive culture, and of guaranteeing that inclusion becomes the norm, rather than an 'add-on' activity within the setting.

Chapter 5: 'Leading, building and maintaining an inclusive learning environment', and Chapter 6: 'Leading and maintaining an emotionally safe environment' focus upon the concept of meaningful participation, and how the environment, supports or hinders this for young children with SEN. These chapters also explore the leadership role in the context of leading, building and maintaining an inclusive learning environment. Using the PEAT model (Moloney & McCarthy, 2010), Chapter 5 focuses on the importance of the physical, aesthetic and temporal aspects of the learning environment, while Chapter 6 is underpinned by the concept of relational pedagogy.

Chapter 5 holds that accessing the physical space is but one step in the journey toward inclusion. It considers what parents might look for when enrolling their child for the first time in an early childhood setting. Regardless of the child's need, however, each of the four aspects of the PEAT model are fundamental to the concept of inclusion, and must be in harmony to effect and maintain inclusive practices within the setting.

Universal design for learning (UDL), which is considered to be the beginning of inclusive education is explored in detail in Chapters 5 and 6. Using the seven principles of UDL, a sample checklist in Chapter 5 helps you to identify whether the physical attributes of the activity areas/rooms in your setting:

- are accessible to all children;
- include equipment and materials that are accessible by, and easy to use by all children;
- are designed with safety in mind.

Children's safety must be a primary concern, and so educators must be able to see and hear what is happening from anywhere in the room (Epstein, 2014). With this in mind, Chapter 5 outlines a comprehensive range of strategies to enable educators to ensure children are safe while attending the setting. Once a safe environment has been established, attention can be directed toward how the space is organised, and the types of learning opportunities and activities that will support children's learning and development. Chapter 5 outlines strategies for intentionally planning and organising an accessible, culturally rich, aesthetic learning environment. It explains how an effective physical, aesthetic and temporal environment helps to promote a sense of identity, belonging, wellbeing and competence for both children and adults.

Chapter 6: 'Leading and maintaining an emotionally safe environment' suggests that a child who feels insecure, anxious or afraid, will be unable to reach his/her optimal stage of development (McMonagle, 2012). Children must feel socially, emotionally and physically safe and valued within the setting. They should be eager to attend the setting, and each day should hold the promise of something new, challenging and exciting. This chapter is underpinned by the concept of relational pedagogy that is characterised by reciprocal interactions and communication. It positions the child as a powerful player in his/her learning, and builds upon an image of the child as 'rich in potential, strong, powerful, competent, and most of all, connected to adults and to other children' (Malaguzzi, 1993, p.10) (see Chapter 3). Relational pedagogy is the bedrock of early childhood education and care.

Discussion of relational pedagogy in Chapter 6 ranges from interpreting and responding to children's communicative cues in infancy, through serve and return exchanges, to sustained shared thinking (Sylva, Melhuish, Sammons, Siraj-Blatchford & Taggart, 2004) from age two approximately, through which educators support the development of children's complex thinking and problem-solving skills. A range of environmental and pedagogical strategies directed towards supporting sustained shared thinking are included, as well as a checklist based upon UDL, which helps you to determine whether the environment in your setting is emotionally safe for all children.

Chapter 7: 'Leadership in planning an inclusive and responsive curriculum' explores a range of topics relating to early childhood curriculum. Following a comprehensive definition of curriculum, the concept of pedagogical framing, which is central to rich diverse early learning opportunities and experiences, is introduced. The chapter examines the central role of play in both children's learning and development, and curriculum planning. Although children have a tremendous propensity for learning from birth, they require support and encouragement from their parents/guardians, educators, peers and other professionals as necessary, throughout their individual learning journey. In the context of ECEC, children's learning is dependent upon purposeful curriculum planning, where careful consideration is given to what children know, what and how they will learn, what resources are required to support their learning, and how their learning will be assessed. The difference between long-, medium- and short-term planning is discussed, and sample plans are included. The concept and importance of integrated learning is explicated throughout this chapter, which also differentiates between pedagogy; pedagogical thinking and pedagogical leadership (Lindon & Lindon, 2012). Throughout Chapter 7, the question of leadership in planning an inclusive and responsive curriculum is continually interrogated.

Planning and assessment are mutually dependent. In addition to providing children with high-quality educational experiences, educators must also provide opportunities for them to demonstrate what they know, what they are able to do and what they are interested in. Chapter 8: 'Leading assessment for learning to support inclusion' explores the role of assessment in informing inclusive practice. As well as defining assessment, this chapter examines the purpose of assessment, describing it as being concerned with what children do and how they do it, as a basis for educational decisions that inform pedagogical approaches, curriculum development and implementation. Further, assessment leads to accommodations, i.e., alteration of the environment, curriculum or equipment/materials, and instruction to enable a child with a disability to participate in and, benefit from the early years curriculum.

In differentiating between formative and summative assessment, this chapter discusses the concept of authentic assessment, which is compatible with a whole-child perspective on learning and development (focusing upon what children do, and how they do it, in the context of their interactions with materials, equipment, peers and adults). A range of authentic assessment tools are examined: observation, learning stories, work portfolios and self-assessment. Crucially, this chapter discusses how to use assessment information to promote children's learning and development. In so doing, it affords primary importance to the role of parents in their child's early education and care. This chapter also addresses reflective practice, which is an essential skill that enables educators to review and analyse their practice in order to improve inclusive provision for children with special educational needs.

Working with others, which involves working with parents, families and a range of other professionals, is a core value of an inclusive culture in ECEC. Chapter 9: 'Leading collaborative working' focuses upon early intervention and collaborative working, which is critical to ensuring that children with special educational needs receive adequate and appropriate supports and resources to maximise their development within the ECEC setting. From its inception, early intervention has involved a multidisciplinary approach to working with a child with special educational needs, such as speech and language, physical and occupational therapists and a psychologist, all working together to support a child and his/her family. Chapter 9 is underpinned by systems theory, which comprises four key components: process, person, context and time, i.e., the PPCT Model (Wachs & Evans, 2010). It interrogates the following components: influence of family, educators and peers, and context, i.e., how interactions between policy, decision and resources at a macro-level, practices within settings including multidisciplinary involvement impact a child's learning and development. An inclusive culture is predicated upon a belief in a parent's right to be included in their child's development and learning, and therefore, the pre-eminent role of parents and families is further elucidated in Chapter 9. Highlighting the manner in which communication with and between children, parents, the early intervention team and the setting's staff team affects all aspect of inclusion, Chapter 9 includes comprehensive strategies for effective communication at multiple levels in the setting.

Further building upon Chapter 8, which discusses confidentiality in terms of storing observation and assessment data detailing concerns about aspects of a child's development, the principle of confidentially is expanded upon in Chapter 9. Although this should be a matter of best practice, many countries have rigorous data protection legislation that protects an individual's right to data protection, such as the Data Protection Act 1998 in England, the Privacy Act 1993 in New Zealand and the Data Protection Act 2017 in Ireland.

The final chapter is a reminder that early childhood is a time of tremendous opportunity for children's learning and development. Opportunities missed in early childhood cannot be made up for later on. Working with young children is an enormous privilege. It is also a tremendous responsibility. It is for all of these reasons that intentional leadership for inclusion is essential.

What is needed is somebody in the setting, a champion and advocate who is committed to turning the vision of offering 'every individual a relevant education and optimal opportunities for development' (UNESCO, 2005, p.16) into reality for children, and working tirelessly to achieve this. Intentional leadership for inclusion must be fostered and supported. It is the 'superglue' (Bolman & Deal, 2008) that unites, motivates and empowers all educators to work towards a common goal; that of creating an inclusive culture within the entire setting.

2

UNDERSTANDING SPECIAL EDUCATIONAL NEEDS AND DISABILITIES

Introduction

This chapter considers what is meant by the term 'special educational needs' (SEN) and their implications for the inclusion of all children in ECEC settings. As discussed in Chapter 3, it is important to remember that a child is a child first and foremost, with his or her own strengths, abilities, interests and talents. We should always approach our work with young children from that positive perspective (NCCA, 2009, p.7). International trends in inclusive and special education have moved away from the practice of labelling children with identified SEN and, instead, focus on identifying the specific and varied needs of the individual child and the ways in which early childhood educators can effectively meet those needs. Ultimately, the goal is to empower those with leadership roles to ensure that all children, with and without special educational needs, can participate fully in their respective ECEC setting.

So we might ask ourselves, why do leaders in ECEC settings need to know about SEN? As an early childhood educator with leadership responsibilities in relation to inclusive provision, it is essential to be aware of the latest evidence-based research about SEN in order to make informed decisions in relation to provision for young children with disabilities. Maintaining current knowledge and an understanding of SEN, supports the inclusion coordinator or SENCO (see Chapter 1) and other leaders within the setting (see Chapter 4) in being able to communicate effectively with parents and other key stakeholders. Furthermore, having an understanding of particular SEN and how they may impact upon a child can assist educators in recognising potential early indicators of SEN and enable him/her to differentiate activities and adapt the learning environment to meet individual needs.

Think 'possibility instead of disability'

As discussed in Chapters 3 and 5, educators' expectations of children with SEN can either support or hinder inclusion. The importance, therefore, of having high expectations for young children with SEN cannot be overstated. Educators and leaders can strive to raise the child's own expectations as well as those of his parents in order to ensure that every child experiences success and realises their full potential (see Chapters 8 and 9). In 2013, Jennie Fenton, mother of a little girl called Mala, highlighted her own transformation in thinking in relation to children with SEN, and emphasised the importance of approaching SEN provision from a positive perspective by 'thinking possibility instead of disability' (Fenton, 2013). Her mantra provides an appropriate underpinning to the focus of this chapter.

Defining special educational needs

As outlined in Chapter 1, the terms 'special educational needs' (SEN) and 'children with disabilities' are used throughout this book. In the UK, the Special Educational Needs and/or Disabilities (SEND) Code of Practice states that a child has SEN if they have a learning difficulty or disability that requires special educational provision; that is, provision that is additional to or different to that which is normally available to children of the same age (DfE, 2017a). In Ireland, children with disabilities are defined as having 'a long-term physical, mental, intellectual or sensory impairment which, in interaction with various barriers, may hinder a child's full and effective participation in society on an equal basis with others' (DCYA, 2016, p.vi). It is important to note, that not every child who has a disability will have a special educational need. Some young children with disabilities may require minor accommodations and will not have any difficulty in accessing the early childhood curriculum (Devarakonda, 2013).

Towards an understanding of special educational needs

In order to understand the potential implications of special educational needs and/ or disabilities for young children, it may be helpful to examine how these can impact upon a child's abilities in the areas illustrated in Figure 2.1.

Communication, language and interaction

There are many reasons why children experience speech and language difficulties. In fact, this is one of the most common developmental problems for children in ECEC settings. Some children may experience a speech and language delay, in which case their speech and language develops normally albeit at a slower pace. Others may have a speech and language disorder, which means that they may have a disordered pattern of language development accompanied by a receptive, expressive

FIGURE 2.1 Areas potentially impacted by SEN and/or disabilities

or global language disorder. These children will require specialist intervention from a speech and language therapist or pathologist. Other children may experience speech, language or interaction difficulties associated with an identified disability such as an autism spectrum disorder (ASD), a hearing impairment, cerebral palsy or Down syndrome (Figure 2.2).

How a communication, language or interaction difficulty can impact a child

Communication is a key foundation to all learning and development. It helps children to understand and make sense of their environment. Chapter 5 illustrates that from birth, children communicate in multiple ways to give and receive information (NCCA, 2009). Young children with special educational needs and/or disabilities may be at the pre-intentional stage of communication, a very early stage of communicative development where the child has not assigned meaning to communication, and is unable to communicate intentionally. Other children may find it difficult to attend to language, they may have difficulty articulating certain sounds, and they may not know how to communicate socially with their peers. Children who have receptive language difficulties usually find attending and listening a challenge. They can experience difficulties with understanding verbal communication, following

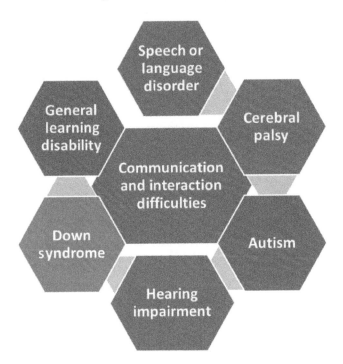

FIGURE 2.2 Causes of communication, language and interaction difficulties

directions and they may have problems with short-term memory. Children who have expressive language difficulties often experience problems with producing and formulating spoken language, may have word retrieval difficulties, can find producing speech sounds and formulating sentences challenging, and may prefer to point or use gestures. Significantly, some children with SEN may have a combination of receptive and expressive language difficulties.

Strategies to support communication, language and interaction in children

There are numerous instructional strategies that can be used to support language development for children with speech, language and communication difficulties. Remember that these strategies can be used with any child in the ECEC setting. Good practice with children with SEN and/or disabilities is usually good practice for all children.

- Use short simple sentences or phrases when communicating with a child who is at the early stages of language development. Speak slowly and exaggerate, using variation in pitch and volume. Use simple vocabulary consistently. Reinforce your message using gestures and/or visual supports, as appropriate;

- Allow enough 'Wait time' for the child to process what has been said or communicated using sign or pictures and also allow enough 'Wait time' for the child to formulate a response;
- Set up the environment to promote communication. For example, place a child's favourite toy out of reach so that the child will have to communicate with someone in order to get it. Encourage children to use speech, sign, symbols or pictures to communicate their needs;
- Set up problem-based scenarios that will require the child to communicate with others to resolve. You might 'forget' to put water in the watering can or leave the lid on the costume box closed too tight for the child to open it for 'dress-up' time. Model words to describe the mistake you have made – for example, 'Uh-oh' – and then wait for the child to ask for help;
- Use stories, songs and rhymes to teach language and communication. Reading to very young children is one of the most effective ways of enhancing language development. Use big books, story sacks and puppets to make the stories interactive. Many children will enjoy tactile learning experiences using 'lift the flap' books with different materials to touch or buttons to press;
- Use *parallel-talk*; that is, use short sentences to describe to the child what they are doing, what they are seeing and what they are hearing; for example, 'Well Christopher… You have a yellow block and a blue block. You are building a big tower!';
- Use *self-talk*, where you describe what you are doing while the child watches and listens; for example, 'I am rolling the ball. Yay!';
- Use *expansion*, where you repeat what the child has said and build on it a little. So if the child says 'Me go', you say 'Yes, you are going for a ride in your car';
- Many young children will mispronounce words, for example, they say 'pollypop' instead of 'lollipop' or 'iscuit' instead of 'biscuit'. An effective strategy is to emphasise the correct pronunciation while providing a positive response to the child's communication;
- Use role play to act out real-life scenarios such as speaking on the phone, going to the shop, making dinner etc., helping to encourage the child to use language in real-life contexts.

PRACTICE SCENARIO

Four-year-old Antoni is from Poland. His family only speak Polish with him at home. He recently had corrective surgery for a tongue tie, which made it difficult for him to speak.

Antoni is not inclined to speak, preferring to gesture, point or make throaty sounds to let the educators know what he needs. When he does speak, the educators find it difficult to understand him, as he tends to mix up words and he has a lot of difficulty with word retrieval and sequencing his ideas.

Consider:

1. What are the main challenges for Antoni in the area of language and communication?
2. How might these challenges impact on the day-to-day activities in the setting?
3. What strategies could the educators use to support Antoni's learning needs?
4. What implications are there, if any, in relation to working with Antoni's family to support his language learning needs?
5. How could an inclusion coordinator/SENCO support and mentor educators in meeting Antoni's needs?

Communicating with a child who is pre-verbal or non-verbal

There are many reasons why a child may be pre-verbal or non-verbal. A physical disability may affect the child's muscle control in vocalisation. In some instances, children become pre-verbal due to an acquired brain injury or stroke. Additionally, some children with an autism spectrum disorder may experience delayed or impaired speech development. Others may be pre-verbal due to a learning disability that has affected their cognitive development. A sensory impairment such as hearing loss or a visual impairment may also impact upon a child's ability to become verbal. It is notable that in the longer-term some of these children will develop meaningful language and clear speech, but they may take longer and need specialist support to do so. While a small number of children may never be able to use recognisable speech, it does not have to stop them from becoming effective communicators; however, they will need special communicative materials and equipment and extra support to learn how to use communicative tools effectively.

Educators can experience challenges in finding effective ways to communicate with children who are pre-verbal or non-verbal. In many cases, where these children are not able to communicate their needs or have those needs met, they can exhibit challenging and even self-injurious behaviours out of pure frustration. Once the educator finds a 'way-in' to communicating with the child, many of these behaviours may reduce or disappear altogether.

Strategies for communicating with a child who is pre-verbal or non-verbal

While there are various strategies that can support communication with a child who is pre-verbal or non-verbal, Augmentative and Alternative Communication (AAC) is particularly effective. AAC provides a range of low-tech to high-tech communicative options for children who are pre-verbal or non-verbal, and may provide a short-term or long-term solution for children whose speech is not developing normally. An AAC system can help educators and extended family and friends to understand the child's communications more clearly. Furthermore, the use of AAC can reduce the risk of a child developing learned helplessness, as there may be a tendency for others to anticipate and sometimes misunderstand the child's needs. AAC can enable the child to make choices, express feelings and achieve independence. Examples of low-tech AAC include using symbols, photos and pictures on printed communication boards or basic voice output devices such as a Big Mack. High-tech AAC supports include complex electronic systems or apps that replace speech such as the Tobii Dynavox or Clicker Communicator AAC app. A speech and language therapist or pathologist usually advises and supports children and families who need access to AAC. When communicating with children who are pre-verbal, the following strategies may provide a useful starting point:

- Find out how the child communicates 'Yes' and 'No'. This could be an eye-gaze upwards or a throaty sound that the child makes consistently. Often parents will be able to provide insights into how their child communicates 'Yes' and 'No';
- Open the conversation by asking the child if he or she would like to talk;
- Position yourself at the child's 'eye-level';
- Allow the child ample time to respond;
- Don't talk while the child is talking;
- Ask the child to repeat or rephrase if you don't understand;
- Once you have succeeded in understanding the child's way of communicating 'Yes' and 'No', you can start to introduce simple choices for the child. Consider using concrete objects or visual supports to represent these choices, as appropriate.

Social communication difficulties

Some children with SEN and/or disabilities experience difficulties with social interaction and communication. This is particularly relevant for children with an ASD who may appear aloof or indifferent to other people, and who may have difficulty with verbal and non-verbal communication. They may use words out of context or they might have echolalia, where they repeat sounds and words they have heard in their environment without communicative intent. Many children with ASDs have difficulty understanding the social aspects of communicating and, consequently, might shout out, interrupt conversations, constantly ask questions or persist in speaking about a favourite topic. A further challenge for children with ASDs is their tendency to have a literal understanding of language. In daily conversations, idioms are often used such as 'get your skates on' or 'it's raining cats and dogs'. These can be especially confusing for children with ASDs and should be avoided if possible.

Children with emotional and behavioural disorders, cognitive difficulties and neurological disorders may also encounter challenges in engaging in positive social interactions with others and establishing acceptance with their peers. Intervention approaches can include a combination of coaching, modelling, role-playing, using puppets, rehearsing and feedback. Sometimes it is necessary to coach a child on a withdrawal basis, working one-to-one with an early childhood educator before the child applies the skill with different partners and ultimately in a larger group setting.

PRACTICE SCENARIO

Arielle has joined the toddler room in her early years setting. She has been diagnosed as having an autism spectrum disorder. While she loves music and lining up blocks and toys, she has difficulties engaging socially with her peers. She also has delayed speech and language development. On the first day in the toddler room, Arielle had a total meltdown when the group were about to engage in story-time. The educator tried to work out what was upsetting Arielle, but Arielle just became increasingly distressed. In the end, the room leader led her out of the room to a quiet space and she stopped crying immediately. As soon as it was suggested that she re-join the group, she started to cry.

The next day the educator observed Arielle closely and noticed that she loved watching the fish in the classroom fish-tank. At story-time she put a chair next to the tank and asked Arielle to sit there for story. Arielle watched the fish during the story but joined in with the songs. Now every day when story-time is about to start, Arielle runs and gets her chair and sits by the tank and enjoys the session.

Consider:

1. Why do you think Arielle became upset?
2. Can you identify alternative strategies that could have been used to encourage Arielle to stay in the room for story-time?
3. How could the educator encourage Arielle to participate with her peers during story-time?
4. How could a SENCO/inclusion coordinator support the educators in addressing Arielle's needs?

Physical and sensory needs

Children may have a physical or sensory disability from birth, or they may acquire a physical or sensory disability through illness or injury later in life. Often these difficulties are identified at birth but occasionally signs of a delay in physical or motor development, sight or hearing may only become evident when a child does not meet expected developmental milestones. Educators are in a good position to observe children's physical and sensory skills, and to watch out for early indicators of delays in children's development. Remember that every child is individual and even typically developing children reach certain milestones at different times. Some infants walk as early as ten months while others may not walk until 18 months. While being cognisant that children develop at different paces, as discussed in Chapter 8, it is still important for educators to observe young children's development, and be able to recognise potential signs that a child may need early intervention or support. Some possible early indicators of motor difficulties are shown in Table 2.1.

TABLE 2.1 Possible early indicators of a motor delay

The child:

- has unusually tight muscle tone;
- cannot hold up his head independently after three months;
- has unusually loose muscle tone;
- does not sit up or bend his knees;
- does not reach across his body even during play;
- does not reach for toys or food;
- cannot pick up or hold objects;
- uses only one hand when feeding himself;
- has difficulty releasing objects from his hands;
- has poor balance and tends to fall frequently;
- has poor hand-eye coordination.

Strategies to support children with physical and motor difficulties

Remember that having a physical disability does not mean that a child will necessarily have an intellectual or learning disability. Children with physical disabilities are children first and foremost, and like all children, they need opportunities to make choices and do things for themselves, within the scope of their ability. Educators should provide appropriate help, but also encourage children to try to do things themselves. This may mean that tasks may take a little more time. Gradually reducing the amount of assistance being provided can enable the child to gradually learn to work independently (Klein, Cook & Richardson-Gibbs, 2001). As highlighted in Chapter 5, doing things independently helps children to build self-confidence and independence. Those in leadership roles can lead by example by being patient, encouraging the child and guiding the educators and other children in the setting to do the same.

Access is one of the key considerations when working with children who have a physical disability or motor difficulty. This may involve adaptations to the learning environment or provision of specialist equipment to enable the child to move independently and fully access activities within the setting (see Chapter 5). Inclusion coordinators/SENCOs or leaders (see Chapter 4) and educators who are working with a child who has a physical disability need to collaborate closely with parents, professionals working with the child and the child him/herself (see Chapter 9). That input can help the ECEC provider and educators to make specific plans to accommodate the child and to know how to differentiate activities to include the child in a meaningful way in the setting. When considering how to meet the needs of a child who has a physical or motor difficulty, the following strategies relating to the environment, use of specialist equipment, and support for play and learning can support inclusion:

Environmental adaptations:
- Make it as easy as possible for the child to move around the setting. Re-organise rooms, if necessary, to ensure that aisles are wide enough to accommodate a wheelchair or walker. Heavy and stable furniture should be used and secured so they cannot be easily moved;
- Remove or securely tape down rugs that could be a tripping hazard;
- Provide a dedicated safe storage space for walkers, crutches and wheelchairs so that children do not trip over them when they are not in use;
- Become familiar with how to seat and position the child safely. Seek advice from the parents and occupational therapist (OT), with parental permission. The OT will be able to advise about the use of foot blocks, sloped tables, seat adjusters, customised cushions, wedges and height-adjustable tables, as appropriate for the child;
- Be alert to feeding difficulties. Poorly developed chewing and swallowing patterns may affect how a child eats certain textures of food. A child with cerebral palsy may not swallow correctly if his head is tilted back. The child's head should be in a central position or slightly forward;
- Seat a child who uses a wheelchair near the corner of a square table, so that an adult can sit and assist comfortably with feeding.

Specialist equipment:
- Provide specialist feeding equipment, i.e., adapted cups, plates and spoons to help a child to eat and drink more easily. Some children will need to be fed by an adult using special feeding techniques, such as, strategies to prevent gagging or biting and strategies to facilitate chewing and swallowing safely. In some cases, children may tongue thrust, have poor lip closure or have food allergies. Always check with parents before introducing a new food;
- Use a mobile hoist to assist in transferring a child from a wheelchair to other spaces, such as a changing table, toilet or for floor activities;

- Keep a full change of clothing in the setting in case of accidents or getting wet during outdoor play, art or water-play activities. As some children with cerebral palsy have difficulty controlling swallowing of saliva, bibs and protective clothing may be required;
- Provide a range of adaptive educational equipment, including chunky crayons, pencil grips, anchorage devices for paper and books, large sponge shapes for artwork and printing, Velcro or Dycem non-slip mats that keep materials from falling off a table easily, and specialist play equipment such as larger, lighter balls, Velcro bats and balls, scoops for catching, foam javelins, soft balls and bowling tunnels;
- Adapt some standard materials to make them more accessible for children with motor difficulties. This can be easily done, for example, by wrapping standard paint brushes in foam or by sticking a square of sponge to the lower outer corner of the page to enable a child with fine motor difficulties to turn the page of a book more easily;
- Consider the accessibility of clothes in the dressing up area. Buttons can be replaced by Velcro strips, shoes can have a section cut out at the back to make them easier to slip on, larger buttons and straps can be included for practising dressing and a selection of wrap-around cloaks and boas can be included for accessibility purposes.

Strategies to support play and learning:
- Seat a child near a socket if he is using a computer or assistive technology devices;
- Provide tools that children with motor difficulties can use for grasping, holding and releasing, such as tongs and large tweezers, and provide materials of different textures; sandpaper, play dough, bubble-wrap, cotton balls, different fabrics, corrugated cardboard and Theraputty to stimulate the child's tactile senses;
- Add wooden or plastic knobs to puzzle pieces and wrap stiff plastic around shoe laces for bead stringing to make them easier to handle;
- Laminate paper materials to protect them from accidental leaks of saliva, and to make them more durable;
- Consider working in a bounded area to keep items contained. For example, play with a ball placed inside a hula hoop on the floor or enclose a space for playing with cars and trucks using cushions and boxes;
- Consider reducing the size of the play area during games, or the length of a race in order to enable all of the children to participate. Remember that wheelchair users can sometimes be at a distinct advantage when it comes to racing against their ambulant peers;
- Choose activities that encourage children with motor difficulties to use all of their body parts. Encourage the whole group to participate in these activities.

PRACTICE SCENARIO

Four-year-old Jacob absolutely loves tractors. He lives on a farm and regularly arrives to the setting with very mucky wheels on his motorised wheelchair. Jacob is small for his age, and can be lifted safely out of his wheelchair. He enjoys engaging in floor work with the other children in his class.

Jacob's three older sisters love to 'help' him and tend to jump up to meet his needs before he has a chance to do things himself. His grandmother, who lives with him, is protective of Jacob and tries to anticipate his needs, reducing his opportunities to gain independence.

An educator in his classroom is also very fond of Jacob, and in her enthusiasm she tends to speak on his behalf and anticipate his needs in the setting. She lifts him out of his chair for floor-time activities before he has a chance to ask, and she provides him with whatever materials the other children collect from the 'movement corner' for these activities. Jacob is becoming quite passive and tends to expect others to do everything for him. The SENCO/inclusion coordinator is concerned about Jacob's growing lack of independence in the setting and at home.

Consider:

1. How can the SENCO/inclusion coordinator encourage the educator to promote Jacob's independence?
2. To what extent can the ECEC staff support Jacob's family in addressing his needs, particularly in relation to making choices and becoming more independent?
3. What role can the educator play in promoting Jacob's independence and child agency?
4. How can Jacob be encouraged to be more assertive and to communicate his needs independently?

Sensory needs: visual loss

Sensory disabilities include visual impairments and hearing impairments, both of which are considered low-incidence disabilities. A visual impairment seriously impacts a child's capacity to see visually presented materials. This does not include children whose visual difficulties can be corrected with glasses. There are many aspects of visual functioning that may be affected:

- Visual acuity: the ability to resolve fine detail;
- Visual accommodation: the ability to focus;

- Field of vision: the area that can be seen;
- Colour vision and adaptability to light.

It is important to be aware that a child who has been assessed as being legally blind may have some capacity to see light, shapes, colours and parts of objects (NICHCY, 2017). Some potential early indicators of a visual impairment are shown in Table 2.2.

TABLE 2.2 Possible early indicators of a visual impairment

The child:

- has eyelid drooping over one or both eyes;
- has an obvious squint or jerky eye movements;
- tends to cover or shut one eye repeatedly;
- holds objects very close or very far away in order to see them;
- turns his head when using his eyes;
- feels for objects on the ground rather than looking with his eyes;
- the child's eyes do not move together when following an object.

Strategies to support children with visual difficulties

Children typically learn a significant amount about the world around them through their sight. However, children who have a visual impairment need to use touch, taste, smell, sound, movement and whatever level of vision they have to learn about and understand their world. This type of sensorial learning is really important to help children with a visual impairment to build understanding and independence. As young children with visual loss may have limited opportunities to learn through observing and copying the actions of their peers, this can impact on their ability to imitate social behaviour and to understand non-verbal cues. When planning to include young children who have a visual loss, pay attention to the following:

- Consider safety and access for children with visual loss. Similar to children who have motor difficulties, children with visual impairments need all areas of the setting to be easily accessible and they need all tripping hazards to be removed. They will need to be familiarised with the layout of the room in advance. A visit to the setting, and to their classroom when there are no other children there can help children to learn to find their way around. Use tactile cues in key areas to assist the child in knowing when they have moved from one area to another, for example, have a tie hanging on a hook near the dressing up area or a paper mobile hanging near the story-time area;
- Try to eliminate glare as much as possible. Appropriate lighting is essential to enable children to use whatever vision they have effectively. Some children may need to be positioned near a window to see an activity. Other children may find bright lights painful and may benefit from wearing tinted glasses or a hat;

- Be aware of shadows that may be cast over an activity. Generally fluorescent lighting is helpful for children with visual loss as it helps to prevent shadows on a surface. Educators must be mindful not to sit or stand with their back to a light source as this can have the effect of causing a silhouette;
- Use colour contrasts to assist a child with a visual impairment by making it easier for the child to see an object. For example, using a navy mat with a yellow plate can make it easier for the child to see the plate;
- Use tactile toys with sensory effects to stimulate the child's senses; for example, toys that have accompanying sound effects or toys that light up in a darkened space. Create tactile books or sensory walls using fabrics, feathers, felt, corrugated cardboard, bubble wrap and cotton balls;
- Allow extra time, as appropriate, for the child to move from one space in the classroom to another, and supplement visual information with verbal explanations to ensure that the child understands what activity is coming up next;
- Announce your presence when you are joining a group activity and equally announce your departure when you are leaving the group.

PRACTICE SCENARIO

Rebecca is four years old and has retinitis pigmentosa, which is slowly causing her retina to deteriorate. She has already lost much of her peripheral vision and her parents have been advised that this will gradually progress to loss of her central vision and acuity and will ultimately result in blindness. Rebecca is cautious about new experiences and is resistant to putting her hands into any unfamiliar substances. Consequently, she tends to become very upset any time that her group is engaged in activities that involve using messy materials, such as, clay, finger paints, glue or papier-mâché.

Consider:

1. What strategies can the inclusion coordinator/SENCO recommend to the early years educators to support Rebecca in overcoming her fear of touching messy substances?
2. What should the educator do if Rebecca refuses to engage in creative activities?
3. Should the parents and family be involved in addressing this issue with Rebecca? If so, how?
4. How can the educators help Rebecca be less fearful of new experiences?

Sensory needs: hearing loss

Hearing ability starts to develop before birth and is nearly fully developed at birth. New born babies recognise the voices of their parents before they recognise their faces and they often turn their heads towards the source of the sound even when they cannot see the person making the sound. There are various levels of hearing impairment ranging from mild to profound. Hearing loss can affect loudness or intensity and pitch and can be experienced in one or both ears. Very few children are completely deaf. In fact, most children with hearing loss have some residual hearing. Some children may have a hearing loss due to having another disability, such as, Down syndrome, Usher syndrome or Alport syndrome.

Significantly, in many cases, the deaf community prefer the term 'deaf' to hearing impairment as they view themselves as a linguistic and cultural minority group rather than a group of people with a disability. Language and communication are a critical consideration in the education and care of young children who have a hearing impairment. Table 2.3 outlines some potential early indicators of a hearing impairment.

TABLE 2.3 Possible early indicators of a hearing impairment

The child:

- does not respond to his name if his back is turned;
- does not startle at loud noises;
- says 'huh?' and asks for things to be repeated;
- has delayed speech;
- has unclear speech;
- does not seem to hear sounds in the environment, such as another child calling him or someone walking up behind him.

(CDC, 2012).

Strategies to support children with a hearing impairment

It is important to identify any hearing loss early so that interventions are put in place to ensure that the child develops effective language and communication skills from an early age. While hearing loss does not affect a child's cognitive ability or ability to learn, children who are hard of hearing may often miss out on important aspects of language learning, leading to difficulties developing vocabulary and grammar, understanding pluralisation and tenses, using sentence structure, understanding idioms and jokes, and delays in developing receptive and expressive communication skills. Children with a hearing impairment often use hearing aids reinforced by lip-reading to achieve fluent communication through speech. Those who cannot hear sounds use sign language as their primary method of communication. If the child is using sign language as their primary mode of communication, the ECEC staff will need to learn basic sign language to communicate with them.

Educators must be mindful that all children can experience fluctuating hearing loss due to having a cold or sinus problem, and that they may also miss out on important messages in the setting during those periods. The following strategies can be helpful in supporting the needs of young children who are experiencing hearing loss:

- Minimise listening distance by positioning the child near you and in a position that allows him to make the most of his residual hearing, for example, with his better ear facing you;
- Minimise environmental noise by using carpets or rugs to absorb noise and avoid unnecessary background noise;
- Be mindful of shadows for children who are lip-reading. Ensure there is good lighting. Face the child directly when you are speaking and avoid moving around. Take care not to cover your face or lips while speaking;
- Use visual aids and demonstrations to clarify meaning. Use concrete objects, pictures and diagrams as much as possible;
- Use natural gestures and model procedures and tasks;
- Speak clearly at a good volume but don't exaggerate your speech. Support with signing, if appropriate;
- Monitor the child's understanding by asking him to repeat or rephrase important information or instructions;
- Identify each speaker clearly and encourage the children to speak one at a time during group discussions. Summarise and repeat other children's answers as required;
- If a child is wearing a hearing aid, ask the parents or guardians to show you how to adjust the volume control, how to replace the battery, how to clean the hearing aid, how to insert it in the child's ear and how to power it on and off;
- Become familiar with how to use assistive technologies such as a sound field amplification system, which can improve sound in the setting for all children.

Social, emotional and behavioural needs

Practically all children exhibit challenging behaviour from time to time, including tantrums, overly anxious behaviours, defiance or aggressive behaviours such as hitting or biting. For most children, these behaviours are temporary. However, children who have a social, emotional or behavioural difficulty exhibit degrees of challenging behaviour on an ongoing basis, which 'act as a barrier to their personal, social, cognitive and emotional development' (National Education Psychological NEPS, 2010, p.4). Children with emotional disturbance may have conditions such as neurosis, childhood psychosis, attention deficit disorder (ADD), attention deficit hyperactivity disorder (ADHD) or conduct disorder. They are also very likely to experience difficulties with communication (O'Leary, 2011) and they often present with negative behaviours that impact upon their social development and learning (Cross, 2011).

TABLE 2.4 Possible early indicators of a social, emotional or behavioural difficulty

The child:

- exhibits aggressive or anti-social behaviours, has difficulty managing anger and frustration and frequently has tantrums;
- demonstrates a general inability to cope with the routine of daily tasks;
- engages in play that seems repetitive or limited;
- has difficulty paying attention and following instructions;
- is easily distracted or impulsive, seems restless and highly active;
- experiences difficulties with social interactions;
- is fearful, anxious or upset most of the time;
- exhibits obsessive and repetitive behaviours;
- has attention-seeking behaviours, such as negative interactions or a poor attitude towards activities, their peers or educators;
- exhibits behaviours, such as withdrawal, self-injurious behaviour or an eating disorder.

They may present with internalising behaviours, such as low self-esteem, anxiety or withdrawal, which limit participation and engagement in activities, or externalising behaviours such as aggressive and attention-seeking behaviours, which impact negatively on their social development or both (CCEA, 2014). Where there are concerns, an assessment will need to be undertaken by a paediatrician, psychiatrist or psychologist to determine if there are any underlying causal factors such as a communication difficulty or learning disability (DfE & DH), 2015). Considerations that may inform the need for assessment include: the frequency and intensity of the behaviour, how extreme the behaviour seems when compared with other children at a similar stage, how well the child has responded to the efforts of parents and educators to support him/her, the extent to which the behaviour is occurring across multiple contexts and how the behaviour is interfering with the child's development. Early identification can ensure that children receive appropriate intervention as early as possible, which in turn can lead to improved behaviour and developmental outcomes, and improved social interactions with their peers.

The term 'social, emotional and behavioural difficulties' encompasses a wide and diverse range of behavioural challenges as presented in Table 2.4.

Strategies to support children with social, emotional and behavioural difficulties

As discussed in Chapter 8: 'Leading assessment for learning to support inclusion', if an educator is concerned about a child's behaviours, it is important to undertake observations of the behaviour during a range of activities throughout the day, and to record specific examples of problematic behaviours when they occur. These observations should be discussed with the SENCO/inclusion coordinator, or other leader for inclusion (see Chapter 4) before raising concerns with parents or guardians. It is essential to work closely with the child's parents in addressing the child's needs (see Chapters 8 and 9). Remember also, that educators can play an important role in providing guidance and support for the child.

Children with social, emotional and behavioural difficulties learn best in well-organised, predictable and structured environments (see Chapter 4). Educators must consider the specific needs of the child when planning activities and build on the child's strengths as much as possible. The following strategies can be helpful in supporting the needs of children with social, emotional and behavioural difficulties:

- Establish and build a positive relationship with the child and incorporate his interests where possible when planning activities;
- Maintain a predictable structure and routine throughout the day;
- Schedule the most attention-demanding tasks as early as possible in the day;
- Praise positive behaviours as much as possible by 'catching the child being good';
- Give clear and concise instructions with a short number of steps;
- Provide advance notice about transitions, for example, 'in five minutes we are going to play outside, so we need to finish up our finger painting';
- Reward and praise positive behaviour towards peers, such as, turn-taking and sharing;
- Be mindful of situations that may cause increased stress or anxiety for the child; for example, being dropped off to the setting in the morning. If possible, modify what happens to make it easier for the child to cope, i.e., produce a favourite toy as a distraction and encourage the parent to leave promptly so that the child settles as quickly as possible;
- Be empathic; let the child know that you are there to listen and offer support when he is anxious or upset.

Cognition and learning ability

When children arrive into the world they start to develop a significant number of skills including holding up their head, smiling, reaching, communicating, rolling over, sitting and crawling. Children who have cognitive disabilities may take longer to develop these skills. In Ireland, a general learning disability is a general developmental delay that affects cognitive ability. This spans a wide continuum of ability ranging from mild to moderate to severe and profound intellectual disabilities. Various terms are used in other countries to represent general learning disabilities; for example, the terms 'intellectual disability' or 'cognitive disability' are widely used in the States. With these different terms in mind, and being cognisant of the move towards using adaptive functioning (which evaluates the social, conceptual and practical life skills of the child) combined with intellectual functioning (IQ) as diagnostic tools, in the context of this book, IQ scores are included solely as a guide to enable the reader to differentiate between mild, moderate, and severe/profound disabilities.

Significantly, children who have intellectual disabilities or general learning disabilities progress through the same developmental stages as their peers albeit at a slower pace. Children with mild intellectual disabilities (with typical IQ scores of between 50 and 70) are not easily distinguishable from their peers and their learning needs may be difficult to define. These children may experience difficulties with memory and language, have a short attention span, experience lower levels of achievement and have social skill deficits. Children with moderate intellectual disabilities (with typical IQ scores of between 35 and 49) are likely to have more significantly impaired development and learning ability in the areas of language and communication, social and personal development, motor coordination, basic literacy skills, numeracy skills and daily living skills. Children with severe and profound intellectual disabilities (with typical IQ scores of 34 and below) have highly individual learning needs and their learning is often at an early developmental level, such as at the stage of a new-born baby or very young infant. These children may have significant communication, motor, sensory, self-care and emotional and behavioural needs. The key focus for children who have severe or profound intellectual disabilities is on attending, responding and initiating.

At the other end of the spectrum of cognition and learning ability are children who are identified as being exceptionally able (with typical IQ scores of over 130), who learn at a much faster pace than their peers and have the ability to process material to a greater depth. They usually learn to read at an unusually young age and may display excellent powers of reasoning and problem-solving. However, many of these children can experience difficulties in the area of social skills, may be overly sensitive and tend to be emotionally intense. Table 2.5 outlines potential early indicators of a cognitive or intellectual disability and indicators of exceptional cognitive ability:

TABLE 2.5 Possible early indicators of a cognitive or intellectual disability and exceptional cognitive ability

Mild intellectual disabilities
The child:

- has a short attention span and may be easily distracted;
- demonstrates a slower pace of learning;
- has poor memory and generalisation skills;
- has difficulty understanding instructions;
- experiences difficulties in the areas of memory, attention and/or language;
- takes longer to acquire daily living skills, such as, feeding, dressing and toilet training;
- has low self-esteem;
- tends to be immature and may have behavioural difficulties.

Moderate intellectual disabilities
The child:

- has speech that is not clear and he has limited vocabulary;
- is slower to walk and talk than his peers;
- has poor fine and gross coordination skills;

(continued)

TABLE 2.5 (*Cont.*)

- has difficulty communicating;
- experiences difficulties generalising and transferring knowledge;
- has significant difficulties with basic literacy and numeracy;
- demonstrates immature behaviour prefers to be with adults or younger children;
- needs assistance in acquiring basic daily living skills.

Severe and profound intellectual disabilities

The child:

- experiences significant delays in reaching developmental milestones;
- has serious speech or communication problems;
- exhibits a severe degree of apathy in relation to the environment and does not respond to visual or auditory stimuli;
- has difficulties with basic physical mobility;
- is unable to remember basic skills;
- cannot generalise skills from one situation to another;
- is dependent on others to satisfy basic needs, such as, feeding and toileting;
- has very loose or tight muscle tone
- is unlikely to be able to live independently and will need support throughout his life.

Exceptional cognitive ability

The child:

- displays incredible intensity in energy, imagination and intellectual ability;
- has a wide range of general knowledge and has an interest in topics that one might expect of an older child;
- has the ability to apply himself to a given task for prolonged periods of time;
- is very articulate and has a well-developed vocabulary that is much more sophisticated than that of his peers;
- displays very good powers of reasoning and problem-solving;
- has an excellent memory, can transfer information and generalises very easily;
- enjoys playing and experimenting with numbers;
- communicates better with adults than his peers;
- may have difficulties with social skills, especially in relating well with his peers.

Strategies to support children with cognitive and intellectual disabilities

A range of strategies can be used to support the learning needs of children who have cognitive or intellectual disabilities. These should be adapted to meet the individual needs of the child, according to where a child is positioned along the intellectual continuum from mild to moderate to severe and profound intellectual disability. It is essential to have high expectations of all children irrespective of their level of intellectual disability, as this helps them strive to learn, and to develop at an appropriate pace. Focusing on the child's own interests when planning activities can be highly motivating for children with cognitive disabilities. For example, if a child loves PAW Patrol or Monster Machines, use those as a theme for his activities. Always start from what the child knows and work at the pace of the child. Use concrete materials and visual aids to support the child's understanding and learning. By ensuring that tasks are within the child's capacity to experience success, the child will be motivated to continue to learn. Aim for a 98 per cent success rate when working with children who have intellectual disabilities. Include as many opportunities as possible for repetition and practice, and provide as much praise and encouragement as possible. For children with intellectual disabilities, the more immediate the praise and reinforcement, the more effective it tends to be. The following strategies can help in supporting the needs of children with intellectual disabilities:

- **Task analysis**: The approach to breaking a task down into small steps and then teaching those steps systematically, in sequence, until the child understands and can complete the task in sequence; for example, putting on a coat, completing a simple jigsaw or building a tower of blocks;
- **Backward chaining**: An approach where you teach a child the steps in a task by working backward through the steps starting with the fully completed task. Take, for example, a jigsaw puzzle. Backward chaining starts by showing the child the jigsaw fully completed apart from one piece. The child is encouraged to insert the last piece. This enables the child to experience immediate success. Once the child is comfortable with putting in one piece, you can give them the puzzle with two pieces missing and so on, building up their confidence and ability until they can complete the full puzzle;
- **A multi-sensory approach**: Involves using as many senses as possible when introducing a new concept. When introducing the colour red, for example, reinforce the concept with a range of sensory experiences: show the child a red ball, eat a red apple, add red food colouring to water and listen to a red fire truck. As children with intellectual disabilities need lots of repetition, teaching the same concept in different contexts while using as many senses as possible is a very effective reinforcement approach;
- **Spacing your practice**: Involves revising the same concept in a variety of ways, using many examples and spacing out the practice. Teach a concept for a short time each day for many days; for example, when teaching a child to take turns, practise this at different stages throughout the daily activities of the setting;
- **Focus on essential skills**: Consider how important it is that a child learns a certain concept or skill. Rather than trying to teach the child with an intellectual disability everything at a lower, slower or simpler level, concentrate on what is important for the child to learn as a base for future learning. Consider the skills that will be essential for the child in later life;
- **Sensory motor integration**: Provide as many opportunities as possible for children to use motor skills in coordination with their senses. Use activities and materials that require the use of two hands; for example, clapping, lacing beads onto string or pipe cleaners, putting together snap construction toys and placing blocks in containers. Provide activities that require different motions of each hand (such as a wind-up toy, where a child has to hold the toy with one hand and wind it up with the other).

Strategies to support children who are exceptionally able

According to the Scottish Network for Able Pupils (SNAP, 2011), it is vital to plan carefully to challenge children with high intellectual abilities as these children also require additional supports to meet their individual needs. Exceptionally able children benefit from open-ended and self-paced activities that challenge and stimulate their thinking. Generally, these children do not need a high level of repetitive work. Once they have grasped a new concept, they are usually keen to move on. The following strategies may be helpful in supporting children who are exceptionally able:

- Provide open-ended, exploratory activities;
- Plan activities that require the child to use thinking strategies, problem-solving and decision-making;
- Provide opportunities for the child to use creativity and imagination through activities involving design and invention; for example, creating a scene using building blocks or Lego;
- Ensure that the child's social and emotional needs are being addressed within the setting;
- Allow extra time for the child to extend or complete work;
- Use questioning techniques that challenge the child to use higher-order thinking skills and direct more complex language towards exceptionally able children;
- Consider using ICT as a tool to extend activities and provide additional challenges for an exceptionally able child, as appropriate.

Intentional leadership: responding to and supporting children with SEN/disabilities

In order to adopt an intentional leadership role in supporting the inclusion of children with SEN in the early years, it is essential that those in a leadership (e.g., SENCO, InCo) have a clear understanding of how SEN and/or disabilities can impact upon a child, and their implications for the meaningful inclusion of that child. It is essential that leaders such as SENCOs lead by example and advise educators about the profiles associated with particular disabilities and potential early indicators that may signal the need for further observation or investigation. Leaders (SENCO/InCo) are in a unique position to support and mentor the ECEC staff in the setting, with a view to ensuring that there is a shared whole-setting commitment to supporting inclusion and that evidence-based decisions are being made to enable children with SEN/disabilities to maximise their full potential. Through leading and embedding an inclusive culture in the ECEC setting, the SENCO/inclusion coordinator can support the ECEC staff to plan for, implement and review inclusive practice and in so doing, meet the individual needs of children with SEN/disabilities and ensure that the ECEC setting is meeting their rights to equal participation alongside their peers.

3

ATTITUDES, VALUES AND BELIEFS

Introduction

As discussed in Chapter 1: 'Introduction', quality inclusive early childhood education and care settings and programmes are underpinned by a series of key components. Underwood and Frankel (2012) identify these as:

1. Accessible to all children and their families;
2. Designed, and implemented with consideration for the unique needs, and abilities of each child;
3. Include ongoing evaluation of programmes to ensure children's full participation.

In addition, inclusive settings are characterised by:

- Policies that promote inclusion;
- Leadership that supports inclusion;
- Staff who believe in inclusion (Underwood, 2013).

This book is concerned with meaningful and effective inclusion. Therefore, as mentioned in Chapter 1, inclusion is not just about physical presence in a setting where a child with a disability is expected to simply fit in (Moloney & McCarthy, 2010). Rather, meaningful inclusion is dependent upon two critical but interrelated factors: staff who understand, believe in and are committed to inclusion, and leadership that supports inclusion. In relation to the latter, this book reinforces the notion that leadership for inclusion is paramount. Accordingly, when it comes to inclusion, robust, intentional leadership is essential in order to progress from tokenistic to meaningful and effective inclusion.

To be intentional is to be deliberate and purposeful in everything you do. When applied to the concept of inclusion, being deliberate and purposeful is critical. It means that inclusion is not left to chance, that somebody – or a number of people – within the ECEC setting (see Chapter 4) takes responsibility for inclusion, ensuring that participation moves beyond being physically present, to enabling all children with and without disabilities to fully participate in all aspects of daily life within the setting. Adopting an 'intentional leadership for inclusion' role, this person/s must be committed to enhancing learning experiences for all children, increasing their own professional learning and development, maintaining 'a high level of professional specialism' (Robertson & Messenger, 2010), as well as motivating and encouraging others to embrace and uphold inclusive practices.

Intentional leadership for inclusion is focused upon challenging stereotypical attitudes and behaviours, supporting and empowering children and families, and where necessary, advocating on their behalf. It is about ensuring that policies that promote inclusion become much more than reference documents lying idly on a shelf. Any policy in the setting that purports to support inclusion must be implemented, reviewed and revised in a systematic way with the entire staff team, children, parents, families and other professionals, so that each child's full and active participation in all aspects of the setting becomes a reality. Intentional leadership for inclusion helps to create and sustain a culture of inclusion within the ECEC setting. This chapter is concerned with attitudes, values and beliefs and how these impact upon the image of the child, the concept of inclusion, and approaches to working with children in early childhood education and care settings.

Attitudes towards inclusion

Although international initiatives (e.g., United Nations, UNESCO, WHO, UNICEF) have contributed to the consensus that children with disabilities should be cared for and educated in inclusive settings, families often face challenges when attempting to secure ECEC for their child (Baker-Ericzén, Mueggenborg, & Shea, 2009; Moloney & McCarthy, 2010) particularly if the child has moderate to severe disabilities (Odom et al., 2004). The reluctance to include children with disabilities may be associated with early years providers' and educators' attitudes towards inclusion, which is considered to be one of the most vital aspects of meaningful inclusion practices (Moloney & McCarthy, 2010; Ostrosky, Laumann & Hsieh, 2006; Purdue, 2009).

With regards to inclusion, everybody has predispositions, some experiences confirm and persuade us in our views, and some repel us. Attitudes towards inclusion, which may be positive or negative, begin in early childhood. They come from within, are deeply ingrained and develop in a myriad of ways and through a range of processes (Mulvihill et al., 2002) including a person's upbringing, education and life experiences. In turn, attitudes shape beliefs relating to the image of the child, how children learn and how adults view themselves in the lives of children (see Figure 3.1).

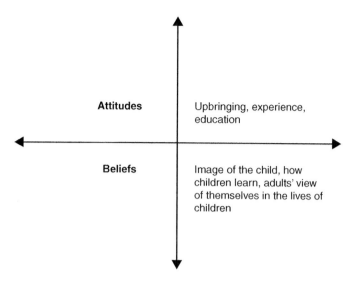

Attitudes

Upbringing, experience, education

Beliefs

Image of the child, how children learn, adults' view of themselves in the lives of children

FIGURE 3.1 Interplay of attitudes and beliefs

In terms of attitudes, Underwood (2013) argues that it is not the diagnosis that defines disability, but the degree to which those working with young children meet the needs of each child, either facilitating their development or creating barriers. Attitudes influence how educators view children and, consequently, shape their approach to working with them, as well as inclusion. Whether consciously or unconsciously educators can either facilitate or create barriers to inclusion. Educators can reinforce negative attitudes and prejudice by the way they act towards children with a disability, the way they draw attention to them or, as discussed in Chapter 2, through their expectations of children. Indeed educators' beliefs about children's abilities transform their behaviours in ways that confirm their initial expectations. Critically, positive attitudes towards inclusion are associated with intentions to act in a positive manner towards children with a disability (Baker-Ericzén et al., 2009), whereas negative attitudes are linked to intentions to act negatively towards children (Levins, Bornholt & Lennon, 2005).

If young children with disabilities are to fully participate and succeed with their peers in the ECEC setting, educators working with them must have corresponding beliefs and skills (Underwood, 2013; Bruns & Mogharreban, 2007). In effect, working with children is significantly influenced by educators' attitudes, values and beliefs, all of which, impact upon inclusion, either enabling or hindering children's participation in all aspects of life within the setting. Such is the importance afforded to attitudes that Lindsay and Dockrell (2002) prioritise them over skills, knowledge and competencies when it comes to successfully including children with disabilities, while UNESCO (2005, p.22) indicate that educator 'attitudes and tolerance are the vehicles for the construction of an inclusive and participatory society'.

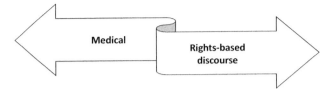

FIGURE 3.2 Opposing discourses associated with the concept of inclusion

Values and beliefs

Although values and beliefs are interrelated, there is a distinctive difference between them. Accordingly, while values relate to principles, ideals or standards of behaviour; beliefs, which are closely linked to attitudes, are deep-rooted convictions that people generally accept as being true. These beliefs influence values and behaviour. As illustrated in Figure 3.1, values and beliefs are influenced by attitudes that are shaped by upbringing, experiences and education. Discussion of values and beliefs inevitably leads to conversations about the concept of inclusion, which is primarily associated with two opposing discourses (Figure 3.2).

Medical discourse results in discrimination, inequity and injustice for children and their families (Booth & Ainscow, 1998; Ballard, 2004). Although we are encouraged to work towards inclusion, Jones (2004) describes how 'the language of SEN, rooted in the medical model of disability, legitimises the idea that some children are normal while others are special' (p.11). Within this construct, Purdue (2009) holds that disability is perceived as a problem that resides within the child. Children with disabilities are seen as different, 'deficient and abnormal, and therefore in need of special and different forms of education and care, preferably in settings other than mainstream education' (Purdue, 2009, p.135). Likewise, Jones (2004) indicates that the medical model allows people to assign specific labels to children, leading to special or segregated provision. Further, Ainscow et al. (2006, p.17) argue that 'categorisation processes, and the practices and language associated with them, act as barriers to the development of a broader view of inclusion'.

PRACTICE SCENARIO

Amelia, a two-year-old, has been attending an early childhood education and care setting for two weeks. Amelia has Apert syndrome, a genetic disorder. She is a happy friendly child, always laughing, and loves other children, who are drawn to her by her sunny disposition. Amelia has webbed hands and feet, and impaired hearing. Because of her webbed feet, she bum-shuffles about the setting. Amelia can hold a cup by grasping it between her hands, using her palms to keep it steady. Her fine motor skills are not well developed, and she is unable to use a spoon for example. She therefore requires her food to be finely cut, so that she can pick it up with her hands.

The manager of the setting has informed Amelia's mother that she will have to source alternative care for her. She explains that setting staff cannot give the time required to cut Amelia's food at meal and snack time, and that she is too slow when eating and, they cannot keep waiting for her to finish.

Consider:

1. What attitudes, values and beliefs are being demonstrated here?
2. What is the barrier to inclusion here?
3. How could this barrier be removed?
4. What role could an inclusion coordinator/SENCO play in supporting the setting to develop inclusive practices?

Rights-based discourse is premised upon the belief that all children have a right to access and avail of quality ECEC in regular settings alongside their peers. Booth and Dyssegaard suggest that

> a concern with 'rights', is seen as an inclusive value, but also depends on the value of equality. People only have rights to the extent that they have them equally. Rights are asserted as a way to stress the fundamental significance of human needs and to persuade others that the recognition of these needs is beyond dispute.
>
> *(Booth & Dyssegaard, 2015, p.8)*

While the Salamanca Statement (UNESCO, 1994) recognises the importance of inclusion of children with a disability in mainstream education, the specific rights of children with a disability are expressed in the UN Convention on the Rights of Persons with Disabilities (UNCRPD, 2006). The UNCRPD is the first internationally legally binding instrument setting minimum standards for rights for people with disabilities, and the first human rights convention to which the EU has become a party.

The UNCRPD, which has 160 signatories has served as a major catalyst in the global movement from viewing people with disabilities as objects of deficit remediation and social protection, towards viewing them as full and equal members of society with human rights. Article 7 of the UNCRPD addresses children with disabilities, placing an obligation upon state parties 'to take all necessary measures to ensure the full enjoyment by children with disabilities of all human rights and fundamental freedoms on an equal basis with other children' (p.7). In addition, the best interests of the child must be a primary consideration in all actions concerning children with disabilities, who have the right to express their views freely on all matters affecting them. They must be provided with 'disability and age-appropriate assistance to realise this right' (p.8).

A child has a fundamental right to be treated as an individual, and not labelled or categorised because of a disability or SEN. In the words of Bray and Gates (2000, p.34) children 'are children first, and their rights, as children, are the most important consideration'. Children therefore, must not be defined by their disability, they are first and foremost children. Accordingly, child-first language is central to inclusion, it shows respect for the child, and puts the child before definitions, descriptions or labels.

Activity: Children-first versus disability-first language

Match the appropriate phase on the right with the disability-first language on the left

He is Down's	She has autism
He is in special education	A child who bites
She is autistic	He has a physical disability
He is physically handicapped	He receives special education services
The biter	He has Down syndrome

This activity demonstrates how language can either reinforce or diminish the message that disabilities reside within the child. To redress this particular obstacle to inclusion, Booth and Dyssegaard (2015) suggest replacing the language of SEN with notions of barriers to learning and participation. This change in language draws attention to the need for educational settings, to remove barriers to inclusion so that they can respond to diversity in a way that values all children equally.

From a rights perspective, the fundamental principle of inclusion is that all children should learn together, regardless of differences or difficulties within mainstream settings. Ainscow et al. (2006) propose that inclusion 'requires us to make explicit the particular values [and] their meanings and implications that we wish to see enacted through education' (p.2). Inclusion is not just about the rights of children with disabilities, it encompasses the rights of all children, families and adults to participate in environments where 'diversity is assumed, welcomed and viewed as a rich resource rather than seen as a problem' (Booth, Nes & Stromstad, 2003, p.2 in Purdue, 2009). Likewise, UNESCO (2005, p.12) promotes the need to see individual differences 'as opportunities for enriching learning'.

Inclusion starts with the premise that an individual has a right to belong to society and its institutions, which therefore implies that others have obligations to ensure that this happens? (Allen, 2005, p. 282).

Think about

1. What are your beliefs about inclusion?
2. Do you believe that children with special educational needs have a right to be cared for and educated in mainstream settings?
3. What role do you play in making sure that this happens?
4. How do you see individual difference? Do you see it as a problem, or as an opportunity to enrich learning? Explain.

The European Agency for Development in Special Needs Education (EADSNE, 2012) identifies four core values relating to teaching and learning that have been identified as the basis for all teachers in inclusive education: valuing leaner diversity; supporting all learners; working with others; and continuing personal professional development. With regards to ECEC specifically, Urban, Robson and Scacchi (2017, p.7) describe professional and personal values 'as the lens through which we interpret professional knowledge [and] orient our making sense of the world and underpin our practices'. They identify a series of values that underpin 'competent professional practice' with young children, families and communities:

1. Children's and human rights to orient towards rights-based pedagogies and practices with all children, families and communities;
2. Democracy as the basis for meaningful participation of all children, families and communities;
3. Respect for diversity as the basis for working towards social justice and more equitable outcomes for all children;
4. Empathy;
5. Early childhood as a public good and public responsibility (Urban et al., 2017, p.7).

While these authors explore ECEC broadly, the values identified are equally pertinent to inclusion discourse. As with any aspect of ECEC, inclusion cannot be left to chance, and achieving the UNESCO (2005) goal as outlined is dependent upon the attitudes, values and beliefs of all those working with young children in the setting. According to UNESCO, 'shared values make cooperation possible' (2005, p.22). This may be problematic if those working with young children in ECEC settings do not hold a shared set of inclusive values and beliefs that are concerned with equality, rights, participation, learning, community, respect for diversity, trust and sustainability, compassion, honesty, courage and joy (Booth & Dyssegaard, 2015) as well as believing in collaboration, and being committed to offering educational opportunities to all children (UNESCO, 2017). In addition, EADSNE (2012) signify the need to work with others and engage in continuing personal professional development as core aspects of inclusion.

Inclusive beliefs are a necessary first step for ECEC educators to provide inclusive services for young children with and without disabilities (Allen & Schwartz, 2001; Stayton, Miller & Dinnebeil, 2003). A shared value system that supports inclusive practices is founded upon the view that diversity in the early years is beneficial for all children. A positive approach to meeting and supporting children's diverse needs within the early years is an essential aspect of the setting's culture and approach to promoting and maintaining inclusive practices. Yet even when educators hold positive beliefs about inclusion, they may not feel confident about their ability to work with children with disabilities (Moloney & McCarthy, 2010). Intentional leadership is essential; somebody in the setting who is committed to turning the vision into reality for children, and working tirelessly to achieve this.

Image of the child

The image of the child is at the very core of inclusion, and cannot be isolated from beliefs about how children learn and develop. Loris Malaguzzi (1993) states that there are hundreds of images of the child, and that as we begin to relate to the child, each of us has an image of the child within us. Where does this image of the child originate? Doubtless it is influenced by cultural beliefs, upbringing, education and experiences. Generally, children are viewed either as full of potential, or as needy and helpless. Consider the contradictory images of the child as proposed by Malaguzzi (1993) shown here:

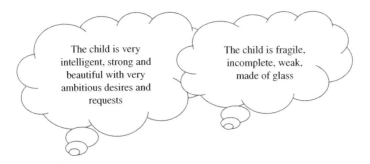

The child is very intelligent, strong and beautiful with very ambitious desires and requests

The child is fragile, incomplete, weak, made of glass

THINK ABOUT

Your image of the child is where your teaching should begin. It pushes you to behave in certain ways towards the child, orients you to talk to, listen to and observe the child (Malaguzzi, 1993).

Question:

1. Which image of the child shown here resonates with you?
2. How was your image of the child shaped?
3. How does it influence your approach to working with children?

In considering your image of the child, it may be that you see children in general as strong, competent, capable and full of potential, while other children, for whatever reason, are perceived by you as needy, vulnerable, helpless and in need of protection.

PRACTICE SCENARIO

Anshul, a 3½-year-old boy, has been diagnosed with autism. He has delayed speech, and communicates using single words. He does not respond to his name being called, even though his hearing is normal. Anshul rejects cuddles and is intolerant of people/children entering his personal space. He has little interest in interacting with people, including children his age, preferring to play alone. He tends to flap his hands repeatedly and plays with toys in a repetitive unimaginative way, lining up blocks by size or colour rather than using them to build. He likes to have a familiar routine, and becomes extremely upset when there are changes to his routine. His parents are anxious about Anshul's social development, and have been searching for an early childhood education and care setting for some time.

Consider:

1. What is your image of Anshul? Why?
2. How would you describe him?
3. What would you say to his parents if they approached you for a place in your setting?

Image of the child within policy

The revised version of *Te Whāriki: Early Childhood Curriculum* in New Zealand was published in 2017. The opening line of the foreword, describes a child as 'a treasure, to be nurtured, to grow to flourish' – 'He taonga te mokopuna, kia whāngaia, kia tipu, kia rea' (Ministry of Education, New Zealand, 2017, p.2). Acknowledging that 'all children are born with immense potential', *Te Whāriki* expresses the vision that 'all children grow up in New Zealand as competent and confident learners, strong in their identity, language and culture' (p.2). Congruent with *Te Whāriki*, early childhood curricula internationally recognise the intrinsic value of early childhood, the uniqueness of each child and promote an image of the child as a competent and confident learner. See for example, *Belonging, Being and Becoming* (Australia, Australian Government Department of Education, 2009); *Aistear: The Early Childhood Curriculum Framework* (Ireland, NCCA, 2009); *Framework Plan for the Content and Tasks of Kindergartens* (Ministry for Education and Research, Norway, 2011); *Curriculum for the Preschool Lpfö 98* (Sweden, Skolverket, 2010) and *National Core Curriculum for Early Childhood Education and Care* (Finland, Finnish National Board of Education, 2016). In addition to the positive image of the child portrayed through these various curricula, they also emphasise a nurturing playful pedagogy (see Chapters 5 and 6) as being paramount to children's learning and development in early childhood. These positive values, when coupled with personal and professional values and beliefs, inform our philosophy of early childhood education and care, and our approach to working with young children. Of course, other factors, including national and international policy agendas are also salient, and play a significant role.

Because of international and national policy agendas and priorities, understandings relating to the purpose of and approaches to early childhood education and care vary greatly between countries. Moloney and Pettersen (2017) argue that 'today, the sector is closely aligned to the discourse of early intervention… eliminating child poverty, and fostering social inclusion within an increasingly diverse population' (p. 2). They further suggest that in many countries, governments have high expectations of the sector in terms of optimising child outcomes in preparation for school readiness. This assertion is increasingly supported by the Organisation for Economic Co-operation and Development (OECD) and by individual government agendas. There is an emerging trend towards formalising early childhood education, typified by prescribed curricula and ongoing standardised assessment. For example, in the UK, a stated objective of the Early Years Foundation Stage (EYFS) is to promote teaching and learning to ensure children's school readiness (DfE, 2017c). Likewise, at the time of writing, the OECD is in the process of initiating the International Early Learning Study (IELS), a cross-national assessment of early learning outcomes involving the testing of children between 4½ to 5½ years in 3–6 participating countries initially (OECD, 2016, p.18). Moloney (2017) argues that the IELS' focus upon comparative education represents a narrow interpretation of early childhood education, as well as a considerable shift away from the concept of holistic child development that recognises that children are not divided up into separate domains, learning styles, intelligences, attitudes, dispositions or creativities. Indeed, the IELS is at odds with the early childhood curricula in countries including New Zealand, Australia, Ireland, Norway, Sweden and Finland as mentioned previously. While it could be argued that the IELS views the child as a confident and competent learner, it nonetheless, 'actively contradicts the rights of children, families and communities to meaningful participation in all matters concerning and affecting the upbringing and education of young children' (Urban & Swadener, 2017, p. 7) as embedded within the UN Convention on the Rights of Persons with Disabilities (UNCRPD, 2006). Furthermore, Moss et al. (2017) argue that the IELS 'rests on the principle that everything can be reduced to a common outcome, standard or measure… [it cannot] accommodate diversity – of paradigm or theory, pedagogy or provision, childhood or culture' (p.348). These authors question how the IELS can be applied to such 'diversity, places and people who do not share its positions, understandings, assumptions and values' (p.348). The initiation of the IELS calls into question the image of the child. Not only are there hundreds of images of the child, Malaguzzi (1993) also proposes that children have 100 languages. Malaguzzi is, of course, referring to the myriad ways in which children learn and express themselves; for example, talking, drawing, writing, clay modelling, dancing, acting, sculpture. The 100 languages of children embodies diversity, allowing for children's individual abilities, interests and needs. Just as the child in the song in Chapter 1, is prevented from seeing the *colours in the rainbow*, the risk with the IELS is that it will 'rob them [children] of ninety-nine, school and culture' (Malaguzzi, 1993).

Rather than emphasising formal learning in early childhood, inclusion is concerned with hands-on, experiential, active and cooperative learning, which is underpinned by a nurturing and responsive pedagogy (see Chapter 6). This has significant implications for ECEC educators, not just in relation to their attitudes, values, beliefs, knowledge and skills, but also their individual and collective roles and responsibilities with regards to inclusion. It also revolves around their image of the child. Educators are tasked with viewing ECEC through an 'inclusive lens' (UNESCO, 2005, p.27), which implies a shift in how we see the child. Rather than viewing the child with disabilities as a problem, we must see him/her as an opportunity to enhance learning experiences, and learning for all children. The challenge is to recognise the problems within the setting that impede inclusion, and to resolve these through inclusive approaches. In ECEC, educators must consider what happens in practice, based upon how we construct our own view of what it is to be inclusive (Nutbrown, Clough & Atherton, 2013).

Empowering early childhood educators

In addition to educators' attitudes, concerns about their competence to support a child with disabilities, and the lack of specialised training and support for them to include children with disabilities is a considerable impediment to inclusion (Mulvihill, Cotton, & Gyaben, 2004; Moloney & McCarthy, 2010; Kaplan & Lewis, 2013). In fact, research (e.g., Mulvihill et al., 2002; Moloney & McCarthy, 2010) points to a strong relationship between training and educators' attitudes towards inclusion. According to Kaplan and Lewis (2013, p.2) training provided during pre-service programmes 'shapes teachers' attitudes, knowledge and competencies, and influences their subsequent work with their own students' leading to better quality care and education (Moloney & McCarthy, 2010).

A study undertaken in San Diego by Baker-Ericzén et al. (2009), in which they utilised a pre- and post-questionnaire, found that educators' attitudes toward and perceived competence of inclusion increased following specialised training. They also found that the more training a provider received, the greater the gains. Thus, providers who attended three or more topic-specific training sessions displayed the most positive attitudes toward inclusion, and demonstrated the greatest perceived competence regarding how to include a children with a disability into their programme. Similarly, a qualitative study undertaken in Ireland, by Moloney and McCarthy (2010), concluded that educators were more positive in their attitudes towards inclusion, felt more confident in their ability to support children with disabilities and had achieved the ultimate goal of enhancing the quality of children's experiences within settings following a 12-week specialised training programme.

The critical factor in their study was the ongoing mentoring provided to educators while engaging in the training programme, which enabled them to change some of the key behaviours that acted as barriers to inclusion, including: organising the learning environment; enhancing communication with children, parents, colleagues and other professionals; observing, documenting and observing children's participation in the day-to-day activities of the setting, and planning for their ongoing learning and development. These findings resonate with Lewis and Bagree (2013) and Kaplan and Lewis (2013) who posit that the concept of inclusion only makes sense once it is seen in practice.

Bridging the theory–practice divide is therefore essential, and while it is vital for educators to grasp the theory behind a concept, inclusion is not a simple concept (Kaplan & Lewis, 2013).

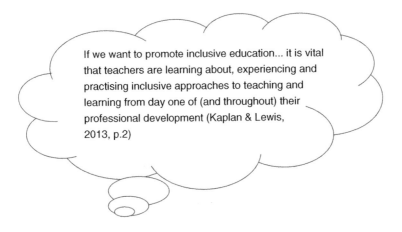

If we want to promote inclusive education... it is vital that teachers are learning about, experiencing and practising inclusive approaches to teaching and learning from day one of (and throughout) their professional development (Kaplan & Lewis, 2013, p.2)

In 2016/17, PLÉ Ireland[1] explored students' perceptions of the practical training component of their undergraduate degree in ECEC. All of the 101 participating students agreed that practical training was critical to enabling them to 'put theory into practice'. They declared that it is not possible to 'learn how to work with young people at lectures alone' and that 'a lot is learned on placement that cannot be learned from books and lectures alone' (Moloney, 2017). When it comes to inclusion, Kaplan and Lewis note that 'like many aspects of good teaching, inclusive education cannot be taught effectively through theory-based approaches alone' (2013, p.13). When undertaking pre-service or in-service training, therefore, it is imperative that students have opportunities to practise inclusive approaches to working with young children; to observe them, identify their particular strengths and learning needs, and ways to support and enhance them. Such practical experiences may reduce the reluctance associated with working with young children with disabilities, as students and educators become familiar with pedagogical strategies, environmental and curricular adaptations etc.

Lewis and Bagree (2013) suggest that a 'twin track' approach to inclusion is required (see Figure 3.3), which involves making ECEC a welcoming and positive

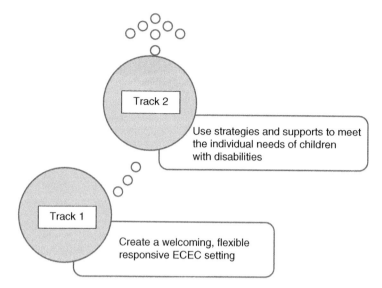

FIGURE 3.3 Twin track approach to inclusion

experience for children, and being sufficiently confident and skilled to meet the specific needs of children with disabilities (p.10).

The practical application of this twin track approach involves educators in knowing how to create a welcoming, flexible and responsive learning environment that meets the learning and participation needs of children with disabilities. This can be achieved through appropriate initial training, continual training and professional development, and ongoing access to adequate high quality support and advice from specialist personnel (Lewis & Bagree, 2013). While it is considered vital that trainee educators learn about inclusion from day one of their training, so that inclusive teaching and learning is seen as a natural aspect of their job, it is equally essential that those already working with children, participate in ongoing professional development that supports them to reflect upon their attitudes and practices and work toward improving the inclusiveness of their settings.

As mentioned in Chapter 1, in an effort to increase access to and the meaningful participation of children with disabilities in ECEC, the Irish government launched the Access and Inclusion Model (AIM) in 2016. This comprehensive, child-centred model involves seven levels of progressive support, moving from universal to targeted, based on the needs of both the child and the setting (see Figure 3.4). Its goal is to empower educators to deliver an inclusive ECEC experience for all children (www.aim.gov.ie). The model is designed to be responsive to the needs of each individual child in the context of his/her ECEC setting.

As shown in Figure 3.4, a qualified and confident workforce is central to the AIM. As part of the model, a new higher education programme, *Leadership for Inclusion in the Early Years* (LINC), commenced in September 2016. Specifically, this programme seeks to address the need for continuing professional development

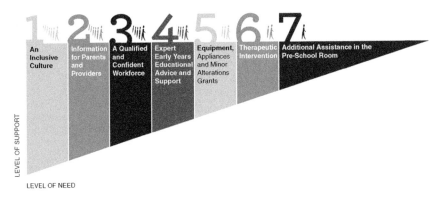

FIGURE 3.4 Access and Inclusion Model
Department of Children and Youth Affairs (DCYA) and Department of Education and
Skills (DES) 2016.

(CPD) within the ECEC sector in Ireland, in relation to the inclusion of children
with disabilities. Its primary objectives are to:

• Equip participants with the knowledge, understanding, skills and competencies to support the participation of children with disabilities in ECEC settings.
• Prepare participants to adopt a leadership role within settings that enables them
to support and supervise other staff in the setting to plan for, implement and
review inclusive practice (adapted from www.linkprogramme.ie).

The DCYA funds up to 900 places per annum on this programme. Participants
must already be working in the sector and be nominated by their employer/setting.

For in-service training to be effective, it must use specific strategies such as
focusing upon specific content areas, allowing opportunities for students to apply
the knowledge and practice, and providing ongoing professional development with
follow-up support. (e.g., Bowman, Donovan & Burns, 2001; Brownell, Ross, Colon
& McCallum, 2005). The LINC programme, which runs for a full academic year,
involves all these elements, offering a suite of topic specific modules: child development; inclusion in early years settings: concepts and strategies; curriculum for
inclusion, promoting collaborative practice for inclusion in early childhood education and care; leadership for inclusion; and a portfolio module. It also provides
a mentoring visit to participants' ECEC setting to support students' professional
learning in leading the inclusion of children with disabilities in the early years.

Intentional leadership relating to attitudes, values and beliefs

Working with children is significantly influenced by educators' attitudes, values and
beliefs, which can either enable or hinder children's meaningful participation in all
aspects of the early childhood education and care setting. Reluctance to include

children with disabilities may be associated with early years providers' and educators' attitudes towards inclusion. Four core values identified by (EADSNE, 2012) relate to: valuing leaner diversity; supporting all learners; working with others; and continuing personal professional development. Lewis and Bagree (2013) propose a twin track approach to inclusion that involves educators in knowing how to create a welcoming, flexible and responsive learning environment that meets the learning and participation needs of young children with disabilities. They further indicate that educators must see inclusive teaching and learning as a natural aspect of their job, and in common with EADSNE (2012), that they participate in ongoing professional development that supports them to reflect upon their attitudes and practices and work toward improving the inclusiveness of their setting.

However, inclusion cannot be left to chance, it is dependent upon intentional leadership. The LINC programme as part of the Access and Inclusion Model (DCYA, 2016) is intended to enable graduates to take on a new leadership role of inclusion coordinator within their ECEC setting. The DCYA (2016, p.79) perceives this role in terms of supporting management by providing leadership in the area of inclusion of children with a disability in the setting: 'Leadership in the early years entails "crafting and implementing the vision of the early childhood service and then leading a team culture which reflects that vision, strives for high performance, and embodies inclusive practice".'

It is also proposed that InCos will support and supervise other staff in the setting to plan for, implement and review inclusive practice. Similarly, in England, settings are required to identify a member of staff to act as special educational needs coordinator (SENCO) who must have regard to the Special Educational Needs Code of Practice (2015), which provides statutory guidance on duties, policies and procedures. There is considerable overlap between the role of the InCo in Ireland, and the role of the SENCO, which involves:

- ensuring all practitioners in the setting understand their responsibilities to children with SEN and the setting's approach to identifying and meeting SEN;
- advising and supporting colleagues;
- ensuring parents are closely involved throughout and that their insights inform action taken by the setting; and
- liaising with professionals or agencies beyond the setting.

Drawing upon both roles, therefore, an initial attempt at delineating the components of intentional leadership for inclusion can be made. It is evident that the role is multifaceted, and involves providing vision and leadership, and garnering support for inclusion. Because attitudes values and beliefs are fundamental to inclusive practices, the intentional leader must model positive attitudes and values, and challenge stereotypical behaviours. To support educators in developing positive attitudes and values, the intentional leader encourages them to participate in ongoing professional development opportunities where they can become familiar with pedagogical approaches, curricular and environmental adaptations, etc., to enhance children's experiences in settings. As mentioned earlier, such practical experiences may reduce the reluctance associated with working with young children with disabilities.

The intentional leader works to empower educators to develop and/or enhance inclusive practice through reflection and cooperative team work within the setting. In this regard, the intentional leader takes responsibility for the development of a culture of inclusion within the setting and the nurturing of critical thinking skills, both of which are essential if inclusion is to become a reality (Myers & Bagree, 2011). Critically, an inclusive culture is dependent upon robust, intentional leadership so that the setting can progress from tokenistic to meaningful, and effective inclusion. Naturally, intentional leaders' own attitudes, values and beliefs about inclusion are critical to aligning the setting's culture with the core values identified in this chapter as being central to inclusion.

Note

1   PLÉ is the national association of third-level institutions in Ireland offering degree-level training in Early Childhood Education and Care in Ireland.

4

LEADING AND SUSTAINING AN INCLUSIVE CULTURE

Introduction

This chapter explores the relationship between leadership and the establishment and maintenance of an inclusive culture in ECEC. While intentional leadership assures the quality of the setting, it is imperative to inclusion. As discussed in Chapter 1, while historically inclusion has been associated with SEN, today it has a wider focus that encompasses all children, including those from ethnic and linguistic minorities, children with HIV, nomadic children, children living in poverty, refugees, rural populations, children with disabilities and any 'at-risk' children (UNESCO, 2009). Accordingly, the vision of the European Agency for Special Needs and Inclusive Education (2015, p.1) is to 'ensure that all learners of any age are provided with meaningful, high-quality educational opportunities in their local community, alongside their friends and peers'. In Ireland, this vision is interpreted as fostering and embedding a strong culture of inclusion 'to support all children's maximum participation' within the setting (Report of the Interdepartmental Group, 2015, p.7). Although culture is not easy to define, Bolman and Deal (2008) provide insight into the variables associated with the concept, describing it as 'the superglue that bonds an organization, unites people, and helps an enterprise accomplish desired ends' (p.253).

Throughout this book, a range of components that underpin inclusive practice are discussed, including professional values and beliefs, the learning environment, curriculum, assessment, support strategies, collaborative working and so on. However, even when these elements are present, they may not ensure that an inclusive culture has been established throughout the entire ECEC setting. Intentional leadership that supports inclusion must therefore be fostered and supported, to provide the 'superglue' that unites, motivates and empowers all early years educators to work towards a common goal; that of creating an inclusive culture within the entire setting. In fact the Division for Early Childhood (DEC, 2015, p.1) underlines a need to 'purposefully build and sustain leadership capital across all domains of practice', from national macro-level through to setting micro-level. This is about much more than developing and publishing macro-level inclusion policies and initiatives. Rather, it is about enabling and supporting those working with young children to translate macro-level policies/initiatives into practice in the daily life of the setting micro-level. It challenges governments in individual countries to commit to the principles of inclusion, to invest heavily in the implementation of macro inclusion policies/initiatives, (e.g., financial incentives to employ additional staff, enable staff to undertake continual professional development, purchase specialised equipment and materials, etc.). Commitment at national level creates a domino effect ensuring that policy documents do not just sit on a shelf gathering dust but become living documents that are proactively enacted within the setting micro-level.

Inclusive culture

As stated, defining culture is not an easy task, and in the context of inclusion in ECEC, a distinction must be drawn between culture that refers to the habits, values, customs, beliefs, procedures, behavioural conventions, artefacts and traditions of various societal groupings (Graham, 2017), and culture as it relates to the setting. ECEC settings generally comprise a diversity of children and families from indigenous and minority ethnic groups, as well as exceptionally able children, children with SEN, refugee children, etc. The staff team working with the children in the setting may also be diverse in its composition across multiple domains; ethnicity, experience and education, all of which influence attitudes, values and beliefs (see Chapter 3) and, by extension, the setting's culture.

Schein (2004) indicates that cultures derive from three sources: the beliefs, values, and assumptions of the founders[1] of the organisation (setting); the learning experiences of group members (staff) as the setting evolves; and new beliefs, values and assumptions brought in by new members and leaders. Whereas Blandford and Knowles (2016) suggest that culture is shaped by the 'social environment, the backdrop against which the processes in the setting take place, the management systems, policies and structures of the setting and, the actions and behaviours of those working in the setting' (pp.341–343), there is little doubt that all six factors identified by Schein (2004) and Blandford and Knowles (2016), which are located within the micro-level (see Chapter 9), are crucial to establishing an inclusive culture. However, macro-level factors, especially government commitment to the principles of inclusion, dedicated fiscal support for enacting inclusive policies and initiatives must not be overlooked. Likewise, at micro setting level, staff qualifications and training, commitment to the principles of inclusion, collaborative working and leadership for inclusion are also critical factors. With this in mind, Figure 4.1 provides an overview of the macro- and micro-level factors that influence the setting's culture.

Establishing an inclusive culture begins with the manager of the setting, whom Schein (2004) considers the most important factor for cultural beginnings. It is

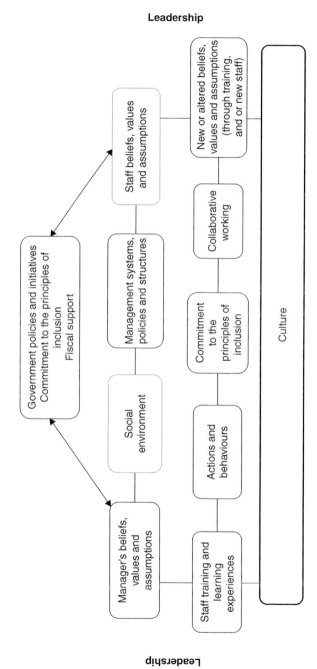

FIGURE 4.1 Overview of macro- and micro-level factors that influence inclusive culture

the manager who not only decides the basic purpose and the environmental context in which the setting operates, s/he also selects the staff team, and invariably imposes his/her assumptions on them (Schein, 2004). If the setting's manager is not committed to the principles of inclusion, it is unlikely that a culture of inclusion will be fostered. It is essential, therefore, that somebody committed to the principles of inclusion assumes a leadership role and takes responsibility for inclusion within the setting.

Becoming more inclusive involves 'thinking and talking, reviewing and refining practice, and making attempts to develop a more inclusive culture' (Muijs, Ainscow, Chapman & West, 2011, p.92). But what is an inclusive culture? How is it defined, and what are its characteristics? One way of looking at an inclusive culture is to think in terms of a set of principles. In Ireland, for example, the DCYA (2016, p.4) outline 11 principles of an inclusive culture in an ECEC setting:

1. Working in partnership and openly communicating with the child's family;
2. Working in partnership with outside agencies that may be involved with the family;
3. Actively promoting equal opportunities and anti-bias practices, so that all children and families feel included and valued;
4. Having robust policies and procedures – inclusion policy, equal opportunities policy;
5. Recognising and valuing that all children are unique and will develop and learn at their own rate;
6. Utilising the AIM programme to meet the needs of children and recognising that not all children with disabilities will require additional support;
7. Encouraging children to recognise their individual qualities and the characteristics they share with peers;
8. Actively engaging children in making decisions about their own learning;
9. Respecting the diversity of the child, their family and community throughout the early childhood service;
10. Understanding that children have individual needs, views, cultures and beliefs, which need to be treated with respect and represented throughout early childhood services;
11. Reflecting on your own attitudes and values.

In keeping with the discussion in Chapter 3, and drawing upon these 11 principles, an inclusive culture is strongly associated with educator values, beliefs and attitudes. Clearly the culture within the setting dictates the atmosphere, and conveys what is valued and what is not valued. The culture determines the extent to which individual difference is embraced as an opportunity for learning, or perceived as a problem within the setting. The culture becomes evident within minutes of entering an ECEC setting. It is apparent in the welcome, how children's work is displayed, the imagery placed about the setting (e.g., showing people of various cultural groups engaged in both similar and different activities; reflecting diversity in family types and configurations; reflecting children of differing abilities), the children's play, the educator's demeanour, the organisation of the learning environment, the interactions between educators and children, with parents and families, and with each other. These observable features are indicative of the shared values and beliefs of the members of the setting, i.e., the staff. This feeling has no metric, it cannot be quantified; it is cultural and derives its success from exemplary leadership (Schubart, 2007).

Chapter 3 suggests that if educators are negative about inclusion, it will reflect upon the culture and practices within the setting. It follows that if educators believe in, and support inclusion, it will be reflected in the setting's philosophy, values and beliefs. Consequently, the setting will have an inclusive participative culture. According to Barr (2016), true inclusion is about more than meeting the needs of unique learners. It involves creating a whole culture in which everyone is valued, included, and able to learn and work together. The overall thrust of an inclusive culture is that all those who engage with the early years setting (e.g., children, families, staff, early intervention team) are respected and valued. Rather than viewing difference as problematic, and reacting to the challenges of inclusion, settings should consider proactively incorporating it, so that all children are welcomed, respected and prepared for the world (Barr, 2016).

As indicted in Figure 4.1, commitment to the principles of inclusion is a core aspect of an inclusive culture. This includes – but is not confined to – recognising and valuing that all children are unique and will develop and learn at their own pace, respecting the diversity of the child, their family and community, promoting equal opportunities and anti-bias practices, so that all children and families feel included and valued. Moreover, collaborative working (which comprises eight elements, see Figure 4.2) involves educators, families and multi-disciplinary teams, for example, working together in the best interests of the child (see Chapter 9), and is fundamental to the establishment and maintenance of an inclusive culture.

Collaboration is demonstrated in teams, where goals are clearly established, there is shared decision-making, and all members of the team feel respected and that their contribution is valued (Bridges et al., 2011). Translating core values and beliefs into practice within the setting is not as simple as it sounds. Teamwork can be difficult to achieve, and the skills of teamwork (see Chapter 9) should be viewed in a leadership context rather than a case of just muddling through on a day-to-day basis. The process of working collaboratively demands leadership *within*, rather than *of*, teams (Read & Rees, 2010).

Defining leadership

The relationship between leadership and quality in the provision of ECEC is unquestionable. Yet, the concept of leadership remains ambiguous, and there is no single universally understood definition. In fact, as noted by Moloney and Pettersen (2017), the literature relating to the early years is underscored by a

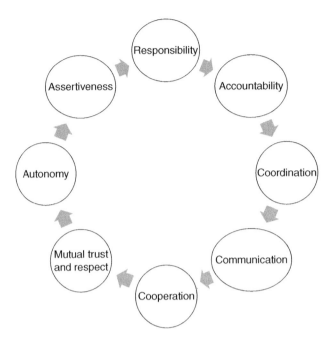

FIGURE 4.2 Elements associated with collaborative working
Adapted from: Bridges, Davidson, Soule Odegard, Maki & Tomkowiak (2011).

leadership/management dichotomy. They suggest that management is concerned with dealing with the different daily tasks in an appropriate manner, whereas leadership is strategic, and focused upon the relationship between the manager and the staff team, and the ability of the manager to create an atmosphere where every individual in the setting works as best they can to achieve agreed aims and objectives. Schein (2004) also identifies a crucial distinction between leadership and management, noting that leaders are concerned with culture, whereas managers are more focused upon processes, structure and control (Moloney & Pettersen, 2017).

According to Schön (1983), leadership tends to be more symbolic in nature; somebody can fulfil the symbolic, inspirational and educational functions of a leader, without any of the burdens of management. Likewise, somebody can manage without leading, monitoring and controlling the activities of the setting, making decisions, allocating resources and so on, without fulfilling the symbolic, inspirational and educational functions of leadership (Schön, 1983). As highlighted by Moloney and Pettersen (2017) Schön's intention was not to distinguish between the role of leader and manager. He went on to say that since we usually expect a manager to lead, it may be permissible to treat management and leadership as one. Indeed many texts relating to leadership and management in the early years adapt this stance, using both concepts interchangeably (e.g., Jones & Pound, 2008; Miller & Cable, 2011). Furthermore, as indicated by Isles-Buck and Newstead (2003), since the distinction between leadership and management may be overdrawn, leadership is seen as part of management.

Pointing to the unprecedented and escalating demands being placed upon those working with young children in ECEC settings, including the introduction of curriculum frameworks, regulatory regimes, inclusion initiatives, funding schemes etc., Fasoli, Scrivens and Woodrow (2007) see leadership as strategic, and associated with vision and values. The field of ECEC is continually changing and increasingly complex (Moloney & Pettersen, 2017), and in the words of Fasoli et al.:

> Roles are changing and expanding. Old solutions to issues and problems do not always work. These 'change challenges' suggest a real imperative for the field to develop new and robust frameworks for leadership that can support people in facing, grappling with, initiating and facilitating change rather than simply reacting.
>
> *(Fasoli et al., 2007, pp.232–233)*

These authors have identified a core aspect of the role and responsibility of a leader within an early years setting; that of supporting colleagues to face, grapple with, initiate and facilitate change. Such actions are part and parcel of establishing and maintaining a setting's culture. As indicated earlier, the leader begins 'the culture creation process and, must also manage and sometimes change the culture' (Schein, 2004, p.223).

In 2006, Janet Moyles developed the Effective Leadership and Management Scheme (ELMS) for the early years, which explored and established a typology of qualities of effective leadership and management. With regards to leading and managing change, she calls upon managers to be culture setters, which involves creating an ethos that is appropriate to the setting, being receptive to the atmosphere of the setting and the attitude of staff, and tuning them into the culture (Moyles, 2006, p.66). The ELMS proposes three further elements of being a culture setter:

1. Being able to understand what is good practice for settings generally, and what is good practice for the setting in particular;
2. Being influential, leading by example and being a transformational leader who transforms values and beliefs into ethos and culture;
3. Identifying and defining values and ethics within the setting – may involve communicating values explicitly and physically through documents such as mission statements and ensuring staff like-mindedness (Moyles, 2006, p.66).

While culture is created by shared experience, it is the leader (e.g., the manager) who initiates the process by imposing his/her beliefs, values and assumptions at the outset (Schein, 2004). In the end, as stated by Waniganayake and Semann (2011, p.24), leadership within the ECEC setting is 'a journey of joint inquiry, exploration and reflection that can involve everyone who believes in making a difference for children'. In the context of inclusion, the DEC (2015) views leadership as a process of mutual influence and shared responsibility. This influence process is enacted by individuals and teams working together to develop a shared vision and purpose. Hence, leadership is both an individual and collective ethical responsibility. It requires deep human qualities that include, but go beyond conventional notions of authority (Lewis & Hill, 2012). Consequently, the traditional concept of a leader as being an individual at the top of a hierarchy is an incomplete appreciation of what true leadership must be (Lewis & Hill, 2012). True leadership, then, is concerned with purpose and, in relation to inclusion that purpose is to establish, support and maintain an inclusive culture. This involves encouraging and supporting the staff team to translate the setting's vision into practice, to lead by example and to make connections with children, families, communities and other relevant organisations. When it comes to children, Jones and Pound (2008) suggest that the quality of leadership and management is paramount in determining the extent to which a setting meets young children's individual needs.

Biddle (2010) identifies three variables, known as the 'three Rs' that affect leadership and contribute to organisational success (see Figure 4.3).

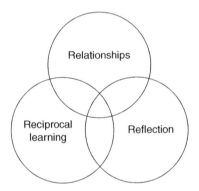

FIGURE 4.3 Overview of the variables that affect leadership

- **Relationships**: Sharing roles and responsibilities among the group creates a strong network of relationships. Leadership must be a collective relationship where individuals are both shapers of and shaped by one another;
- **Reciprocal learning:** Leadership is about learning together and constructing meaning and knowledge collectively and collaboratively;
- **Reflection:** In the process of leadership, individuals collectively reflect upon their work to gain insight and to create effective action (Biddle, 2010).

Yukl (2013) associates leadership with the 'process of influencing others to understand and agree about what needs to be done and how to do it, and the process of facilitating individual and collective efforts to accomplish shared objectives'(p.7). Kagan (2013) proposes an alternative perspective, that resonates with Biddle (2010) stating that leadership involves individuals engaging colleagues in 'reflective, dynamic, value-based planning and organising that provides vision, inspiration, structure and direction' (p.34). Regardless of how leadership is defined, in terms of establishing and maintaining an inclusive culture within ECEC settings, who leads and how they lead is critical. While the concept of leadership is located at the interface of relationships – shared vision, values, beliefs, planning, enacting and reflection – it is also underpinned by leadership theory that addresses the question of what makes certain people become leaders. It determines leadership style and is linked to professional values and beliefs.

Leadership theory

The eight major theories of leadership can be summarised as: great man, trait, contingency, situational, behavioural, participative, transactional and relationship theories.

1. **Great man theory**: Associated with the concept of 'born leaders', this theory was popularised in the 1840s by Thomas Carlyle. It suggests that great leaders are simply born with inherent characteristics such as charisma, confidence, intelligence and social skills that make them natural-born leaders. Hence leaders are born, not made. This theory often portrays leaders as heroic, mythic and destined to rise to leadership when required. The term 'great man' was used, because at the time, leadership was primarily thought of as a male quality, especially in terms of military leadership;

2. **Trait theory**: Similar in some ways to great man theory, trait theory assumes that people inherit certain qualities and traits that make them better suited to leadership. This theory is associated with personality, social, physical or intellectual traits (e.g., ambition, energy, a desire to lead, intelligence, self-confidence) that differentiate leaders from non-leaders. Although it is similar to great man theory, trait theory is more systematic in its analysis of leaders, but its fundamental premise assumes that the leader's personal traits are key to leadership success;

3. **Contingency theory** (also known as Fiedler's contingency theory) argues that there is no one best way of leading, and that a leadership style that is effective in some situations may not be successful in others. The leader's ability to lead, is therefore contingent upon particular variables related to the environment that might determine which particular style of leadership is best suited for the situation. Success is dependent upon on a number of variables, including leadership style, the qualities of the followers and aspects of the situation;

4. **Situational theory** is founded on the notion that there is no one perfect style of leadership. It proposes that leaders choose the best course of action based upon situational conditions or circumstances. According to Hersey and Blanchard (1982), the motivation and the abilities of the leader affects his/her decision in a given situation. Hersey and Blanchard group leadership into four styles of leadership: delegating, supporting, coaching and directing. Each of

these leadership styles can be effective, depending on the developmental level of the individual or group that is being led. Different styles of leadership may therefore be more appropriate for certain types of decision-making. How you lead is not just a question of your skills and abilities, it also depends on your followers' abilities and attitudes;

5. **Behavioural theory** contests both great man and trait theories. It attempts to describe leadership in terms of what leaders *do*, rather than emphasising what leaders *are*. Rooted in behaviourism, this theory focuses upon the actions of leaders, suggesting that leadership ability is defined by what the leader does. According to behavioural theory, people can learn to become leaders through training and observation (Amanchukwu, Stanley & Ololube, 2015). The LINC training currently being rolled out in Ireland, and discussed in Chapter 3, is an example of such an attempt to train inclusion coordinators (leaders). Naylor (1999, in Amanchukwu et al., 2015) notes that interest in leader's behaviour has been stimulated by a systematic comparison of autocratic and democratic leadership styles. Groups under these types of leadership perform differently:
    - Groups led by autocratic leaders work well while the leader is present. However, group members tend to be unhappy with the leadership style and express hostility;
    - Although democratically led groups do almost as well as the autocratic group, members tend to be more positive. Critically, the efforts of the group members continue even when the leader is absent (Amanchukwu et al., 2015, p.8);

6. **Participative theory** involves consultation, joint decision-making, power-sharing, decentralisation and democratic management (Filosa, 2012, p.15), as well as empowerment (Yukl, 2013). It suggest that the ideal leadership style is one that takes the input of others into account. These leaders encourage participation and contributions from group members and, help them feel more relevant and committed to the decision-making process. The leader, however, retains the right to allow the input of others;

7. **Transactional theory** (also known as managerial leadership) assumes that people are motivated by reward and punishment. It focuses upon the role of supervision, organisation and group performance. This is an authoritative model of leadership, where the leader is required to 'set goals, articulate explicit agreements regarding what the leader expects from organizational members and how they will be rewarded for their efforts and commitment, and provide constructive feedback to keep everybody on task' (Vera & Crossan, 2004, p.224). The primary focus is upon maintaining the status quo, and the followers are expected to obey the instructions and commands of the leader. Kolzow (2014) asserts that the transactional leader is more a manager than a leader, and is unable to embody qualities such as empowerment and development of employees;

8. **Relationship theory** (also known as transformational leadership) 'grows out of the assumption that people will follow a leader who inspires and motivates

them' (Kolzow, 2014, p.43). It is also associated with change, developing a vision for the future, and mobilising others to achieve results beyond those that would normally be expected (Spreitzer, Sutcliffe, Dutton, Sonenshein & Grant, 2005). As mentioned earlier, Moyles (2006) associates transformational leadership with transforming values and beliefs into ethos and culture. In addition, Cherry (2012, in Amanchukwu et al., 2015) indicates that these leaders are focused upon the performance of group members, and upon each person fulfilling his/her potential and, they often have high ethical and moral standards. Building on earlier work on transformational leadership, Copeland (2014) focuses on 'value based' criteria. When identifying leaders, organisations must consider ethical and moral values, or 'values based leadership' (VBL), because when leaders demonstrate these VBL behaviours, they are evaluated 'as more effective by subordinates' (Copeland, 2014, p.105). In recognition of the need to promote sharing of organisational vision and goals, Pearce, Wassenaar and Manz (2014) indicate that organisations increasingly use a transformational leadership style to encourage personal and team improvement to enhance organisational performance. They also suggest that sharing of power is increasingly encouraged by leaders, as is recognising, understanding and capitalising on each employee's best qualities; involving him/her in the decision-making process, leading to empowerment and collaboration.

In summary, leadership theory focuses upon leaders' traits and styles, which are particularly evident in many of the aforementioned theories (i.e., participative, transformational, and transactive). The following activity provides an overview of other common leadership styles, and asks you to identify the matching leadership theory, as well as the advantages and disadvantages of each style.

Activity: Leadership styles

Leadership style	Identify the leadership theory	Identify the advantages	Identify the disadvantages
Authoritative (also known as autocratic): Centred on the boss/manager who holds all the authority and responsibility. Leaders make decisions on their own without consulting with staff. They decide what needs to be done, when and how it should be done. This leadership style is synonymous with 'Do as I say', and, it is strongly focused upon both command by the leader and control of the followers			

Leadership style	Identify the leadership theory	Identify the advantages	Identify the disadvantages
Democratic (also known as consultative or participative): Achieves consensus through participation. The democratic leader involves staff in making decisions and, will ask 'What do you think?' This leader holds final responsibility, but will delegate responsibility to others			
Laissez-faire: Means 'let it be' (translated from French). This leader 'exercises little control over the staff team. Staff are left to sort out their own roles and tackle their own work' without participation from the leader (Moloney & Pettersen, 2017, p.47). The laissez-faire leader takes a hands-off approach, but is available when advice and input is needed.			

Communicative leadership

A recurring theme throughout the leadership literature is the relationship between leadership and vision. Kelley (2014), for example, asserts that vision, communication and empowerment are three principle factors required in leaders. Thus, while leaders must be able to communicate the vision to both motivate and empower team members to share in and, enact the vision in daily practice, Bryman, Collinson, Grint, Jackson and Uhl-Bien (2011) argue that the communication aspects of leadership are largely overlooked and neglected.

Blandford and Knowles (2016, p.72) assert that the essentials of good leadership hinge on the effective and appropriate management of people. But what does this mean, and how can it be achieved? One way of achieving this may be through communicative leadership (Johansson, Miller & Hamrin, 2014). In fact Johansson et al. (2014) see 'communication as constitutive of leadership' (p.5), and they define communicative leadership in terms of engaging employees in dialogue, actively sharing and seeking feedback, practicing participative decision-making, and perceived as open and involved. They suggest that this 'tentative definition' comprises leader behaviours that are socially co-constructed and constituted in discourse, which enables and shapes interactions between leaders and members (p.11). Their definition underscores the relational nature of leadership, and the manner in which it can foster staff agency with regards to encouraging and, empowering them to actively co-participate in decision-making and problem-solving processes, as they translate the setting's vision into practice.

The characteristics of communicative leadership are embodied in the four central communicative behaviours of leaders as determined by Johansson et al., (2014) (Figure 4.4).

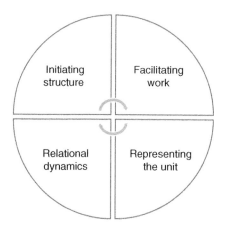

FIGURE 4.4 Central communicative behaviours of leaders
Adapted from: Johansson et al., 2014, p.6.

These communicative behaviours occur at manager/leader–employee-level interactions, and then across the team level (Johansson et al., 2014, p.6) (see Table 4.1)

Johansson (2015) refers to communicative leadership as a 'bottom-up' approach to leadership that involves dialogue and responsive communication behaviours that invite employees to make their voice heard, and participate in decision-making, contributing to a greater level of employee empowerment. This type of leadership encourages employee autonomy and contrasts with approaches to leadership that focus upon influencing employees in order to create engagement (Johansson, 2015). This suggests that a core element of leadership is the leader's interpersonal communication style, which will either motivate and encourage staff, or serve to impede their efforts to establish inclusive practices. Focusing upon inclusion specifically, it is important to bear in mind that leadership is not just about efficiency and effectiveness, it is also about what is good, what is right, what makes sense and what is worth doing (Sergiovanni, 2009). An intentional leader communicates these ideas to the staff team, actively seeks, listens to and incorporates their voice into decision-making processes, and motivates, encourages and empowers the team to develop, implement and sustain inclusive practice.

Distributed leadership

Leadership and management is endorsed through legislation as a professional responsibility of educators in Australia, Ireland and England. With regards to Ireland, it is a core aspect of the Early Years Services Regulations, (Department of Health & Children (DHC), 2016), as well as the Early Years Education Focused Inspections (Department of Education and Skills (DES), 2016). The former emphasises governance as it relates to recruitment practices for example, while the latter is

TABLE 4.1 Communicative behaviour across manager/leader–employee level and across the team

Behaviour	Manager-employee level	Team Level
Initiating work	Manager/leader plans and allocates tasks as well as setting goals and expectations for individual employees.	Manager defines the mission, plans and allocates tasks to maximise coordination efficiencies, sets goals and expectations for the team. Manager also selects appropriate team members, and provides sense-making of events for team members.
Facilitating work	Manager/leader coaches and trains employees, and provides performance feedback.	Leaders: coach and train employees to work in teams; provide timely and relevant feedback to the team so they can modify their actions, if necessary; engage employees in problem-solving (often in participatory decision-making manner) encourage independence and team self-management on appropriate matters.
Relational dynamics	Managers/leaders are perceived to be open (e.g., approachable for asking questions, good listeners, giving positive or negative feedback, and trustworthy). They are also seen as supportive, approaching conflict in a constructive, respectful, balanced manner.	Managers/leaders enacting these behaviours are perceived as considerate by individual employees and by the team as a whole.
Represent	Managers/leaders must be able to exert upward influence and be seen as capable of obtaining resources from upper management.	Managers/leaders are perceived as actively monitoring the external environment for opportunities and threat. They also: participate in networking opportunities to develop strategic information, and cooperative links; manage boundaries by leading the team to cooperate with other teams in a professional manner; provide resources for their team.

Adapted from Johansson et al. (2014, p.7).

predominantly concerned with pedagogical leadership (see Chapter 7). Adding to the complexity of ECEC in Ireland, is the renewed focus upon inclusion and the introduction of InCos in ECEC settings participating in the Early Childhood Care and Education (ECCE) scheme.[2] This gives rise to a pertinent question: can one person, such as the ECEC manager, the InCo or the SENCO, fulfil these various roles and responsibilities? Commenting upon schools, Fullan (2002, p.14) cautions that 'an organisation cannot flourish-at least, not for long on the actions of the top leader alone'. He goes on to say that 'Sustainable improvement must be nurtured up close in the dailiness of organisational behaviour, and for that to happen there needs to be many leaders around us. Leaders at many levels' (p.14). Applying this to the field of ECEC; settings tend to follow a traditional model of leadership, where the manager is the leader. In this hierarchical structure, and depending upon the size or nature of the setting, the manager may be assisted by a deputy or an assistant manager. The manager takes responsibility for developing policy and for all decision-making processes, expecting the educators to act upon and implement these policies and decisions in their practice with children and families. Given the increasingly complex nature of ECEC, it is questionable whether this approach to leadership is suitable, or sustainable.

Siraj-Blatchford and Manni (2007) call for a shift away from the traditional view of leadership as being vested in one key individual, to a more collective vision where the responsibility for leadership rests within formal and informal leaders. This approach to leadership looks beyond the overall leadership of one person in the setting and looks instead towards a model of distributed leadership. The intention here is not to diminish the invaluable central role played by the setting manager, rather it is to acknowledge and recognise the funds of knowledge, experience and expertise that others in the setting hold, while also creating an environment where they can share this, in the best interests of children and families.

It is thought that distributed leadership has become the most pervasive model of leadership in the early years. Yet its meaning is ambiguous with terms such as 'distributed', 'shared' and 'dispersed' leadership often used interchangeably. However, it is important to note that in relation to distributed leadership, emphasis must be placed upon leadership practices, relational aspects and relocation of power relations. In their 1995 description, Knutton and Ireson succinctly include these various aspects, describing it as a process where: 'Leaders and senior managers relocate their power, and are then freed to guide new developments. Those within the team are given ownership in some significant parts of their own working environment and are consequently empowered to act' (p. 61).

This definition of distributed leadership supports the notion that leadership practice extends beyond the roles and responsibilities style of leadership usually associated with the manager, a point captured by Harris (2013) who suggests that distributed leadership 'is primarily concerned with the interactions and dynamics of leadership practice rather than a pre-occupation with the formal roles and responsibilities traditionally associated with those who lead' (p.vii). There is no doubt that distributed leadership is concerned with the practice of leadership. It suggests that there are spheres of influence within the setting with concomitant layers of leadership and, it underpins the need to mobilise leadership expertise at all levels within the setting. Unlike formal leadership roles, which tend to focus upon individual, independent actions, distributed leadership emphasises interdependent interaction and practice.

Lindon and Lindon (2012, p.119) describe distributed leadership as a 'deliberate process' of sharing leadership behaviour, so that team members other than the manager can take an active lead, and accept responsibility for some areas of the work, and developing best practice. They see this as a 'critical point, it is not about being the overall leader of the setting, but of practitioners adopting a leadership role' (p.119). Referring to distributed leadership in a school context, Spillane, Halverson and Diamond (2001) refer to distributed leadership practice as being 'stretched over' the whole school. Certainly from our perspective, ECEC lends itself to a model of distributed leadership that stretches over the entire setting. Moreover, with regards to inclusion, leadership for inclusion seems like a logical place to start. Indeed, as discussed in Chapter 1, the role of the InCo in Ireland, and the SENCO in England are both examples of a leadership role within ECEC settings, developed specifically to support the inclusion of children with a disability.

InCos are responsible for: assessment and planning for the adaptation of the ECEC environment; mediation of the curriculum to support inclusion; liaison with parents and multidisciplinary professionals; provision of support for other staff in the setting; observation and evaluation of children's participation; and preparation of reports for stakeholders as required. This is just one model of leadership relating to inclusion. However, given the many aspects of inclusion, there is a danger that a single leadership for inclusion role may be spread too thinly across too many areas. Consequently, other leadership roles such as pedagogical and advocacy leadership may be required (see Chapters 7 and 9). In relation to pedagogical leadership, Nutbrown (2012) found that 'evidence for the positive impact of good pedagogical leadership in the early years is overwhelming' (p.56). Distributed leadership can therefore create opportunities to tap into staff funds of knowledge, expertise and interests, serving to sustain an inclusive culture and achieve the setting's vision through the actions and interactions of many leaders.

Jones, Lefoe, Harvey and Ryland (2012) identified five key dimensions of distributed leadership as illustrated in Figure 4.5.

1. **Context:** Leadership moves from a reliance on power to that of influence. This involves collaborative working between people who trust and respect each other's contribution;
2. **Culture:** Leadership moves from a reliance on control to one of autonomy. This can be achieved through an open culture of acceptance and recognition of staff expertise within the setting;
3. **Change:** Leadership is from the bottom up and encourages greater participation by more staff. This includes encouraging interdependent multi-level involvement by creating processes that provide opportunity for staff to

influence policy, rather than policy being simply developed from the top and devolved down for implementation;

4. **Relationship management:** Leadership focuses on collective rather than individual identities. Staff members are encouraged to self-identify as leaders;
5. **Activity:** Leadership assumes a shared purpose through cycles of change. Staff are encouraged to engage in cycles of planning, acting, observing and reflecting (adapted from Jones et al., 2012).

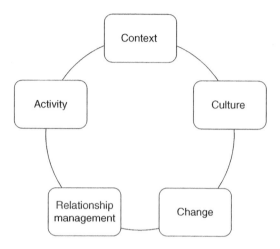

FIGURE 4.5 Dimensions of distributed leadership

The emphasis here is upon the relational aspects of leadership that, according to Jones et al. (2012, p.12), are dependent upon four practices:

1. **Self-in-relation** – emphasis on interdependence;
2. **Social interaction** – ability to create conditions for collective learning by exercising certain strengths, abilities and relational skills;
3. **Collective learning** – through learning conversations progressing through a four stage dialogue of 'talking nice', 'talking tough', 'reflective dialogue' and 'generative dialogue';
4. **Growth-in-connection** – focus on mutuality where the boundary between self and others is more fluid and multi-directional. Movement occurs from mutual authenticity (bringing self into the interaction) to mutual empathy (hold onto self but also experience other's reality) to mutual empowerment (each is in some way influenced or affected by the other) so that something new is created.

This change in emphasis 'from personal capabilities (skills, traits, behaviours) to practices, recognises the fundamental change from an emphasis on leaders to leadership' (Jones et al., 2012, p.12), and, as noted by Harris and Spillane (2008, p.33) 'it is the nature and quality of leadership practice that matters'. While developing a leadership for inclusion role can enable settings to establish and sustain an inclusive culture, this should not necessarily be vested in one individual, who is then left to deal with all inclusion issues within the setting. Potentially this role could be further strengthened by developing a pedagogical leadership role for example.

Intentional leadership relating to inclusive culture

Culture derives from the beliefs, values and assumptions of the founders of the setting; the learning experiences of staff as their organisation evolves; and new beliefs, values and assumptions brought in by new members and leaders (Schein, 2004). Moreover it is shaped by the social environment, the backdrop against which the processes in the setting take place, the management systems, policies and structures of the setting, and the actions and behaviours of setting staff (Blandford & Knowles, 2016). These micro-level factors are greatly influenced by factors at macro-level, in particular government commitment to the principles of inclusion. which determines fiscal support for enacting inclusive policies. Macro-level policies drive the move towards inclusion within ECEC. The DCYA (2016) for instance, charges those working in settings to establish an inclusive, participative culture and environment that is culturally sensitive, inclusive and, celebrates difference. This begins with the setting's manager who decides the basic purpose and the environmental context in which the setting operates. From the outset, culture dictates the atmosphere of the setting and the behaviour of those working within it.

Inclusion involves much more than meeting the needs of unique learners, it is about creating a whole culture in which everyone is valued, included and able to learn and work together (Barr, 2016). The overall thrust of an inclusive culture is that all those who engage with the ECEC setting (e.g., children, families, staff, multidisciplinary teams) are respected and valued. Therefore, if the manager is not committed to the principles of inclusion, it is unlikely that a culture of inclusion will be fostered.

This chapter indicates that there may be more than one intentional leader within an ECEC setting. This suggestion draws upon the concept of distributed leadership that is aligned to spheres of influence within the setting with concomitant layers of leadership. It underscores the need to mobilise leadership expertise at all levels within the setting. Unlike formal leadership roles, which tend to focus upon individual, independent actions, distributed leadership emphasises interdependent interaction and practice.

Distributed leadership can create opportunities to tap into staff expertise and interests, serving to sustain an inclusive culture and achieve the setting's vision through the actions, and interactions of many leaders (e.g., manager, pedagogical leader, advocacy leader). Each leader, however, in whatever capacity, must lead intentionally in the best interests of children in establishing and, maintaining an inclusive culture within the setting. The intentional leader(s) must:

- establish, promote and sustain an inclusive culture throughout the setting;
- identify and define values and ethics within the setting (may involve communicating values explicitly and physically through documents such as mission statements, and ensuring staff like-mindedness) (Moyles, 2006, p.66);

- lead by example and be a transformational leader who transforms values and beliefs into ethos and culture (Moyles, 2006, p.66);
- support the staff team to see that inclusion is an integral part of their role and responsibility;
- ensure that the setting's curriculum is based upon the principles of inclusion (involving collaborative working with parents and others), and is responsive to the collective and individual needs of children;
- develop inclusive policies and practices in collaboration with management, staff, parents, families and others as necessary;
- advocate for children and families;
- account for actions to multiple stakeholders; children, families, staff team, community, funders.

While this is by no means a definitive list of responsibilities, it provides insight into the complexity of an intentional leadership for inclusion role. Moreover, building upon the discussion in Chapter 3, it is apparent that intentional leadership is concerned with relationships, reciprocal learning and reflection (Biddle, 2010), and with vision, communication and empowerment (Bryman et al., 2011). As indicated in the present chapter, while an intentional leader must be an effective communicator, this aspect of leadership is largely overlooked and neglected. Yet, a core element of intentional leadership is the leader's interpersonal communication style, which either motivates and encourages educators, or impedes them in their attempt to establish inclusive practices. When it comes to inclusion, leadership is not just about efficiency and effectiveness, it is also about what is good, what is right, what makes sense and what is worth doing (Sergiovanni, 2009). An intentional leader: communicates these ideas to the staff team; actively seeks, listens to and incorporates their voice into decision-making processes; and motivates, encourages and empowers them to develop, implement and sustain inclusive practice.

Thus, intentional leadership that supports inclusion must be fostered and supported. Intentional leadership becomes the 'superglue' that unites, motivates and empowers all educators to work towards a common goal; that of creating an inclusive culture within the entire setting. In borrowing from Waniganayake and Semann (2011, p.24), we suggest that intentional leadership is 'a journey of joint inquiry, exploration and reflection that can involve everyone who believes in making a difference for children'. Thus, distributed leadership can be used as an effective means of embedding intentional leadership practice within ECEC, of ensuring the development of an inclusive culture and of guaranteeing that inclusion becomes the norm, rather than an 'add-on' activity within the setting.

Notes

1 In this book, the founder is taken to mean the manager of the early childhood education and care setting
2 The ECCE scheme was introduced in 2010. It entitles all children aged between three and five years old access to up to two years of free pre-school (15 hours per week).

5

LEADING, BUILDING AND MAINTAINING AN INCLUSIVE LEARNING ENVIRONMENT

Introduction

All children, regardless of ability, have the same need for care, attention and love. They need caring, consistent, respectful interactions and relationships, opportunities for play and exploration, communication, choice and meaningful participating. This chapter focuses upon the concept of meaningful participation, and how the environment, supports or hinders this for young children with SEN. Furthermore, it explores the leadership role in the context of leading, building and maintaining an inclusive learning environment.

As with all aspects of inclusion, positive attitudes, shared values and beliefs are fundamental to establishing and maintaining an inclusive environment, and, as mentioned in Chapter 3, they determine the expectations that educators have for children. Let us pause and think about what those expectations might be for young children in an ECEC setting: will children be expected to take off and hang up their coat independently? Put on and fasten their coat? Put on and take off their shoes by themselves? Will they be expected to use a spoon to feed themselves without help? Or perhaps they will be expected to master personal care skills such as toileting and handwashing? Whatever the expectations, they exist for all children. The simple tasks outlined pose limited challenges for the majority of children, who generally accomplish them in their own way and at their own pace. There are children, however, for whom these tasks are difficult, and who, therefore, require a greater level of support from adults or peers to accomplish them, thus ensuring meaningful participation and inclusion for all children. When children master a task, they experience a feeling of success – an 'I can do it' attitude. This encourages them to keep trying, thereby gaining confidence in their abilities, developing independence, a stronger sense of self and, a greater sense of belonging within the early years setting. Ultimately, when children experience success, they want to achieve more.

Creating a supportive learning environment is fundamental to enabling children achieve their goals.

Using the PEAT model (Moloney & McCarthy, 2010), this chapter discusses the learning environment, indoor and outdoor, with a particular emphasis upon how the physical, aesthetic and temporal aspects contribute to effective and meaningful participation and inclusion in an early childhood context. While the emotional environment is touched upon, it is peripheral to the present chapter. Consequently, Chapter 6 focuses specifically upon the establishment of an emotionally safe learning environment and emphasises the centrality of a nurturing pedagogy.

The PEAT model

When thinking of the environment, the physical attributes (design, access, equipment and materials) are usually uppermost in people's minds. This is not surprising, as the physical space is the first point of contact for parents, children, families and other stakeholders. It speaks a language that leaves a lasting impression on parents, children and other users in terms of accessibility, welcome and safety, for example. However, the physical space, is just one aspect of the overall environment, which is multi-dimensional, comprising also emotional, aesthetic and temporal aspects (see Figure 5.1).

Accessing the physical space, is but one step in the journey toward inclusion. It can be viewed as the key to unlocking the door to the other, related and interconnected, emotional, aesthetic and temporal aspects of the environment. Think about the many special educational needs and disabilities presented in Chapter 2. What will parents of a child with a special educational need look for when enrolling their child for the first time in an ECEC setting? Depending upon their child's particular needs, parents may initially focus upon different aspects of the environment. They will be

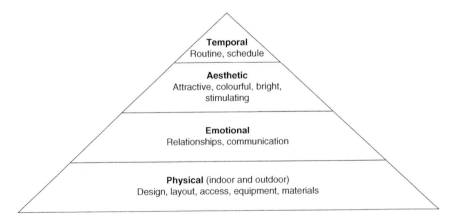

FIGURE 5.1 PEAT model
Source: Moloney & McCarthy (2010, p.26).

mindful of how a child with a physical disability, for instance, can enter, and leave the building, navigate corridors, play spaces, toileting areas, as well as the outdoor area/s. In the case of a child with a visual impairment, parents may be more interested in the aesthetic aspects; how the building is lit, the sources and balance of natural and artificial lighting. They may be attentive to shiny and glossy surfaces, which can result in glare or intense reflection, which pose challenges for a child with a visual impairment. The parents of a child with attachment issues will clearly be focused upon the emotional environment and, be concerned with caring, nurturing and responsive relationships between educators and their child, while for the parents of a child with autism, the temporal aspects of the environment – routines, schedules and transitions – may be paramount. Regardless of the child's need, however, each of the four aspects of the PEAT model are fundamental to the concept of inclusion, and must be in harmony to effect and maintain inclusive practices within the setting.

Meaningful participation

In a joint statement on early childhood inclusion, the Division for Early Childhood and the National Association for the Education of Young Children (DEC & NAEYC, 2009) in the US identify participation as one of the three defining features of inclusion; the others being access and supports. In their statement, the DEC and NAEYC stress that even if environments and early childhood programmes are designed to facilitate access, some children will require 'additional individualized accommodations and supports to participate fully in play and learning activities with peers and adults' (p.2). There is evidence that, without purposeful adaptations and strategies, children with disabilities are not involved in as many activities as other children (Odom, Buysse & Soukakou, 2011). Purposeful adaptations and supports are fundamental to the concept of meaningful participation, which is increasingly used in relation to inclusion. Meaningful participation is therefore, correlated with attitudes, values and beliefs, and, as mentioned in Chapter 3, these are influenced and changed through education, training and direct hands-on work with children.

Commenting upon how values can change over time, Moore (2012) highlights a change in thinking about the outcomes that we want for children with SEN, which, he claims, are increasingly formulated in terms of 'developing capabilities (rather than reaching potential), meaningful participation (rather than social exclusion or marginalisation), and quality of life' (p.12). For him, meaningful participation 'is the engine of development and the key to attaining a true sense of belonging and a satisfactory quality of life' (p.10). For participation to be meaningful, the person's role and contribution must be valued by all those involved in the activity, including the person themselves. Therefore the interactions between the child and his/her immediate surroundings are fundamental to the child's wellbeing and competences. In the words of Bronfenbrenner (1999):

> Child development takes place through processes of progressively more com-
> plex interaction between an active child and the persons, objects, and symbols

in it immediate environment. To be effective, the interaction must occur on a fairly regular basis over an extended period of time.

These multiple interactions relate to proximal processes considered as one aspect of the PPCT model: process, person, context and time (Wachs & Evans, 2010). While this model is interrogated in Chapter 9, proximal processes that are instrumental in shaping the child's learning and development are embedded in the reciprocal relationships between the child and his environment.

Ensuring that each child's role and contribution is valued rests with the educators working with children in the daily life of the setting. At a minimum, educators and others working with children must understand and be knowledgeable about the circumstances of children's lives, the contexts for their learning, how they learn and how best to support and facilitate their learning.

PRACTICE SCENARIO

Jawad is three years old. He lives with his mother, his eight-year-old brother and his nine-month-old sister. Jawad is a quiet boy. Although his mother describes him as chatty, stating that he talks to her and his siblings at home all the time, he has not spoken to anybody in ECEC setting, since he started attending six months ago. He likes to play alone, seldom engaging with other children, whom he likes to observe from a distance. He smiles, gestures, nods, and sometimes he even giggles, but he does not talk while in the setting.

Consider:

1. What might you need to know about Jawad to enable you to support his needs and his meaningful participation in the daily routines of the setting?
2. How would you gather information to help you identify and support Jawad's needs?
3. Who should be involved in supporting Jawad to meaningfully participate in the setting?
4. What role could the InCo/SENCO play in supporting Jawad's inclusion in the setting?

Because Jawad is a quiet child, who smiles, gestures, nods, and giggles occasionally, his lack of conversation, and interaction with other children may go unnoticed by the educators. In this scenario, intentional leadership is paramount. In the absence of somebody taking responsibility for inclusion, shaping and influencing others (e.g., the staff team, parents) to support Jawad's development, the opportunities for his meaningful participation will be minimal at best and non-existent at worse.

In keeping with the notion of distributed leadership in the field of ECEC (see Chapter 4), intentional leadership for inclusion, as discussed throughout this book, involves leadership at a number of levels, beginning with the setting's manager who is responsible for demonstrating inclusive values, working with the staff team, parents and others, to develop a positive ethos and inclusive practices. Progressing from the manager to individual areas within the setting, there may be other leadership roles, such as the appointment of a key worker to observe Jawad, identify his abilities and his needs, and to reflect and work in collaboration with his parents and the other educators, to plan how to encourage and support his meaningful participation with and alongside other children.

King et al. (2002) view meaningful participation along two dimensions:

1. The context for children's learning;
2. The ultimate goal of intervention services; it is therefore, both a process and an outcome (King et al., 2002) (see Figure 5.2).

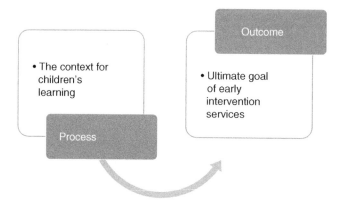

FIGURE 5.2 Dimensions of meaningful participation
Adapted from: King et al. (2002).

Meaningful participation in activities provides the context where 'people develop competencies, gain an understanding of their strengths and abilities, form friendships and relationships, and make a contribution to their worlds' (King et al., 2002, p.63). Congruent with this notion of participation, *Aistear: the Early Childhood Curriculum Framework* in Ireland places children's learning in the context of loving, trusting and respectful relationships (NCCA, 2009). In simple terms, children learn through relationships that are premised upon sensitive, responsive and nurturing environments (Moloney & McCarthy, 2010).

An emotionally safe environment is inextricably linked to relationships at multiple levels within the setting, and is critical to supporting children to develop their autonomy in the form of basic skill development, including independent mobility and self-care during early childhood. In fact, Moore (2012, p.9) suggests that the overall outcome we want for children, with or without disabilities, is that they 'gain the functional skills or capabilities they need to participate meaningfully in their daily environment'. Mastery of these early skills produces feelings of pride and success, and lays the foundations on which later successes and love of learning are built. Enabling children to become autonomous is part and parcel of inclusive practice, and it begins with a supportive, inclusive learning environment.

Buildings for everybody

In their article, 'The universal design of early education: Moving all children forward', Conn-Powers, Conn-Powers, Traub & Hutter-Pishgahi (2006) pose a series of pertinent questions: How well have we conceived early education programmes to support and respond to all young children? Do they welcome and include every child? Are activity areas and materials physically accessible to each child? Do all families have opportunities to be involved in their children's education? Is every child engaged and learning? They argue that 'the goal for educators is to design early education programs that meet the needs of all learners within a common setting and begin to move away from specialized programs' (p.1). This approach, known as universal design, relates to the design and composition of an environment so that it may be accessed, understood, and used:

> to the greatest extent possible, in the most independent and natural manner possible, in the widest possible range of situations, and without the need for adaptation, modification, assistive devices or specialised devises or solutions, by any persons of any age or size or having any particular physical, sensory, mental health or intellectual ability or disability.
>
> *(Government of Ireland, Disability Act, 2005)*

Universal design is the beginning of inclusive education. Thus, when flexibility is factored into the design stage from the beginning, all children regardless of ability, can access the setting and the early childhood curriculum, and they can process information in a way that works for them and demonstrate what they know (Conn-Powers et al., 2006).

Universal design began in the US, in the field of architecture, following the adoption of the Americans with Disabilities Act (ADA, 1990),[1] when buildings were retrofitted with ramps, elevators, etc., to accommodate individuals with disabilities (Brillante, 2017). However, these modifications also benefited others, such as the elderly and parents with baby strollers. As a result, architects realised that it was more economical to build accessibility into the design of new buildings, rather than to retrofit the changes later on.

THINK ABOUT

Following an accident in a swimming pool, Naomi, aged five years, is now quadriplegic. Her life is very different to what it was before her accident. One major difference is accessibility. Can you think of any aspects of universal design that would help Naomi to access her home, ECEC setting and other public spaces?

Think about the benefits of automatic doors that open by themselves when somebody approaches. While these doors automatically enable more people to access a building, they also ensure that somebody with reduced mobility (e.g., a wheelchair user) can enter and leave without difficulty. Likewise, a parent pushing a stroller or somebody carrying lots of shopping bags may find it easier to use automatic doors.

Universal design results in more user-friendly accessible environments that can be used by everyone in a similar manner

The seven principles of universal design

Universal design calls for educators to value the importance of planning learning environments and activities for a diverse population of children; creating a universally designed setting where all children can actively and fully participate and learn (Blagojevic, Twomey & Labas, 2002). It is underpinned by seven key principles – these are set out in Table 5.1, which provides an overview of each principle, together with an explanation of how it relates to education and care for young children and an example of its application in universal design for learning (UDL) in an ECEC environment.

As illustrated in Table 5.1, the application of universal design is not about a focus on people with disabilities, but about making environments accessible to them, which ultimately benefits others also. It places a high importance on diversity, equality and inclusiveness, and, as the examples shown in Table 5.1 illustrate, it can equally be applied to learning.

Establishing an inclusive environment and culture in early childhood requires those working with children to think about all those who access and use the building: children, parents, families, setting staff and external stakeholders. In addition, careful consideration must be given to the activity areas/rooms within the setting. Table 5.2 provides a sample checklist to help you identify whether the physical attributes of the activity areas/rooms in your setting:

- are accessible to all children;
- include equipment and materials that are accessible by, and easy to use by all children;
- are designed with safety in mind.

It also provides some examples of how to address any concerns identified.

TABLE 5.1 Seven principles of universal design

Principle	Explanation	Example
Equitable use	The design works for children with diverse abilities. All children with and without disabilities can use equivalent ways of using the material, equipment, curricula or assessment.	Instead of an easel for a child who uses a wheelchair and a table for everyone else, easels are set up for all children.
Flexible use	The design accommodates a wide range of individual preferences and abilities. Children use the same materials and curriculum as everyone else, but in varied ways or with modifications to accommodate personal preference or a disability.	Books with paper clips, or sponges added to the pages enable a child to turn the pages more easily. Children learn concepts and practise skills at their own pace.
Simple and intuitive	The design of the space and the materials is easy for everyone to understand regardless of the child's experience, knowledge, language skills or concentration levels.	Use a one-way circulation system for ease of movement, and ready access to space and materials. Every material has a specific place and is labelled in different ways, making finding and tidying up easy to understand and accomplish.
Perceptible information	The design communicates information effectively to the child, regardless of ambient conditions (noise levels, distractions) or the user's sensory abilities.	Pictures, words (in English and children's home language) and braille are used together to bring meaning to children with language delays or vision impairments, and to dual language learners. Lights flicker when the fire alarm goes off, so that children with hearing impairments understand the same information as everybody else in the setting.
Tolerance for error	The design minimises hazards and the adverse consequences of accidental or unintended actions.	Attaching felt to wooden blocks so they are less likely to fall over if a child inadvertently knocks into them when building.
Low physical effort	Spaces and materials are set up so they are easier to use by children, with a minimum of effort and fatigue.	All materials are placed within the child's reach or at eye-level. Providing a sink that turns on and off when children place their hands under the faucet reduces the physical effort needed by children with low strength.

TABLE 5.1 (*Cont.*)

Principle	Explanation	Example
Appropriate size and space	Appropriate size and space is provided for approach, reach, manipulation and use regardless of the child's body size, posture or mobility.	Chairs and tables are of varying heights to accommodate all children. Outdoor areas have ramps. There are spaces for small and large group activities, places for one or two children to work together, and quiet retreat areas

Adapted from: Brillante (2017) & TATS (2009).

Drawing upon the work of Conn-Powers et al. (2006); Brillante (2017) urges those who wish to effectively support the needs of all children in the ECEC setting to consider ways to design the space, routines and activities so that they are adaptable and can be used with, and by, as many children as possible. For children with disabilities, meaningful participation requires educators to utilise a range of instructional and intervention approaches to promote engagement, and a sense of belonging for each child (Buysse & Peisner-Feinberg, 2013). Without adaptations and strategies, children with disabilities may be restricted in terms of movement, choice, flexibility and meaningful participation in activities and routines within the setting.

Establishing and leading the physical learning environment

Chapter 3 proposes that a 'twin track' approach to inclusion is required. This involves making ECEC a welcoming and positive experience for children, and being sufficiently confident and skilled to meet the specific needs of children with disabilities (Lewis & Bagree, 2013, p. 10). Consequently, the physical learning environment should be welcoming, attractive, stimulating and challenging; a place where both children and adults (educators and parents) wish to spend time. It requires considerable attention. Epstein (2014) holds that the setting must 'promote not only children's learning, but also their pleasure in learning, and the motivation to pursue it' (p.13).

Bearing in mind the need for intentional leadership, the learning environment must be set up each day, before the children even arrive at the setting. Think about what this involves and who is responsible for ensuring the environment is ready for children as they arrive to the setting each day. What messages are conveyed to children and parents when the environment is untidy, cluttered, lacking in equipment and materials, or full of broken, and unkempt toys?

When preparing the learning environment, the primary consideration must be the children's safety. Across the globe, children's safety while attending ECEC settings is governed by statutory regulations, such as the Education (Early Childhood Services) Regulations, 2008 in New Zealand, the Childcare Act, 1991 (Early Years Services) Regulations, 2016 in Ireland, and the Childcare (Welfare and Registration Requirements) (Amendment) Regulations 2014 in the UK. These

TABLE 5.2 Universal design checklist for use in activity rooms

Does/is my activity room…	What can I do?
Accessible for all children?	Ensure that children can use each part of the area in a similar way;
	Provide easels for painting so that such activities are accessible by all children;
	Adapt a table to accommodate a child in a wheelchair to sit comfortably into the table to engage in an activity. Kidney-shaped tables are ideal for this purpose;
	Use sound-absorbing materials such as rugs, curtains, pillows and soft toys to reduce noise, distraction and sensory overload for children;
Include equipment and materials that are easy to use by all children?	Group similar furnishings and equipment together. Keep colours neutral to reduce distraction and sensory overload for children. Label shelves or use pictorial cues so that non-verbal children, children with English as a Second Language (EAL), or those with a language impairment can choose activities independently;
	Rotate materials on shelves rather than crowding all materials together at one time. Crowded shelves are confusing for children, and discourage them from choosing materials independently. Use storage containers, transparent crates, wooden boxes or baskets. Place a pictorial cue on the outside so that children know what it contains. This also makes it easier for children to tidy up and maintain order in the environment;
	Encourage children to be responsible. Model appropriate behaviour such as maintaining the environment in a clean and orderly manner. Encourage children to return materials to where they belong once they are finished with them;
Designed with safety in mind?	Establish clear unobstructed traffic patterns and pathways to ensure safety and maximum mobility when entering and leaving the room, navigating within the area when putting belongings away and moving between activities;
	Develop evacuation procedures in collaboration with colleagues, families and others (i.e., members of the multidisciplinary team);
	Develop materials, such as pictorial books, with braille to help children understand what to expect during a fire drill.

Source: Moloney & McCarthy (2010), Brillante, (2017).

regulations provide for adult/child ratios, space requirements, ventilation, heating, lighting, sanitation, temperature control and so on. Although compliance with regulatory requirements, establishes a basic minimum standard of quality, Epstein (2014) argues that children's safety depends on educators being able to see and hear what is happening from anywhere in the room. With this in mind, the educator's location within the indoor and outdoor environment is critical, so that they can see and hear children at all times. This means that educators must:

- position themselves where they can see all children all the time (i.e., not have their back to any child, at any stage);
- constantly 'scan' the environment, taking note of where children are located, what they are doing, who they are playing with and what equipment and materials they are working with;
- remain alert to the need to intervene as and when required to ensure children's safety.

While safety is clearly a primary concern in ECEC settings; it is all too easy to become complacent as people become comfortable within their surroundings. Again, in this context, intentional leadership is required, to ensure, for example, that:

- equipment and materials are in good repair, and that broken toys, equipment and furniture are removed and/or repaired;
- furniture and equipment is arranged to allow for visual and auditory supervision;
- unused electrical outlets are covered;
- circulation areas are clear of electrical cords and clutter;
- exits are clearly marked and kept free of clutter at all times;
- materials and equipment are chosen with children's safety in mind (e.g., non-toxic, washable and free of choking hazards) – it is useful to familiarise yourself with the International Safety Standards for Toys available at www.toy-icti.org/info/toysafetystandards.html;
- cleaning products and hazardous materials are stored in areas/cabinets that are inaccessible to children.

Once a safe environment has been established, attention can be directed toward how the space is organised and the types of learning opportunities and activities that will support children's learning and development. The Centre for Early Childhood Development and Education (CECDE, 2006) indicates that the learning environment (indoor and outdoor) should motivate and appeal to all children, and that the equipment, materials and activities should be reflective of the diversity of children's needs, interests and background experiences. Educators must intentionally structure both the learning environment, and the activities within it, to facilitate and maximise each child's active and meaningful participation (Willis, 2009). Careful planning and organising of the physical space '[h]elps children to pursue their individual interests; provides cues and directions that help children understand the purpose of the environment, what is expected of them, while supporting their active participation and interaction within the setting' (Moloney & McCarthy, 2010, p.28). Through Article 31 of the UNCRC (1989), every child is entitled to have the chance to join in a wide range of activities, and children with disabilities have a right to access the same activities as other children (UNESCO, 2005). The challenge for educators is in knowing how to create an environment that supports the rights of children with disabilities to access the same activities as other children.

According to Isbell and Isbell (2005), early years settings must support a wide range of activity choices (e.g., art, construction, language), diverse forms of interaction (e.g., solitary, small group, large group) and different activity types (e.g., exploration, guided discovery, problem-solving, discussion, demonstration and direct instruction). One way of achieving this is to establish a number of activity centres, which are designed to actively engage children in their learning while building on individual interests and abilities. Activity centres have the capacity to invite children's meaningful participation and develop their skills in 'personally meaningful ways' (Isbell & Isbell, 2005, p.13), inviting them 'to make choices, cooperate with others, share, follow their individual interests, discover new interests, enhance skills, work at their individual level and above all experience success' (Moloney & McCarthy, 2010, p.35) while also 'expanding the range of content children are enticed to pursue' (Epstein, 2014, p.13).

If activity centres are to appeal to and, support children's learning and be inclusive of all children with and without disabilities, intentional leadership is paramount. In this regard, the leader, who is focused upon meaningful participation for all children, takes responsibility for:

- establishing areas that match the developmental level, interests and experiences of the individual children in the setting;
- designing areas in a way that work for all children, paying attention to layout, materials, furniture, lighting and access;
- rotating materials, and collecting additional materials, items and equipment to maintain interest;
- talking with children about the areas, their likes, preferences, dislikes and so on – this reflection helps children to build communication skills, and to recognise that their viewpoint matters and is of interest to practitioners and peers;
- reviewing areas to identify those that should be replaced, closed for renovation or need to be re-energised;
- undertaking observations of children working in different areas to demonstrate real learning, use of and enhancement of skills, and as a means of identifying any areas of concern to inform future planning for their learning (see Chapter 8);
- creating a chart where children can record where they worked during the day and with whom they worked. This can be in pictorial format, where children simply tick a box to indicate what they did and with whom. It can be used to help children and educators to recognise patterns, preferences and avoidance of areas and of children (adapted from Isbell, 2008).

Typical activity centres found in the indoor environment include:

- **Construction area** with an array of blocks and other construction materials;
- **Literacy area** comprising books, magazines, notebooks, Post-Its, different types of paper and card, pencils, chalk, markers and crayons;
- **Home area** using real-life materials and equipment;

Block area

Through participation in the block area, children with a disability will

- Manipulate blocks of various sizes, shapes, weights and textures
- Develop gross and fine motor skills and visual-perception skills
- Construct objects using blocks and other materials
- Enhance social skills
- Develop communication skills
- Work cooperatively with others
- Learn to problem-solve

FIGURE 5.3 Block area learning objectives
Adapted from: Isbell and Isbell (2005).

- **Music and movement area** with a diverse range of musical instruments, music books, pencils, paper, headphones, recording equipment and CD player;
- **Sand and water area**, where children have access to these materials, as well as equipment for pouring, scooping, measuring, weighing, etc.

The following areas might be included in the outdoor play spaces:

- Physical activity/gross motor development including climbing frames, slides, tricycles;
- Sand and water;
- Areas for gardening, observing wildlife (plant and animal), art and construction.

Using the block area, Figures 5.3 and 5.4 provide an overview of the learning objectives associated with block play and how it supports integrated learning. Although the learning objectives shown in Figure 5.4 apply to all children, they are even more important for a child with a disability.

The design and layout of the learning environment cannot be divorced from the aesthetics of the environment. From the outset, when designing a building, an architect will already be focused upon the aesthetics; window size, length and shape, aspect, shadow and light. So too, when preparing the learning environment for young children, spaces that sustain children's attention, provide opportunities for play, exploration, collaboration and learning, and which reflect the rich diversity of children's backgrounds are important. You can intentionally prepare an accessible, culturally rich, aesthetic learning environment as illustrated in Table 5.3, which provides an overview of some key considerations when planning the aesthetic learning environment.

When we pay attention to the physical layout, and the aesthetic aspects of the learning environment, we design inspiring spaces that support sustained shared thinking (Sylva et al., 2004) (see Chapter 6). In addition, an effective physical and

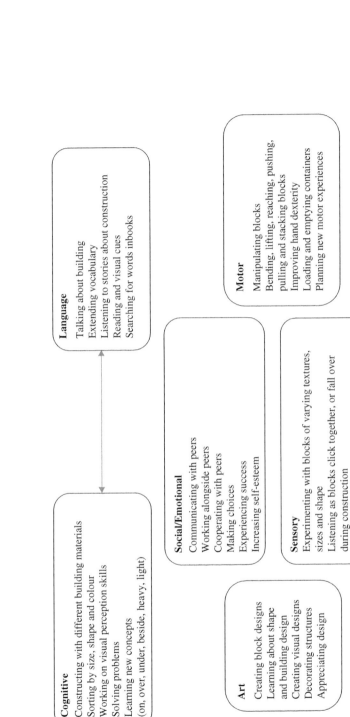

Cognitive
Constructing with different building materials
Sorting by size, shape and colour
Working on visual perception skills
Solving problems
Learning new concepts
(on, over, under, beside, heavy, light)

Language
Talking about building
Extending vocabulary
Listening to stories about construction
Reading and visual cues
Searching for words inbooks

Social/Emotional
Communicating with peers
Working alongside peers
Cooperating with peers
Making choices
Experiencing success
Increasing self-esteem

Art
Creating block designs
Learning about shape
and building design
Creating visual designs
Decorating structures
Appreciating design

Sensory
Experimenting with blocks of varying textures,
sizes and shape
Listening as blocks click together, or fall over
during construction
Experiencing a variety of coloured materials

Motor
Manipulating blocks
Bending, lifting, reaching, pushing,
pulling and stacking blocks
Improving hand dexterity
Loading and emptying containers
Planning new motor experiences

FIGURE 5.4 Block area: web of integrated learning

TABLE 5.3 Key considerations for planning the aesthetic learning environment

Colour helps to create a warm, friendly, and calm environment. Select soft, light, neutral colours for walls and ceilings. Bright colours dominate and detract from art and the natural aesthetics of the environment, while also distracting and over-stimulating children, which is problematic for some children with special educational needs. Neutral colours provide a good background for displaying children's work, and make it easier to mount visual cues and displays, which enable children to read and make sense of routines and schedules;

Light: natural light sources should be used where possible for activities such as reading, art and planting areas. This is especially important for children with a visual impairment. Dimmer switches on lights help to reduce glare and alter the mood in a room, making it more restful and relaxing. Likewise, lamps are a useful way to create a sense of calm and peace. The brightness of fluorescent lights, and the accompanying flickering and humming can be overly stimulating for a child on the autistic spectrum, or with attention deficit disorder. Conversely, a child with a visual impairment may find fluorescent lighting helpful;

Texture in the environment appeals to children's tactile and visual sensations. Hanging drapes, such as net or shower curtains, from the ceiling helps to create quiet, cosy, relaxing spaces. These spaces also work well as withdrawal areas for children who are overwhelmed by noise, large numbers of children, excessive activity, etc. They allow for one-to-one adult/child interactions. Using blinds on windows helps to reduce glare from glass. Fabrics – such as cushions during story-time – absorb sound, thus reducing noise within the environment. They also provide a sensory feast for children's eyes, and hands, and can also be representative of different backgrounds and cultures;

Pathways provide direction and are essential within a busy learning environment. They can be used to establish safe boundaries, communicating how to move and what to do within the environment. Plan pathways carefully. Use colour-coding or adhesive tape to delineate pathways to ensure the smooth flow of children and adults within the environment. Fix pictures and numbers to shelving to indicate the purpose of different areas and the numbers of children that can be accommodated in a particular space. Use fences, paved areas, curbs or grass to define boundaries in the outdoor environment. Cones, for example, can be used to delineate temporary boundaries for specific activities such as ball games, simple obstacle courses, or hula hoops;

Plants and natural materials (e.g., shells, sponges and herbs) create a welcoming and inspiring environment. Plants can also be strategically placed to create cosy/quiet relaxing areas for individual or small group work. Encourage children to collect twigs, tree branches, shells, etc. when out walking with parents or during ECEC activities. Children can decorate and mount these items on walls and ceilings to display their work, and to enhance the sensorial impact for children. While these artefacts represent the world outside the setting, they also make the environment into a living, breathing, inviting and welcoming space;

Landscaped areas are an effective way of enabling children to sit near shrubs or under trees in the outdoor space. These are also useful to enhance children's sensory development (smells, colours, textures), and can be used for children to take time out, away from activities they find overwhelming.

Adapted from: Moloney and McCarthy, 2010.

aesthetic environment helps to promote a sense of identity, belonging, wellbeing and competence for both children and adults.

Temporal environment

The child's day in the setting is made up of a series of routines and activities. The temporal environment refers therefore to the timing, sequence and length of routines and activities. It is about how educators use the time available throughout the day to ensure that children's basic needs are being met and that they have sufficient time for activities that support their learning and development. Educators establish a schedule that takes account of opportunities to move, interact, relax, explore, create and engage in a range of activities throughout the day. The schedule takes account of the amount of time and the level of flexibility and choice children have with regards to arrival to the setting, play time, meal time, rest time, individual activities, as well as small- and large-group activities, and the many transitions they experience as they move from one activity to another throughout the day. The importance of play as a conduit for children's learning and development is discussed in Chapter 7: 'Leadership in planning an inclusive and responsive curriculum', at this point, however, it is important to note that children need considerable blocks of time to develop play themes and ideas, and this must be accounted for within the temporal environment.

Predictable schedules and routines are essential for children. They create a sense of security and belonging, helping children to learn about their world and adjust to new situations. They are instrumental in managing children's expectations and preventing challenging behaviours. For example, a predictable daily routine coupled with the support of an encouraging and nurturing educator helps children to say goodbye to parents and to feel safe and secure within the setting. Knowing what is expected of them upon arrival to the setting, such as where to leave their bag and hang their coat, creates a sense of predictability while also fostering children's growing autonomy and sense of identity and belonging.

The temporal environment is closely aligned with short-term planning, which in Chapter 7 is described as the working document that supports daily practice within the setting and outlines the ingredients required for specific learning experiences including equipment, materials, pedagogical strategies and time. Different activities will require different ingredients; some activities will be child-led, some adult-led, some require more time to enable children to meaningfully engage and participate, while others will be complete in minutes. A critical aspect of short-term planning and, by extension, the daily schedule relates to the concept of pace; the speed at which activities occur within the setting.

Pace

In 2010, we advised that 'it is critical that the schedule is not dominated by the clock... [Rather] it should allow sufficient time for children to begin an activity, engage in it and, complete it at their leisure' (Moloney & McCarthy, 2010, p.102). This means that children must not be rushed to complete an activity, but allowed to enjoy the process of engaging in it. At all times, engaging in activities must be an enjoyable learning experience for children, so as to foster positive learning dispositions. It is important to strike a balance between child-led, and educator-led activities. This ensures that you introduce content you want children to learn, focusing upon areas you notice require particular attention or support, as well as following children's current and emerging interests and abilities. The importance of choice and flexibility within the schedule cannot be overemphasised.

Remember one of the most important skills any child requires is a sense of autonomy/independence. It is essential to keep this in mind when considering the pace of activities. If the pace is always set by the educator, it creates an unsustainable level of child-dependency, as s/he will continually require the educator to change the activity. This can be frustrating for children as it tends to overlook their individual abilities and needs. Given the many differences between children with regards to ability, interest, concentration levels and needs, some children will finish an activity quickly and want to move onto something else within a few minutes, whereas others may just be settling into the activity when they are asked to tidy up. It is all too easy for an educator to become impatient with a child who is slow to complete an activity. Equally, educators can become frustrated with children who finish an activity quickly. This points to the need for flexibility within the schedule, so that an activity can be extended or reduced by 10 to 15 minutes as necessary.

Drawing upon the short-term plan, the schedule should clearly show the times for specific activities; for example, all children might be expected to come together for story-time at a particular time in the day. The schedule will take account of this. Sometimes children will set their own pace, i.e., when some activities are scheduled for small groups of children alongside optional activities over a prolonged period of time, children can set their own pace of moving through the planned activities (Kostelnik, Soderman & Whiren, 2007). You may find that one child will only complete one activity, while another has completed two or three within the same time frame, yet another child may not complete any task and may need to return to the activity the following day (Moloney & McCarthy, 2010). This is quite normal, as children vary considerably in their attention span, ability, task completion, need for repetition, understanding and learning pace. Flexibility of pace can provide opportunities for educators, or others such as a special needs assistants, to provide support and to scaffold individual children's learning.

Intentional leadership in the learning environment

The learning environment conveys a strong message to children and parents about their value within the setting. It is essential that the learning environment is warm and inviting for children and parents, and that they develop a sense of identity and belonging. In the context of intentional leadership, there are numerous considerations, all relating to children's safety, access to and use of equipment and materials, rich learning experiences, level of comfort within the setting, as well as timing and pacing of activities.

Again, concepts such as professional development and reflection are critical components in establishing and maintaining an inclusive learning environment. It is highly unlikely that any educator working with young children does not hold a minimum basic qualification and is therefore somewhat familiar with how children learn and develop, the context for their learning and how to support it. Accordingly, in relation to the learning environment, the intentional leader can be hands-on in preparing the learning environment, and/or have an overseeing role in terms of being alert to:

- environmental safety, paying particular attention to children's safety in line with legislative requirements relating to adult/child ratios, space requirements, ventilation, heating, lighting, sanitation, temperature control, etc.;
- layout and design of areas within the setting to ensure children can navigate areas with ease;
- accessibility of equipment and materials, and ease of use by all children;
- pedagogical framing, how the environment and activities are set up before children arrive to the setting each day, for example;
- educator's location within the indoor and outdoor environment in terms of their ability see and hear children at all times;
- timing, sequence and length of routines and activities.

The ultimate purpose of intentional leadership as it relates to the learning environment is to ensure children's access to meaningful participation and inclusion in the setting. The intentional leader identifies gaps in educator knowledge and skills with regards to maintaining an inclusive learning environment. Through positive role modelling, s/he can motivate and support staff to develop an inclusive environment, embrace diversity, affirm children's efforts, scaffold their learning and use peer support to encourage and foster participation, and engender feelings of success, pride and achievement in young children. They can further organise professional development opportunities for educators or invite specialists into the setting to engage in capacity-building with the staff team.

Engaging educators in regular reflection with regards to environmental adaptations (e.g., rotating materials, changing lighting, re-energising interest areas, altering the pace/timing of activities) is also a crucial aspect of intentional leadership. As mentioned, without adaptations and strategies, children with disabilities may be restricted in terms of movement, choice, flexibility and meaningful participation in activities and routines within the setting.

A core aspect of an inclusive learning environment, however, is concerned with the relationships and specifically with the establishment and maintenance of emotional safety, upon which Chapter 6 is premised.

Note

1   The ADA is a civil rights law that prohibits discrimination on the basis of disability in all areas of public life, including jobs, schools, transportation and all public and private places that are open to the general public.

6

LEADING AND MAINTAINING AN EMOTIONALLY SAFE ENVIRONMENT

Introduction

Chapter 5 explored the need for a physically safe environment. However, safety is not just about creating a harm-free environment, ensuring materials are non-toxic or keeping hazardous substances out of children's reach. A physically safe and an emotionally safe environment are intertwined. Regardless of the learning opportunities provided for in the setting, a child who feels insecure, anxious or afraid, will be unable to reach his/her optimal stage of development (McMonagle, 2012).

It is widely acknowledged that children's early experiences influence brain architecture, shaping neural connections and pathways. Babies are born with almost all of the neurons they will ever have, and during the early years connections between these neurons are formed and reinforced. Educators play an essential role in supporting these neural connections, and they must be consistent in responding to children's needs and provide opportunities for them to gain experience and practise their emerging skills (e.g., talking, reading, playing, exploring). In the absence of a stimulating and safe environment, there is a risk that some of these potential brain circuits will die away (Maggi, Irwin, Siddiqi & Hertzman, 2010) thus impeding brain development.

As discussed in Chapter 3, the concept of holistic child development recognises that children are not divided up into separate domains, learning styles, intelligences, attitudes, dispositions or creativities. On the contrary, children learn lots of things at the same time and in many different ways (NCCA, 2009). In this chapter, social-emotional development that is shaped in early childhood is explored. This refers to the developing capacity of the child to:

- form close and secure adult and peer relationships;
- experience, manage and express a full range of emotions;

- explore the environment and learn – all in the context of family, community and culture (Cohen, Oser & Quigley, 2012, p.1).

Early experiences 'determine the course of children's social-emotional development, which in turn, affects early learning, behaviour, relationships, and the ways in which children react and respond to the world around them' (Cohen et al., 2012, p.3). Social-emotional development is the 'cornerstone of healthy development' and underscores all future development: physical growth and health, cognitive skills, and communication. Darling-Churchill and Lippman (2016) assert that social and emotional 'experiences with primary caregivers as well as interactions with other children and adults early in life' are correlated with other areas of development including 'the confidence and competence needed to build relationships, problem-solve, and cope with emotions' (p.2). Conversely, failure to develop secure attachments with caregivers 'may lead to later difficulties in communicating or managing emotions, or developing positive relationships with peers' (Sroufe, 2005, in Darling-Churchill and Lippman, 2016, p.2).

The role of the educator in establishing an emotionally safe environment that fosters and scaffolds children's social and emotional development is essential. A lacklustre approach to planning the learning environment in both the physical and emotional domains represents a failure to protect children, places them at risk, undermines their social-emotional development and impedes their learning and development. Children must feel safe and secure within the learning environment. They need to learn how to express and control their feelings; know they belong and, that all adults in the setting are there for them. They need to feel visible, valued and supported.

Defining an emotionally safe environment

An emotionally safe environment ensures that children can feel socially, emotionally and physically safe and valued. It is where children can take risks, are challenged but not overly stressed, and where play, pleasure and fun are facilitated (Bluestein, 2001). Such an environment is founded upon respect, trust, honesty, acceptance, protection, positive interactions and responsive, consistent, caring relationships (see Figure 6.1). At the most fundamental level, children should be eager to attend the setting, and each day should hold the promise of something new, challenging and exciting.

Figure 6.1 illustrates the interplay between a number of factors, including the range and type of material and equipment, and the level of choice and flexibility that are central to establishing an emotionally safe environment. In addition to the design and organisation of the environment, attitudes, values, beliefs, positive interactions and reciprocal relationships are essential ingredients.

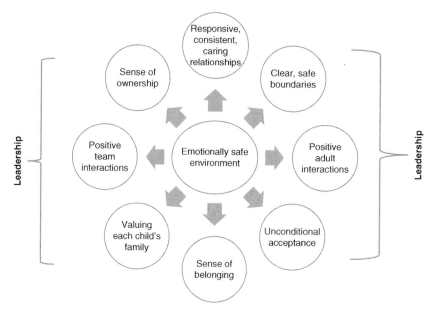

FIGURE 6.1 Components of an emotionally safe environment

Jane Bluestein's (2001) work relating to emotional safety identifies the following benefits of an emotionally safe environment for young children:

- A sense of belonging, of being welcomed and valued, being treated with respect and dignity, acceptance;
- Freedom to not be good at a particular task;
- Freedom to make mistakes, to forget, to need additional practice and still be treated respectfully and with acceptance;
- Having one's own unique talents, skills and qualities valued, recognised and acknowledged;
- Freedom to have and express one's own feelings and opinions, and to have them valued, recognised, acknowledged and acted upon where possible;
- Freedom from prejudice, judgement and discrimination based on cognitive, physical, creative or social-emotional capabilities;
- Freedom from prejudice, judgement and discrimination based on physical characteristics;
- Freedom from prejudice, judgement and discrimination based on background; religious, racial or cultural;
- Encouragement and success; recognition, instruction, guidance and resources according to need and regardless of need (adapted from Bluestein, 2001, pp.31–32).

The benefits outlined here are dependent upon how educators foster and maintain positive reciprocal relationships with children, which, in turn, determines children's behaviour and, consequently, the level of emotional security within the environment.

Relational pedagogy

Becker and Becker, (2008, p.147) suggest that from birth, relationships with adults are the 'critical determinants' of children's social and emotional development. They are also the foundation for the construction of identity: 'Who I am, how do I belong, and what is my influence?' (DEEWR, 2010, p.20). Other contemporary early childhood curriculum documents, such the *Early Years Foundation Stage* (UK), *Te Whāriki* (New Zealand) and *Aistear* (Ireland), reflect the principle that children learn through loving, trusting and respectful relationships during early childhood, and that relationships are the foundation for learning and development (see Table 6.1).

Each of these curriculum documents places a premium on the educator's 'understanding of children's interests and prior experiences by listening and watching them closely, interpreting their multiple languages and talking with their families' (White, 2016, p.45). In Ireland, for instance, the NCCA (2009) acknowledges that

> early learning takes place through a reciprocal relationship between the adult and the child… Sometimes the adult leads the learning and sometimes the child leads. The adult enhances learning through a respectful understanding of the child's uniqueness. He/she alters the type and amount of support as the child grows in confidence and competence, and achieves new things.
>
> *(NCCA, 2009, p.9)*

TABLE 6.1 The importance of relationships across curriculum documents in four countries

Aistear: Ireland	Children have a fundamental need to be with other people. They learn and develop through loving and nurturing relationships with adults and other children, and the quality of these interactions impacts on their learning and development (NCCA, 2009, p.9);
EYFS: UK	Children learn to be strong and independent through **positive relationships** [and they] learn and develop well in **enabling environments**, in which their experiences respond to their individual needs and there is a strong partnership between practitioners and parents and/or carers (DfE, 2017c, p.6);
Te Whāriki: New Zealand	Children learn through responsive and reciprocal relationships with people, places and things [through which] children have opportunities to try out their ideas and refine their working theories (MoE, 2017, p.21);
EYLF: Australia	Through a widening network of secure relationships, children develop confidence and feel respected and valued. They become increasingly able to recognise and respect the feelings of others and to interact positively with them (DEEWR, 2010, p.12).

The EYLF in Australia, defines the adult's role in terms of giving priority to nurturing relationships:

> Providing children with consistent emotional support can assist children to develop the skills and understandings they need to interact positively with others. They also help children to learn about their responsibilities to others, to appreciate their connectedness and interdependence as learners, and to value collaboration and teamwork.
>
> *(DEEWR, 2010, p.12)*

As these descriptions signify, the concept of relational pedagogy, which is characterised by interactions and communication (Papatheodorou, 2009) has become the bedrock of early childhood education and care. Critically, it underscores the establishment of an emotionally safe environment for young children.

Dineen (2009) describes relational pedagogy as a reflective and negotiative process that requires reciprocity, initiation and sustained shared thinking. In this respect, building and sustaining warm, caring, reciprocal relationships with all children requires an environment that allows for growth and learning of both children and adults. Relational pedagogy is therefore perceived as a dialogic process where educators and children embark on a learning journey together. Similar sentiments are expressed through the Early Childhood Curriculum Framework in Ireland (NCCA, 2009) where the Irish word *Aistear* translates as 'journey'. Throughout the learning journey, the educator facilitates and supports children's learning rather than setting a predetermined path (Papatheodorou, 2009; NCCA, 2009). The most explicit example of this is found in Reggio Emilia pre-schools where the approach to working with children is underpinned by a relational pedagogy. In the Reggio approach, interactions between children and adults are paramount, and are viewed as more important than curriculum content. Rather, as proposed by the Australian Children's Education and Care Quality Authority (ACECQA, 2011), 'Educators are actively engaged in children's learning and share decision making with them. They use everyday interactions with children during play, routines and ongoing projects to stimulate children's thinking and to enrich their learning' (p.214). Because learning results from interactions in the everyday routines that occur naturally within the ECEC setting, children and educators jointly construct the learning and have the freedom to both drive and alter the pace of learning depending upon abilities, interests and particular needs. Learning in this sense is a carefully negotiated territory between adults (including parents, educators, early intervention team, etc.) and children.

Brownlee (2004) defines relational pedagogy in terms of three parameters:

1. Respecting the child as a knower;
2. Providing learning experiences that relate to the child's own experience;
3. Articulating and facilitating a constructivist approach to learning by emphasising meaning-making rather than knowledge accumulation.

This understanding of relational pedagogy positions the child as a powerful player in his/her learning. It provokes and builds upon an image of the child as 'rich in potential, strong, powerful, competent, and most of all, connected to adults and to other children' (Malaguzzi, 1993, p.10) (see Chapter 3). Moreover, it negates the image of the educator as simply a transmitter of knowledge, viewing him/her instead, as a co-constructor of knowledge with the children. Co-construction places an emphasis on educators and children working together to generate shared understandings and meanings, rather than acquiring facts. It requires educators and children to make sense of the world, interpreting and understanding activities and observations as they interact with each other.

The early stages of relational pedagogy

Relational pedagogy, and co-construction begin from birth. During the first year of life in particular, children are totally dependent upon adults to interpret their communicative cues. Capturing the intensity of the relationship between a parent and child, Bronfenbrenner (1991) states that 'human development occurs 'in the context of an escalating psychological ping-pong between two people who are crazy about each other' (p.3). He further suggests that 'in order to develop normally, a child needs the enduring, irrational involvement of one or more adults in care and joint activity with that child. In short, someone has to be crazy about that kid' (in Weisner, 2008, p.259). Bronfenbrenner's reference to being crazy about a child, succinctly describes the unique bond that exists between parent and child/children. While the majority of parents are indeed 'crazy' about their children, and will overcome any obstacle to ensure their healthy development, those working with young children in ECEC settings, are tasked with providing the best possible experiences for children, so that they can optimise their development and learning. The way in which educators interact with young children is vitally important in supporting social-emotional development, fostering learning dispositions and, laying the foundations for lifelong learning.

Drawing upon the work of Bronfenbrenner, neuroscience uses the 'serve and return' metaphor as a way of helping us to recognise and understand the types of experiences that build strong brain architecture in the first years of life (Harvard Centre on the Developing Child, n.d). Serve and return works like a game of ping-pong or tennis between the child and the adult, where the child 'serves' by reaching for interaction, through babbling, gestures, facial expressions, eye-contact, crying or touching. According to White, Peter and Redder (2015, p.160) infants are 'highly social communicators capable of using whatever is at their disposal (usually their bodies) to engage with others', they are also 'active and competent contributors to their relationships with caregivers [and] their social competence is influenced by how successful they are in getting a response from their environments' (Smith, 2013, p.134). When a child 'serves' it is imperative that the adult 'returns the serve' by responding appropriately to the child's cues, including speaking back, giving a hug, playing peek-a-boo, laughing or sharing a toy. Smith (2013) highlights the reciprocal nature of the relationship and asserts that it is essential to recognise the importance of dialogic interactions between children and adults, and that both parties play a role in the relationship.

Children thrive in the context of stable, caring and positive relationships with adults who provide love and nurturance, security and responsive interactions. Serve and return interactions help children learn how to control their emotions, cope with stress, and develop skills that serve as a foundation for later development (Harvard Centre on the Developing Child, n.d). Educators who are attuned and sensitive to children's cues, thoughts and feelings support the development of a strong sense of wellbeing, belonging and identity, all of which are identified as key components of contemporary early childhood curriculum documents as outlined in Table 6.1. When educators establish an emotionally safe, responsive environment, children can develop secure attachments that enhance their resilience and long-term social competence.

Over time, the back and forth, ping-pong-like exchanges between children and educators become more robust, expanding in duration, frequency, affect and content (Brandt, 2014, p.10). Ideally, interactions are increasingly characterised by 'sustained shared thinking' (Sylva et al., 2004) through which educators support the development of children's complex thinking and problem-solving skills.

With regards to sustained shared thinking, findings from the Effective Provision of Pre-School Education (EPPE) project in the UK, which followed 3,000 children as they moved from pre-school to school, identified the 'quality of adult child verbal interactions' as a critical component in ECEC programmes (Sylva et al., 2004, p.5). Contingent upon the EPPE findings, the researchers coined the term 'sustained shared thinking' to describe the type of interactions that best support and extend children's learning. Accordingly, the concept of sustained shared thinking is defined as 'when two or more individuals work together in an intellectual way to solve a problem, clarify a concept, evaluate activities, extend a narrative etc. Both parties must contribute to the thinking and it must develop and extend the understanding' (Sylva et al., 2004, p.6). This means that both children and educators engage in open-ended, exploratory conversations to discuss and think about problems or challenges in a serious way.

PRACTICE SCENARIO

Sahar and Adham (both five years old) are making a cake for their friend's birthday. They both have different ideas about the cake, and as they begin, their differences become apparent

SAHAR: First we have to put the eggs in the bowl with the sugar.

ADHAM: No, that's wrong, we need the butter and sugar first, don't we teacher?

EDUCATOR: You both have different ideas. What type of cake are you making?

ADHAM: It's going to be a Madeira cake, just like my mother makes. That's why we need butter and sugar first.

EDUCATOR: What do you think Sahar?

SAHAR: But is that like a sponge? My mother made a sponge for my birthday, and we had eggs and sugar but no butter. I want to make a sponge.

EDUCATOR: What ingredients do you have?

SAHAR AND ADHAM [TOGETHER]: 12 eggs, butter, flour, sugar, vanilla, baking powder, and chocolate powder.

EDUCATOR: That's a lot of ingredients. How can you find out what you need to make the cake?

ADHAM: I know. Let's look in the baking book. There's lots of cakes there. We might make a different cake… two cakes.

SAHAR: That's a good idea Adham. Let's get the book.

Here the educator guides the children's learning through gentle probing and careful questioning. The children are not being told what is needed or how to make the cake. They are engaged in an open-ended, exploratory conversation with the educator to discuss and think about the problem of what kind of cake to make, and what ingredients they will need, in a serious way. This helps them to clarify the problem, share knowledge and agree on a solution, i.e., the need to use a 'baking' (recipe) book to help them. To support sustained shared thinking, it is best to use open questions that help to extend the narrative, clarify a concept and engage in in-depth conversation with the children.

PRACTICE SCENARIO

Jack (four years old) is working with play dough. The educator joins him at the table.

EDUCATOR: Do you like playing with the play dough Jack?

JACK: I love play dough, look, I made trees, and a wood cutter man.

EDUCATOR: Oh you made trees, good. What colour are the trees?

JACK: Green.

EDUCATOR: Good boy [as she moves onto the next table].

Unlike the previous example, it is apparent that Jack and the educator are not engaged in sustained shared thinking; the narrative has not been extended, and there is only the briefest sharing of knowledge. Based upon the brief interaction, we know that Jack loves play dough; that he made 'trees and a wood cutter man' and that he can identify the colour 'green'. As illustrated, closed questions, such as: 'What colour is the play dough' tend to reduce a child's communicative role to short, often one-word responses, and rely only on a child's capacity to recall information, so diminishing their opportunity for thinking, reflecting and/or speculating (Siraj-Blatchford & Manni, 2004).

In Jack's case, the educator could have supported sustained shared thinking by engaging him in a deeper discussion relating to what 'a wood cutter man' does? Where has Jack seen him? S/he could introduce an element of wonder to affirm Jack's efforts while also encouraging conversation and knowledge construction. Instead of simply saying 'what colour are the trees?', the practitioner could perhaps, say 'I wonder how you made those trees'. This approach shows genuine interest, attunement and engagement, ultimately leading to sustained reciprocal discussion, and co-construction of knowledge. Table 6.2 provides an overview of the many strategies that can be used to support sustained shared thinking.

TABLE 6.2 Strategies to support sustained shared thinking

Active listening/ tuning in	Getting down to the child's level, listening carefully to what is being said, observing the child's body language, and what s/he is doing. It also involves using positive, open body language and giving children your full attention.
Showing genuine interest	Giving your whole attention, maintaining eye-contact, affirming, smiling, nodding.
Respecting children's own decisions	'That's a wonderful suggestion, let's try it.'
Inviting children to elaborate	'I really want to know more about this.'
Re-capping	'So you think that…'
Offering/sharing personal experience	'I like to swim in the evenings when I finish work.'
Clarifying ideas	'OK Ruby, so you think if you mix the yellow paint with the green paint, you will make black paint.'
Suggesting	'You might like to try doing it this way.'
Reminding	'Don't forget that you said you would put on your apron first.'
Using encouragement to further thinking	'You have thought really hard about where to plant the sunflowers, but where will you hang the bird feeder?'
Speculating	'What do you think will happen if you play in the snow without wearing your gloves?'
Reciprocating	'Thank goodness, you wore your gloves when you played in the show. Look at my fingers Jim, they're frozen.'
Asking questions	'What do you think?' 'What would happen if…?' 'How did you…?' 'Why does this…?'
Modelling thinking	'I wonder what the sand will feel like when I add the water. It feels different now, look it won't run through my fingers like before.'

Adapted from: Siraj-Blatchford (2005).

Although questioning is a critical aspect of sustained shared thinking, it is important not to ask too many questions, or to ask questions in quick succession. Children need time to think, formulate an answer and extend their knowledge (Moloney & McCarthy, 2010). Rather than bombarding children with questions, Brodie (2015) recommends that children should be gently encouraged to think beyond the obvious.

Of course, not all conversations will result in sustained shared thinking. During a busy day, educators will always have fleeting/casual conversations with children (a quick hello or a passing comment). However, if that is the extent of your interactions with children, there is limited opportunity to connect seriously with their learning and thinking (NQS-PLP, 2012). The critical factor here is time. Building relationships with children takes time, and engaging in sustained shared thinking takes time. Therefore, as mentioned in Chapter 5, pacing is vital.

Getting to know children and building relationships with them involves spending extended time in their company, observing them, engaging in conversations with them, reflecting upon how they think, learn, participate in activities and engage with their peers. When you take the time to listen to a child, and demonstrate that what s/he has to say is important, you send a powerful message to the child about his/her importance. In the same way, when you interrupt a child who is trying to explain or tell you something, when you appear ready to leave at the first possible opportunity, you demonstrate a lack of interest that does little to make a child feel visible, valued or respected in the environment.

When you take time to get to know children well, you may learn things about their background, culture, needs, abilities and interests that enable you to better support their ongoing learning and development. With this in mind, look again at the practice scenario involving Sahar and Adham. Would you be surprised to learn that both Sahar and Adham are Syrian refugees? Both carry trauma – war, separation, loss, a new country, new language, social barriers, isolation, loneliness, and great uncertainty about their future. Does this information matter? How does it affect the creation of a physically and emotionally safe environment? How does it affect inclusive practice within the early years setting?

There are many things you might wish to know about Sahar and Adham, but you would be wise to tread cautiously. You would be prudent to take as much time as possible in getting to know them. In effect, this means that you may need to deliberately plan for meaningful conversations and episodes of sustained shared thinking. The following strategies recommended for educators by NQS-PLP (2012) are especially salient in the context of intentional leadership for inclusion. We recommend that the leader for inclusion within the early years setting works collaboratively with management and educators to put these strategies in place, to ensure that meaningful conversations and sustained shared thinking do actually happen:

- **Arrange the daily routine** to ensure there are blocks of time where educators and children can become deeply involved in learning and conversations about learning;

- **Make deliberate use of routine times** such as arrival and snack times, as opportunities to engage children in meaningful conversations;
- **Plan rosters** and educator shift-working arrangements to ensure that as many staff as possible are available to interact with children rather than doing other tasks (e.g., cleaning);
- **Ensure that educators understand** how vital conversational interactions are, so that they are more likely to initiate and engage in them;
- **Consider how supervision is managed** so that educators can focus on their interactions with individual children or small groups, rather than feeling that they always need to be monitoring the entire group;
- **Provide a rich and engaging environment** that provokes ideas and encourages conversations in the first place.

Universal design

As discussed in Chapter 5, the application of universal design is not about focusing on people with disabilities, but about making environments accessible to them. It places a high importance on diversity, equality and inclusiveness. UDL is just as applicable to the emotional as it is to the physical environment. Table 6.3 provides a sample checklist to help you identify whether the environment in your setting is emotionally safe for all children. It examines core aspects of emotional safety: how children are welcomed, level of structure and routine; stereotyping, segregation and stigmatising; educator-led communication; and ways for children to communicate as well as work cooperatively.

The actions identified in Table 6.3 that are intended to ensure that children feel emotionally safe in the setting indicate the need for educators to proactively engage with children in a positive and supportive manner. As with all other aspects of inclusion, these actions will not happen without the support and encouragement of a key staff member with responsibility for inclusion in the setting. Therefore, the intentional leader for inclusion must be attentive to how educators meet and greet children upon arrival to the setting and how they relate to them throughout the day, paying attention to the tone of voice used, the pace of interactions and the modes of communication that are utilised and supported. Moreover, attention must be paid to the structure and routine in the setting in terms of how time is allocated for different activities, to ensure a balance between adult- and child-led activities, and between individual, small- and large-group activities, with particular emphasis being placed upon the time needed for sustained shared thinking, and for children to develop their play themes and ideas.

The educator's role in boosting or detracting from children's social and emotional development should not be taken lightly. To have the most positive effect, you must understand how adult behaviours contribute to establishing relationships with children; how children's emerging capabilities in early childhood influence their connections to you, their peers and others; and how to translate your understandings into meaningful inclusive practice within the daily life of the setting.

TABLE 6.3 Universal design checklist for emotional safety

Does/is my activity room...?	*What can I do?*
Welcome all children, including those who attend part-time (couple of hours per day, or one/two days per week)?	Treat every child as a member of the group. Work with the children's other educators, members of the multidisciplinary team, special needs assistant and parents to make educational decisions together.
	Display each child's work and creations in the activity room/setting.
	Include everyone in group photos, and events in the setting, ensuring that children who attend part-time are included.
	Provide sufficient tables and chairs so that each child has their own space, and feel included during whole group, and small group activities.
Establish routine and security?	Establish the daily routine and communicate it clearly to the children. This creates a sense of security as children become familiar with your expectations in terms of their behaviour and learning; for example, time for snacks and lunch, going outdoors, play, story-time and going home.
Avoid stereotyping?	Do not assume that a child with a disability needs assistance with a particular activity or routine. Always give the child sufficient time to try to accomplish the task as independently as possible.
Avoid segregating or stigmatising any child?	Encourage educators not to draw unnecessary or unwarranted attention to a child with a disability, a gifted child or a child from a minority background.
	Avoid having an adult always by the side of a child with a disability. This hinders the child's sense of autonomy, and can prevent development and learning.
	Establish a peer-buddy programme so that children have peers to play with during non-structured times.
Enable effective teacher-led communication?	Pay attention to your tone of voice and word choice. Speak firmly and directly when dealing with challenging behaviour, for example. This is much more likely to be absorbed than when you raise your voice unnecessarily. This approach sets an example of calm and control and reinforces that fact that children are emotionally safe in the environment.
	Speak directly to the child with a disability, just as you would any other child. Give a child with a disability enough time to process what you are saying and allow time for a response. Do not ask too many questions or give too many instructions.
	Model the behaviour you expect from children; return equipment and materials, smile, say thank you, close the door gently, etc. Actions speak louder than words, so ensure you are communicating the message you want children to receive.

TABLE 6.3 (*Cont.*)

Does/is my activity room...?	What can I do?
Have multiple ways for children to communicate with each other?	Provide ways for a child who is non-verbal or who has little or no speech to communicate with educators and children without adult assistance. Teach all children in the group to use the child's preferred way of communicating – picture symbols, sign-language etc. – and model it with everyone.
	Assign peer buddies to help a children with English as a second language.
	Encourage all children to contribute to activities and discussions using their preferred method of communication.
Encourage cooperative work?	Design activities that require more than one child's participation to accomplish the task. This does not have to be done on a grand scale, but can begin with two children working together, gradually leading to small group work involving three or four children. Assign peer buddies, instead of an educator, to assist children with disabilities.

Adapted from: Moloney and McCarthy (2010); Brillante (2017).

Intentional leadership in maintaining an emotionally safe environment

This chapter, which is aligned with Chapter 5, highlights the role of the educator in establishing an emotionally safe environment that fosters and scaffolds children's social and emotional development. Against the backdrop of the Reggio approach to children's learning and development, where interactions between children are paramount and viewed as more important than curriculum content, this chapter affords equal importance to the physical and the emotionally safe environment for children. It suggests that a lacklustre approach to planning in either domain represents a failure to protect children, places them at risk, undermines their social-emotional development and impedes their learning and development.

The concept of relational pedagogy, which is characterised by interactions and communication has become the bedrock of ECEC, and, therefore, the manner in which educators interact with young children is central to supporting social-emotional development, fostering learning dispositions and laying the foundations for lifelong learning. As indicated, children thrive in the context of stable, caring and positive relationships with adults, who provide love and nurturance, security and responsive interactions. Educators who are attuned to and sensitive to children's cues, thoughts and feelings support the development of a strong sense of wellbeing, belonging and identity.

With regards to the intentional leader for inclusion, it is essential that s/he works collaboratively with management and educators to create the optimal conditions to support educator–child relationships, to ensure that meaningful conversations, and sustained shared thinking do actually happen. However, when it comes to the emotionally safe environment, certain aspects of the intentional leader's role overlap with those outlined in Chapter 5. Accordingly, the intentional leader is attentive to the structure and routine in the setting in terms of how time is allocated for different activities, to ensure a balance between adult- and child-led activities, and between individual, small- and large-group activities, with particular emphasis being placed upon the time needed for sustained shared thinking, and for children to develop their play themes and ideas. S/he is also attentive to how educators meet and greet children upon arrival to the setting and how they relate to them throughout the day.

Educators must be supported to understand how vital conversational interactions with children are, and how to make deliberate use of routines, such as arrival and snack times, as opportunities to engage children in meaningful conversations. The intentional leader can demonstrate this through modelling and mentoring, and by supporting staff to engage in continual professional development.

Given the centrality of the emotionally safe environment and its relationship with relational pedagogy, the intentional leader must pay attention to and, carefully plan staff rosters so that as many educators as possible are available to interact with children at all times. Not only does this involve organising staff rosters, it involves staff supervision and monitoring, as well as positive role modelling and interpersonal relationships with staff.

7

LEADERSHIP IN PLANNING AN INCLUSIVE AND RESPONSIVE CURRICULUM

Introduction

The concept of curriculum is clearly articulated and understood in the field of formal education, where it is associated with a course of study in school or college. This notion of curriculum is generally highly structured, prescriptive and subject-based. When it comes to ECEC, where it is thought that children learn best through play, hands-on experiences and interacting with the environment, the concept of curriculum can be problematic. After all, play is a nebulous concept that defies definition, as there are multiple types of play and ways of playing. Furthermore, there can be a tension between the idea of learning through play and what is considered 'real learning', involving activities that are targeted at cognitive development and with an emphasis on literacy and numeracy. Unlike the situation that prevails in relation to formal education, early childhood curricula, generally, emphasise learning experiences, the types of environments in which children's learning occurs and the ways in which opportunities for learning can be optimised. This broad, seemingly unstructured approach to young children's learning and development raises many questions pertaining to how curriculum is defined in early childhood, the kinds of learning experiences children should be engaged in, the types of environment in which learning takes place, and the role of the educator in facilitating and supporting learning and development.

Howard Gardner proposes that people possess unique capabilities and intelligences. For example, some children learn best by doing, others by listening and others by seeing, while others prefer a combination of all these intelligences. In relation to children with special educational needs, Dinnebeil, Boat and Bae (2013) note that certain young children '[f]ind communication difficult or challenging, others may have difficulty maintaining relationships with peers, while still others may have difficulty staying engaged in meaningful learning activities' (p.4). The goal for ECEC then is to design early childhood programmes that meet the needs of all learners within a common setting while also focusing on standards and programme accountability (Conn-Powers et al., 2006, p.1). Because 'even typical young learners vary so much in terms of their interests and abilities' (Dinnebeil et al., 2013, p.3), the principles of universal design (see Chapters 5 and 6) provide a framework to support all young children's learning and development.

In utilising UDL, the focus shifts from the right of a child to be physically present in the setting, to the right of all children to be in the setting and engaged in the general curriculum (Bertling, Darrah, Lyon & Jackson, n.d., p.2). Universal design does not remove challenges, it removes barriers (Bauer & Kroeger, 2004), and consequently, UDL 'involves the conscious and deliberate creation of lessons and outcomes by the educator that enable all children access to and participation in the same curriculum' (Moloney & McCarthy, 2010, p.136). Educators must therefore anticipate learning differences and, design the curriculum to meet the needs of all children, rather than adapting curriculum solely for children with SEN. When options and choice are built into the curriculum from the outset, fewer modifications are required for individual differences. Consequently, planning is more efficient and, provides for differentiation in the curriculum as children can access information in diverse ways, demonstrate skills through flexible curricula and, find multiple ways to be successful – key components within a universally designed classroom (Rose, Harbour, Johnston, Daley & Abarbanell, 2006).

This chapter explores a range of topics relating to early childhood curriculum. Drawing upon *Te Whāriki* (New Zealand, 2017), *Belonging, Being and Becoming: The Early Years Learning Framework* (Australia, 2016); the *Early Years Foundation Stage* (UK, 2017) and, *Aistear* (Ireland, 2009) it explores how curriculum is defined or described in each of these countries. Readers are introduced to the concept of pedagogical framing, which is central to rich diverse early learning opportunities and experiences. The chapter also examines the central role of play in children's learning and development, as well as curriculum planning. Although children have a tremendous propensity for learning from birth, they require support and encouragement from their parents/guardians, ECEC educators, peers and others, as necessary throughout their individual learning journey. In the context of early childhood education and care provision, children's learning is dependent upon purposeful curriculum planning, where careful consideration is given to what children will learn, how they will learn, what resources are required and how their learning will be assessed. Throughout this chapter, the question of leadership in planning an inclusive and responsive curriculum is continually interrogated.

Defining early childhood curriculum

Early childhood curriculum means different things to different people. For many, it is a particular educational approach or method, such as High-Scope, Montessori, Steiner or Reggio, for instance, each of which adopts a specific approach to curriculum planning, implementation and evaluation. Outside of these specific curricular approaches, the concept of curriculum for young children is open to interpretation. Some people, therefore, see curriculum in ECEC settings as the programme of activities, the routine, the plan or the schedule that encompasses everything a child experiences within the setting from the time they arrive to the time they leave.

As discussed in Chapter 3, governments in many countries view early childhood curriculum as a mechanism to optimise child outcomes through structured academic experiences in preparation for school readiness. However, as discussed, such a viewpoint fails to take account of education in its broadest sense, associating it solely with prescriptive cognitive based activities and with standardised testing, which does little to foster children's learning dispositions, curiosity, perseverance, resilience, enthusiasm, etc. Congruent with Gardner's theory of multiple intelligences, there is no doubt that the curriculum should provide opportunities for development in areas other than intellectual or cognitive development, ensuring that children's holistic development is paramount.

The Australian Early Years Learning Framework, *Belonging, Being and Becoming* (2009), proposes a broad definition of curriculum, describing it as 'All the interactions, experiences, activities, routines and events, planned and unplanned, that occur in an environment designed to foster children's learning and development' (p.45). In the same way, *Te Whāriki* (MoE NZ, 2017) and *Aistear* (NCCA, 2009) also interpret the concept of curriculum broadly, taking it to include all the learning experiences, activities and events, whether formal or informal, planned or unplanned, that occur within the ECEC setting that contribute to a child's development. Interpreted in this way, the message is clear: those working with young children must intentionally foster and contribute to their learning and development.

It is clear also, that the 'hidden curriculum' – the subliminal messages that children receive while participating in the setting – plays a key role. The hidden curriculum happens throughout the day and permeates all activities and areas of the setting. It is evident in the culture within the setting (see Chapter 4), in how children are greeted upon arrival to the setting, how they are treated by comparison to their peers, how educators interact with parents and each other. Because it is hidden, the curriculum implicitly conveys attitudes and values to children, conveying what is important and unimportant, who is respected and valued, and who is not.

PRACTICE SCENARIO

Three-year-old Jack struggles to open his coat upon arrival to the setting. All about him, other children open, take off and, hang up their coats independently. As he continues to struggle with the buttons, Jack becomes upset. Olivia, an educator approaches. Seeing Jack struggle, she says 'you're a big boy now, you should be well able to take off your coat'. She turns to June who has just hung her coat on a peg, 'well done June, good girl'. She then walks away, leaving Jack upset, and still unable to open the buttons of his coat.

Consider:

1. What is the hidden curriculum in this scenario?
2. What has Jack learned?
3. How do you think he feels?
4. What has June learned?
5. What could the educator have done differently to support Jack's learning and development?
6. How would Jack benefit from the support of an InCo or SENCO?

Te Whāriki acknowledges that all children have rights to protection and promotion of their health and wellbeing, to equitable access to learning opportunities, to recognition of their language, culture and identity and, increasingly, to agency in their own lives (MoE NZ, 2017, p.12). Children's agency – their ability to make decisions and choices, to influence events, to act upon their own ideas, to develop knowledge and skills in areas that interest them – is also reflected in *Aistear* in Ireland, the EYFS in the UK, the *Framework Plan for the Content and Tasks of Kindergartens*, Norway, *Curriculum for the Preschool Lpfö 98*, Sweden and the *National Core Curriculum for Early Childhood Education and Care*, Finland. The agentic child is interrelated with the image that each of us holds of the child (see Chapter 4), and it therefore has implications for how we perceive the curriculum. If we believe in the agentic child, every effort will be made to consult with and, incorporate children's ideas and interests into the curriculum, and as mentioned previously, doing this has been identified as a core principle of an inclusive culture in ECEC.

Curricular documents in the countries outlined provide a framework or a blueprint that guides educators with regards to what and how to plan for young children's learning and development. In the words of Goodfellow (2009), it is like a 'skeleton that gives shape to our bodies, or the physical support that holds a building together' (p.7). As a conceptual skeleton, it is both a guide and a planning framework that guides how educators view children, their capabilities and how they learn, and provides the shape for, or scaffolds the ways educators think about and work with children and their families (p.7).

When thinking about curriculum, there is much to learn from Jerome Bruner's questions: *What shall we teach, and to what end, when and how?* These questions suggest that we must consider how children learn, what they need to know, what it is we want to teach them, and how, as educators, we can support their learning. If we are to plan effectively for children's learning and development, it is imperative that we understand child development and how to foster it through the curriculum, pedagogy (how to promote children's development) and assessment whereby we determine how children are progressing and, identify any areas of development that require attention and additional support. Crucially, we must recognise and respect that children will take many different pathways in their learning, and that we support and encourage them to meet the curriculum goals in their own way and, in their own time.

The role of play in children's learning and development

Influenced by the work of pioneering educators such as Froebel, Dewey, McMillan and Steiner, ECEC is underpinned by a strong tradition that regards play as essential to children's wellbeing, development and learning. More recently, the child's right to play, rest and leisure is enshrined within Article 31 of the UNCRC (1989). Accordingly, children should not be denied their right to play in early childhood. Instead, play must be the cornerstone of learning and development. It is the foundation of learning in all domains and, across multiple ages, enabling children to interact with, explore and make sense of the world around them.

> Play is a source of joy and fulfilment for the child. It provides an important context and opportunity to enhance and optimise quality early childhood experiences. As such, play will be a primary focus in quality early childhood settings.
>
> *(CECDE, 2006, p. 9)*

The NCCA (2009) reminds us that relevant and meaningful experiences make learning more enjoyable and positive for children. There is nothing more relevant and meaningful in the life of a child than play and hands-on experiences, through which children explore social, physical and imaginary worlds. Play helps children to manage their feelings, build their confidence as they learn to explore, think about problems and relate to others (NCCA, 2009; DfE, 2017c).

As indicated in Figure 7.1, play is classified in two ways, style and types. The multiplicity of play types and, the complexity of play is clearly demonstrated in Hughes (2002) taxonomy of 15 play types which are summarised in Table 7.1.

Not only must educators understand these different types of play, they must also recognise and understand the need for both structured and free play for children. Table 7.2 illustrates the differences between structured and free play.

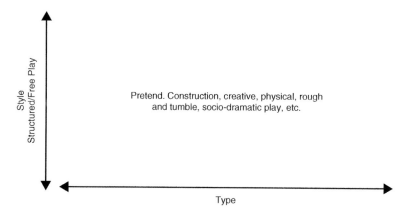

FIGURE 7.1 Classification of play

TABLE 7.1 Overview of the different types of play

Type of play	Description
Symbolic play	Using items to represent something else (e.g., a banana can be used as a phone).
Rough and tumble play	Playful fighting, chasing, wrestling (playful and non-aggressive).
Socio-dramatic play	The enactment of real and potential experiences that are personal, social, domestic or interpersonal in nature (e.g., visiting the doctor, playing house, going shopping, putting the baby (doll) to sleep).
Social play	Any social situation where there is an expectation that all participants (children) will abide by the rules (e.g., games with rules, making something together).
Creative play	Creating pictures or artefacts using a range of materials (e.g., clay, paint, paper, card, crayons, pencils).
Communication play	Using words, nuances or gestures (e.g., mime, singing, poetry, jokes).
Object play	Using objects for their intended or unintended purpose (e.g., sweeping brush).
Role play	Exploring ways of being (usually not of a personal, social, domestic or interpersonal nature), examples include driving a car, talking on the telephone.
Dramatic play	Dramatising events in which the child is not a direct participant (e.g., presentation of a TV show).
Deep play	Engaging in risky experiences to develop survival skills and conquer fear (e.g., climbing, balancing on a beam).
Exploratory play	Exploring objects and what they can do (mixing substances together to see what will happen, stacking bricks or sticks as in Jenga).
Fantasy play	Pretending to be someone unlikely, or enacting far-fetched occurrences (e.g., fire fighter, racing driver or princess).
Imaginative play	The conventional rules that govern the physical world so not apply (e.g., children imagining they are dinosaurs or Batman).
Locomotor play	Movement in any and every direction for its own sake (walking, running, hopping, sliding, sliding).
Mastery play	Controlling physical and affective aspects of the environment (e.g., digging holes, building huts).

As indicated in Table 7.2, in structured play, the educator has a specific learning intention in mind, which influences the nature and extent of his/her intervention. This is a complex task, requiring tremendous skill on the part of the educator who must strike a delicate balance between knowing when and how to intervene, and taking over the children's play. When the educator takes over, play becomes adult-led, which reduces children's choice and autonomy.

TABLE 7.2 Difference between free play and structured play

Free play	The children use and, choose toys, materials and equipment. They initiate and lead the play experience, developing their own ideas and themes. Children decide what to play, how to play and for how long.
Structured play, also known as guided play	Play experiences where the educator has more of an input, either initiating the play, controlling the resources available, or intervening or participating during the course of the play. Educators provide a significant amount of direction and guidance, offering suggestions, and purposefully teaching children. For example, the educator may introduce the concept of size and space during a ball game.

At all times, the educator must be sensitive to children's needs, interests and abilities. Although educators generally intervene in play to extend and support learning, they must be sensitive to what children are trying to achieve and, consider carefully how best to support them.

PRACTICE SCENARIO

Monika, a curious 3½-year-old is playing outside. She loves exploring her surroundings, frequently bending down to pick up a leaf 'for mama', admiring the 'fowers' and pointing to 'yukky mud' on the ground. She picks up a bird's feather from the grass, shows it to Joe, the educator 'big, birdie fy', as she stretches her arms wide in imitation of flying. She rubs the feather along the side of her face and laughs 'dickle me, soft' before placing it into her pocket. After a few minutes she bends again. She picks up a small white feather, dropping it quickly, she says 'not nice, doty'. Joey picks up the feather, brushes off a small piece of mud, and hands it to Monika who says 'cean, not doty'. She places the feather into her pocket 'for mama'. Beside her, two children are jumping in and out of a pool of water. Joe invites Monika to 'come and jump in the water, it's fun'. Monika shakes her head, 'no, doty, not nice'.

Consider:

1. What does this scenario tell you about Monika's development and learning?
2. What are her particular strengths and abilities?
3. What are her particular learning needs?
4. What structured activity would you plan to foster Monika's learning?
5. How would you support her learning?

The CECDE (2006) advise that

> Promoting play requires that each child has ample time to engage in freely available and accessible, developmentally appropriate and well-resourced opportunities for exploration, creativity and 'meaning making' in the company of other children, with participating and supportive adults and alone, where appropriate.
>
> *(CECDE (2006, p.49)*

Children's learning and development must be implemented through planned, purposeful play, and through a mix of adult-led and child-initiated activity (DfE, 2017c). There is no argument here; however, the question has to be asked, where does responsibility lie for planning and supporting children's learning and development in this way? Drawing upon Chapter 4: 'Leading and sustaining an inclusive culture', we suggest that curriculum planning is based upon participative theory involving consultation, joint decision-making, power-sharing, decentralisation and democratic management (Filosa, 2012, p.15), as well as empowerment (Yukl, 2013). In keeping with this concept, the intentional leader (e.g., the manager, the InCo, SENCO, pedagogical leader) actively seeks and takes the input of others into account. S/he encourages participation and contribution from all educators in the setting, helping them to feel valued, respected and committed to the planning process. The intentional leader, however, takes responsibility for ensuring that a plan for children's learning and development is drawn up, implemented and regularly evaluated.

Pedagogical framing

When, where and how does curriculum planning begin? Bearing in mind the importance of UDL (see Chapters 5 and 6) and the hidden curriculum, planning begins ever before a child enters the setting. Universal design ensures that the setting and the curriculum is accessible to all children, including equipment and materials that are easy to use by all children, and designed with safety in mind.

Critically, the relationship between pedagogical framing (Siraj-Blatchford et al., 2004) and curriculum planning should not be overlooked. What is pedagogical framing? It is described as the 'behind the scenes' work that educators do with regards to the provision of materials, the arrangement of space and the establishment of daily routines to support learning through exploration, cooperation and the equitable use of resources (Siraj-Blatchford et al., 2004). It also involves making informed decisions about the structure and content of the curriculum.

Let us consider for a moment the pedagogical framing associated with organising the learning environment in readiness for children's arrival to the ECEC setting each day. Behind the scenes, educators engage in a multiplicity of tasks to ensure that the environment is inviting and welcoming for all children and families. As demonstrated in Table 7.3, this includes risk assessment of the outdoor environment, checking that

TABLE 7.3 Pedagogical framing

Setting the scene	Pedagogical framing
Meera, Anna and Jan have arrived early to the setting to ensure everything is ready for the children's arrival and participation;	1. Pick up toys and replace on shelves, or into containers;
	2. Remove food items from the top of the cupboard;
Some toys are strewn about the floor, and the remnants of the previous evening's snack are sitting on the top of a cupboard, with crumbs scattered about the floor. The children's bathrooms require fresh hand towels and soap;	3. Wipe down the cupboard with disinfectant solution;
	4. Sweep and wash floor;
	5. Check and if necessary empty rubbish bins in the activity rooms;
	6. Check that all furniture and equipment is fit for use by children;
Upon checking the plan for the day, Millie, Anna and Jan see that a painting activity is scheduled for 10.00am, followed by an hour of outdoor play before the children's lunch time at 1.00pm.	7. Replenish supply of paper towels and soap in bathrooms;
	8. Check that heating is turned on;
	9. Check there is sufficient supply of paint for the painting activity;
	10. Ensure paint trays are available, as well as containers for water for each child;
	11. Ensure there is a plentiful supply of paintbrushes, sponges, rollers, paper and other items necessary for painting;
	12. Check the availability of T-shirts for use by children to protect clothes;
	13. Undertake a risk assessment of the outdoor play area.

all equipment and furniture is in a suitable state of repair and fit for purpose, ensuring that heating has been turned on or off, as necessary, and replenishing supplies.

As illustrated, the ECEC educator plays a fundamental role in the behind-the-scenes work in resourcing and organising the learning environment. Pedagogical framing is premised upon educator values and beliefs. Thus, if the educator believes in the child's right to a prepared, welcoming environment, pedagogical framing becomes a core aspect of his/her work, rather than an add-on. When it comes to pedagogical framing, intentional leadership comes from within, rather than being imposed by others; manager, demands of regulators and so on.

It is important to remember that pedagogical framing does not mean the educator is in control of everything that happens in the setting. On the contrary, it facilitates children's autonomy and agency within the environment. When the environment is in a state of readiness, children are primed for learning and will want to interact with and, act upon the environment.

Curriculum planning

Within the ECEC setting, children's learning and development is founded upon effective planning. As mentioned earlier, curriculum holds great meaning for children when it is relevant and meaningful (NCCA, 2009) and, when it connects them to real-world experiences, including their culture, home-life, interests and community. Furthermore, when children have opportunities to share in planning and evaluation, the curriculum is even more relevant and meaningful.

Each early childhood curriculum or curriculum framework outlined in this book places an equally strong emphasis on planning and assessment. In the words of the CECDE (2006) 'Enriching and informing all aspects of practice within the setting requires cycles of observation, planning, action and evaluation, undertaken on regular basis' (p.57). Assessment (see Chapter 8) enables educators to determine children's progress over time, and, plan accordingly for their future learning experiences.

Curriculum planning is a multi-layered process that provides a blueprint for what happens in the setting in the long, medium and short term. It involves a series of steps as shown in Figure 7.2. Furthermore, curriculum planning is a whole-team process involving all staff, full and part-time, involved directly with the children in the setting (Moloney & McCarthy, 2010). A whole-team approach ensures a sense of ownership and a consistent approach to curriculum throughout the early years setting, and is in keeping with the principles of inclusion. However, somebody must take responsibility for the planning process, deciding when and how it occurs. Whoever takes on this intentional leadership role decides the schedule of planning meetings, facilitating the staff team to come together to brainstorm, to identify curriculum goals, determine content (what to teach), plan activities aligned to curriculum goals and, ascertain how best to assess children's learning and development. In consultation with the staff team, the intentional leader also assigns roles and responsibilities with regards to sourcing and adapting resources, and 'writing up' the curriculum so that it becomes a working document that staff can repeatedly draw upon to guide and inform practice on a daily basis. Finally, the intentional leader ensures that the curriculum is implemented within the setting.

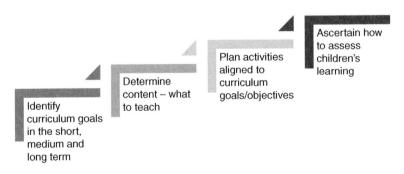

FIGURE 7.2 Steps involved in the planning process

This is not about rigid implementation. Rather, that the curriculum is used as a guide to inform practice, on the understanding that it is flexible enough to follow the child's lead when something captures his/her attention, as new interests emerge, or when it is evident that children are not ready to move on, but need more time to explore a particular concept or enhance a particular skill.

Long-, medium- and short-term curriculum goals are essential. They provide 'a natural gradation in the planning process, leading the teacher and practitioner from a broad overview to a more precise focus on the individual child' (Blandford & Knowles, 2016, p.182). When considering the long-term goals, think about what you might say to a parent/guardian when enrolling their child in your early years setting. What would you say to a parent/guardian who asks what their child will achieve while attending the setting? Would you be able to explain the approach to children's learning and development? At this early stage, you can tell parents about the overarching goals (long-term), what concepts children will be introduced to (medium-term), and provide examples of the types of activities and experiences (short-term) children are exposed to while attending the setting. Figure 7.3 highlights the difference between long-, medium- and short-term planning.

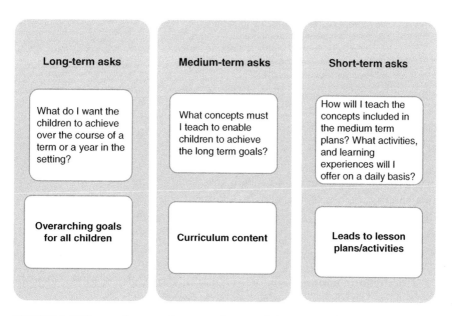

FIGURE 7.3 Difference between long-, medium- and short-term planning

Long-term planning

The long-term plan serves as a guide for the ECEC educator. It considers aspects of children's learning and development based upon national standards as in the

Early Years Foundation Stage in the UK, or in the particular areas outlined within a national curriculum framework such as the *Framework Plan for the Content and Tasks of Kindergartens* (Norway), *Te Whāriki* (New Zealand) and *Aistear: the Early Childhood Curriculum Framework* (Ireland). Additionally, the long-term plan is based upon in-depth knowledge of child development, as well as what you know about the children in the early years setting, including knowledge of any special educational needs and/or disabilities (see Chapter 2). Often, the long-term plan is developed before children actually attend the setting. As a result, it is guided by your knowledge of child development, as well as information provided by parents/guardians about their child. Taking all of these factors into account – knowledge of child development, national standards or curriculum framework goals and information from parents – long-term planning may set broad goals relating to communication, literacy, physical development, creativity, social and emotional development, identity, belonging and wellbeing, for example.

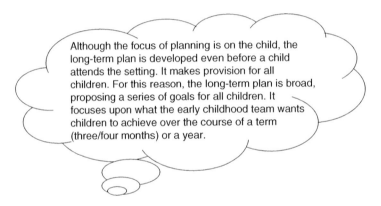

Although the focus of planning is on the child, the long-term plan is developed even before a child attends the setting. It makes provision for all children. For this reason, the long-term plan is broad, proposing a series of goals for all children. It focuses upon what the early childhood team wants children to achieve over the course of a term (three/four months) or a year.

Long-term planning is concerned with children's entitlement to a broad and balanced curriculum. This means that children are not subjected to an unrelenting diet of academic activities, but that equal attention is given to the arts, to music, to movement and so on. Both the medium-term and the short-term plans are informed by the long-term plan. The long-term plan leads to questions about:

- **Curriculum content** – what concepts children will be introduced to in order to help them achieve the long-term goals;
- **Activities and experiences** – how content will be taught.

In the following activity, which uses 'wellbeing' as an example, you are asked to identify a corresponding long-term goal for each of the following areas of learning and development: social development, language, literacy, physical development and creativity.

Activity: Identify the long-term goal

Area of learning and development	Corresponding long-term goal
Example: Wellbeing	Children will be confident, happy and healthy individuals
1 Social development	
2. Language	
3. Literacy	
4. Physical development	
5. Creativity	

One of the benefits of long-term planning is that educators have goals in mind for children's learning and development. In effect, they become 'intentional' educators (Epstein, 2014).

> Intentional teachers 'act with specific outcomes or goals in mind for all domains of children's development and learning. Academic domains (literacy, mathematics, science and social studies) as well as what have traditionally been considered early learning domains (social and emotional, cognitive physical, and creative development) all consist of important knowledge and skills that young children want and need to master.
>
> *(Epstein, 2014, p.1)*

Medium-term planning

It can be tempting for educators to develop short-term daily or weekly plans without any long- or medium-term planning. However, such 'off the cuff' planning is inadequate (Moloney & McCarthy, 2010). It does not capture the breadth and depth of children's learning as envisaged in the long-term planning process, and it can degenerate into nothing more than 'filling in time'. It holds little meaning or relevance for children. While more comprehensive broader planning is essential for all children, it is even more so for children with SEN.

Medium–term plans are derived from the long-term plan, and they are concerned with continuity and progression in children's learning over a term or a month. They identify the concepts, skills, knowledge and attitudes children will be introduced to over a specified time. All of this adds up to curriculum content, or as Epstein terms it, the 'substance or subject matter' that educators will teach (2014, p.7), which requires the educator to think carefully about what to teach children in order to achieve the stated goals of the long-term plan.

At this stage, different areas of learning can be linked through themes or topic. Using the theme Exploring and Thinking from *Aistear* (NCCA, 2009) as an example, Table 7.4 provides an overview of long-term and medium-term planning.

TABLE 7.4 Example of long-term and medium-term planning

Long-term plan	Medium-term plan	When
Children will acquire and use skills and strategies for observing, questioning, thinking, exploring, experimenting, understanding, negotiating and problem-solving	Provide opportunities for children to: • Explore **patterns** so that they can make connections and associations between new learning and what they already know; • **Explore and make sense of the world**: question, plan, predict, put into action, think, manipulate, reflect on, remember, modify, discuss, explain, wonder, speculate; • **Collaborate** with others to confidently solve problems and share interests; • Demonstrate their ability to **reason logically**; • Use their **creativity** and **imagination** to think of new ways to **problem-solve**; • **Gather information** in different ways (adapted from NCCA, 2009).	**Term 1: September to December**

Clearly, the medium-term plan is focused upon domains of learning and content areas, it covers specific areas/themes of learning. Significantly, the medium-term plan guides the short-term, supporting the educator to plan daily and weekly activities.

Early childhood education emphasises integrated learning and, as illustrated in Figure 7.4, the curriculum content identified during medium-term planning cuts across multiple domains of leaning and development. With this in mind, let us explore the benefits of introducing children to 'pattern'. Figure 7.4 provides an overview of the relationship between pattern and integrated learning.

Although pattern is aligned to the theme of wellbeing in *Aistear* (NCCA, 2009), it connects with, and supports children's learning and development in multiple areas. It is not just a one-off activity, it is all around us. Pattern then can become a theme in the medium-term plan, leading to a variety of activities across multiple domains of learning and development. When thinking about medium-term planning, it is important to take account of the knowledge, skills and understanding you want children to learn, as well as the types of skills and attitudes children should develop, including independence, motivation and resilience (Blandford & Knowles, 2016).

Given that pattern supports integrated learning, it is pertinent to ask, what does it look like in the context of a short-term plan? The answer to this question lies in our understanding of what is meant by short-term planning.

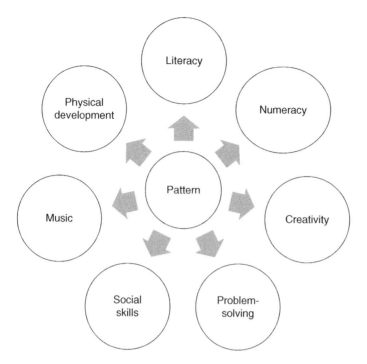

FIGURE 7.4 Relationship between pattern and integrated learning

Short-term planning

The short-term plan is the working document that supports daily practice within the setting. It is drawn from the medium-term plan, and, is generally prepared a week in advance. It

- is concerned with differentiation and planning for the specific needs of specific groups and individual children;
- is flexible and fluid – it changes daily as educators observe children, and learn something new about their learning, development, interests and abilities;
- provides details of activities that support long- and medium-term curriculum goals;
- provides details of resources, groupings for activities and pedagogical strategies.

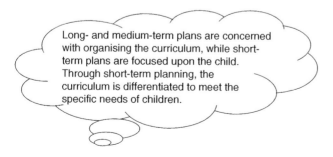

Long- and medium-term plans are concerned with organising the curriculum, while short-term plans are focused upon the child. Through short-term planning, the curriculum is differentiated to meet the specific needs of children.

The short-term plan is like a recipe that outlines the ingredients required for specific learning experiences, including equipment, materials and, pedagogical strategies. It enables you to plan particular learning experiences for specific children. Using the recipe analogy, different activities will require different ingredients. When applied to short-term planning, this means that there will be a balance of child-led and adult-led activities, and that some will require blocks of time to enable children to meaningfully engage and participate, while others will be shorter and completed in minutes. There will be a balance between indoor and outdoor activities, between large and small group times, etc. Although the principles of universal design outlined in Chapters 5 and 6 reduce the need for individualised supports, some children will require specific intervention to access the curriculum, participate fully in the activities and make progress (see Chapter 2 for particular strategies).

Let us now return to the concept of pattern, and consider what it looks like within the short-term plan. Pattern helps children to learn sequencing and, to make predictions that lead to mathematical skills, logical thinking and to establishing order in life. Young children regularly sort blocks by colour shape and size. They begin to build towers using blocks of colour, or alternating colours to form a pattern. They show an interest in knowing the days of the week, months of the year and the rhythm of the seasons, odd and even numbering. Different musical genres introduce children to other forms of pattern, where they clap, tap their feet and move their bodies to a musical beat. Modelling how to read from left to right during story-time introduces children to the pattern in writing.

Table 7.5 provides an overview of pattern in the short-term plan, showing a range of activities that introduce the concept of pattern to children, while also supporting integrated learning, and consolidating their learning.

TABLE 7.5 The concept of pattern in the short-term plan

Monday	Tuesday	Wednesday	Thursday	Friday
Sorting buttons	Threading	Reading from left to right	Matching socks	Finger painting

Remember that while this example has been drawn from the medium-term plan, it is not written in stone. It is continuously informed by observations (see Chapter 8) and may change as children's interest increases or diminishes, or as difficulty in undertaking or engaging in activities emerges. For example, a child with dyspraxia will have weak fine motor skills that make it difficult for him/her to sort buttons, hold a crayon or zip up their coat. Activities such as threading, matching socks or sorting buttons may also be challenging for a child with dyspraxia, and accommodations (see Chapter 8) will be required. The simple adaptations introduced in Chapter 2, such as providing large chunky buttons or adding a grip to crayons or paintbrushes can make it much easier for a child with dyspraxia to participate in activities. These simple adaptations, which are based upon children's abilities, interests and needs, ensure that the curriculum is used as a tool for inclusion that supports access to and participation in all learning activities and routines in the setting.

Decisions about curriculum are continually informed by systematic observations of children (see Chapter 8), which often result in alterations to curriculum content and, to the educator's particular pedagogy. Fisher (2010) suggests that 'any teacher who is planning to meet the learning needs of children using their daily observations cannot know on Monday what a child might be learning on Friday' (p.160). The following practice scenario illustrates this point.

PRACTICE SCENARIO

Ruby, who is three years and seven months old, is sitting at a table sorting buttons. She has a bowl of mixed red, yellow and blue buttons, and is sorting by colour into three clear bowls. Observing her, the educator Gerry, notices that Ruby finds it difficult to pick the buttons up between her thumb and forefinger, and that she is becoming frustrated. As soon as she grasps a button it falls back into the bowl. Ruby turns the bowl over scattering the buttons onto the table. She now uses her hand to slide buttons into piles, naming the buttons as she does so. Gerry notices that Ruby is confused about the colours, as she repeatedly mixes them up, calling the red buttons 'blue' and vice versa.

Consider:

1. How would you characterise Ruby's approach to this sorting activity?
2. What strengths is Ruby displaying in this scenario?
3. What specific learning needs is Ruby displaying?
4. What are the implications for Ruby's learning and development?
5. What are the implications for the weekly short-term plan?
6. What change, if any, would you make to the weekly short-term plan to support Ruby's learning and development?
7. How could an InCo or a SENCO support Ruby in this activity?

Even though Table 7.5 focuses upon the short-term plan over the course of a week in the life of the ECEC setting, it tells us little about how the activities will be structured, or what pedagogical strategies will be utilised to support children's meaningful participation.

Planning allows educators to think and act long-term and systematically with regard to their pedagogical practices. It helps ensure continuity and progression for each child and for the group of children as a whole. Planning shows how the setting interprets and utilises the early childhood curriculum as a starting point for reflection and for developing the setting over time (see Chapter 8). Planning must be based on knowledge of the children's wellbeing and all-round development, individually and, as a group. It must also be based on observation, documentation, reflection, systematic evaluation and conversations with children and parents, all of which are discussed in Chapter 8.

TABLE 7.6 Sample short-term plan

Activity	Purpose	Resources and who is responsible for sourcing and organising	Grouping and number of educators	Pedagogical strategies
Patterns	Children will become familiar with and, create patterns and sequence.	Multi-coloured beads, laces, wooden sticks and blocks, pegs and boards, writing materials (crayons, pencils, markers, pens), an assortment of paper and card, collage making materials. **Responsibility:** Carl (room leader)	Children will be in three groups of six. Three educators: one educator will work with each group of children.	**Positioning** **Describing** **Questioning** **Listening** **Modelling** **Co-constructing** **Scaffolding** (MacNaughton & Williams, 2008)

Intentional leadership in planning an inclusive and responsive curriculum

This book calls for and, supports the need for intentional leadership, to ensure effective and meaningful inclusion. Chapter 4 discussed the concept of distributed leadership, suggesting that there are spheres of influence within the setting, with associated layers of leadership. As mentioned, distributed leadership underscores the need to mobilise leadership expertise at all levels within the setting. One such level must be in the area of pedagogical leadership, which is concerned with supporting and promoting quality early learning experiences for young children. It is focused upon curriculum planning, implementation, assessment including family engagement and review.

It is important at this point, to explore the term pedagogy, and what it means. While it is usually described as the art or the craft of teaching, Lindon and Lindon (2012) differentiate between pedagogy; pedagogical thinking and pedagogical leadership.

- Pedagogy: The details of the individual or team approach about how to support children's learning wherever they spend their day. The core values, principles and chosen strategies creates the pedagogical base for your practice;
- Pedagogical thinking: An exploration to enable deeper understanding of what informs your practice, and the reasons why you work in a particular way;
- Pedagogical leadership: Active support, guidance, explanation and setting a best practice example to other team members over a developmentally sound approach to supporting children's learning (Lindon & Lindon, 2012, p.133).

Abel (2016) combines each of these aspects into his description of pedagogical leadership in terms of impacting teaching and learning by establishing organisational norms of continuous quality improvement: 'Pedagogical leaders influence children's learning by fostering family engagement, ensuring fidelity to the organisations curricular philosophy, using data to evaluate the effectiveness of the learning program, and meeting standards established to optimize learning environments.' The pedagogical leader is focused upon planning and assessment, parental engagement, and, with ensuring the quality of early childhood education and care.

Who can be a pedagogical leader? Coughlin and Baird (2013) indicate that anyone who has a deep understanding of early learning and development may take on the role of the pedagogical leader. These individuals see themselves as partners, facilitators, observers and co-learners alongside educators, children and families. 'Most importantly, pedagogical leaders challenge others to see themselves as researchers in the teaching and learning process. In turn, this practice builds a culture of reflective teaching that helps us to sort through the complexities of our work' (Coughlin & Baird, 2013, p.1). The role of pedagogical leader, which is well established in Norway, is defined by the Norwegian Directorate for Education and Training (2017, p.17), which identifies the following dimensions:

- Implement and oversee the kindergarten's pedagogical practices using sound professional judgement;
- Offer guidance and ensure that the Kindergarten Act and the Framework Plan are observed in the kindergarten's pedagogical practices;
- Oversee the process of planning, implementing, documenting, assessing and developing the work taking place amongst the group of children or in the areas he/she is tasked with supervising.

In relation to inclusion, the pedagogical leader takes responsibility for ensuring that a plan for children's learning and development is drawn up, implemented and regularly evaluated. Alongside this, the pedagogical leader plays a key role working with educators in the behind-the-scenes work in resourcing and organising the learning environment. Thus, the pedagogical leader recognises the child's right to a prepared, welcoming environment, and ensures that pedagogical framing is a core aspect of the educator's work, rather than an add-on. As discussed in this chapter, when the environment is in a state of readiness, children are primed for learning, and will want to interact with and act upon the environment.

Like all other aspects of leadership for inclusion, the pedagogical leader acts with intent, to make things happen. S/he therefore takes responsibility for the planning process, deciding when and how it occurs, facilitating the staff team to come together to brainstorm, to identify curriculum goals, determine content (what to teach), plan activities aligned to curriculum goals and ascertain how best to assess children's learning and development. Furthermore, in consultation with the staff team, the intentional pedagogical leader assigns roles and responsibilities with regards to sourcing and adapting resources, and 'writing up' the curriculum, so that it becomes a working document that educators can repeatedly draw upon to guide and inform practice on a daily basis, and s/he ensures that the curriculum is implemented within the setting.

The intentional pedagogical leader 'nurtures dispositions that are useful for educators' in their daily practice, such as curiosity, openness, resiliency and determination, which help to 'create a culture where there is less focus on teaching and more on how learning takes place for both the child and the adult' (Coughlin & Baird, 2013, p.2). This involves ensuring that educators have time to reflect on their own practices, to observe children and to engage with parents. Clearly, intentional pedagogical leadership is not all about the children – as important as this is, but as noted by Lindon and Lindon (2012, p.134) 'children's experiences are dependent upon adult choices over their own behaviour'. An intentional pedagogical leader is tasked with building up the educators' confidence and view of themselves as learners, and to supporting them in understanding their current skills, identifying any gaps in their knowledge/skills, and working with them to redress these gaps in the best interests of supporting children's learning and development. The role of the intentional pedagogical leader, which is inextricably linked to reflective practice, is further explored and developed in Chapter 8: 'Leading assessment for learning to support inclusion'.

8

LEADING ASSESSMENT FOR LEARNING TO SUPPORT INCLUSION

Introduction

As discussed throughout this book, within any ECEC setting, children are at different stages in their development and learning. They learn at vastly different rates and their developmental and learning patters can be episodic, uneven and rapid (Ackerman & Coley, 2012), with some children lagging behind in their development, while others are exceptionally talented or able. Children, therefore, take many different pathways in their learning. However, as proposed by the European Agency for Special Needs and Inclusive Education (2015, p.1) inclusive education is about ensuring that all children, 'are provided with meaningful, high quality educational opportunities in their local community alongside their friends and peers'. Such opportunities begin with consideration of the learning environment (see Chapters 5 and 6); curriculum planning (Chapter 7) and with assessment for learning, which is the focus of the present chapter.

Planning and assessment are mutually dependent. In addition to providing children with high-quality educational experiences, educators must also provide opportunities for them to demonstrate what they know, what they are able to do and, what they are interested in. Just as children learn in different ways, they also demonstrate their knowledge in different ways (Dinnebeil et al., 2013). Assessment then, is an integral aspect of the learning and development process. It is key to helping educators *inter alia* to:

- appreciate children's unique qualities;
- plan appropriate, relevant and meaningful learning experiences for children;
- identify necessary supports to enhance children's learning and development;
- reflect upon and improve their own practice.

To optimise learning opportunities for all children, authentic assessment and ongoing monitoring of their learning and development is essential. As with other aspects of inclusive practice, assessment is influenced by

- educators' attitudes, values and beliefs;
- educators' image of the child;
- intentional leadership.

Let us revisit the predominant and contradictory images of the child proposed in Chapter 3: a) the child as a competent and confident learner, and b) the child as fragile, incomplete, weak and made of glass. The former image leads to a strengths-based approach to assessment that celebrates what the child can do, while the latter operates from a deficit model that emphasises what the child cannot do.

This chapter explores the role of assessment in informing inclusive practice in ECEC. It examines the need for educators to undertake systematic assessments of children's learning and development, so that they can determine what children know and understand, identify priority learning needs, plan and implement appropriate, relevant and motivating learning experiences for each child. It discusses the concept of authentic assessment, which is compatible with a whole-child perspective on learning and development (focusing upon what children do, and how they do it, in the context of their interactions with materials, equipment, peers and adults). This chapter also addresses reflective practice, which is an essential skill that enables early childhood educators to review and analyse their practice in order to improve inclusive provision for children with SEN. The need for intentional leadership is further developed in this chapter.

What is assessment?

Assessment is not the same as testing (Hearron & Hildebrand, 2011). It involves collecting information from multiple sources that may or may not include standardised or formal testing. Along a continuum, it is defined as 'building a picture of children's individual strengths, interests, abilities, and needs and using this to support and plan for their future learning and development' (NCCA, 2009, p.11), and as the 'process of observing, recording and documenting what children do, and how they do it as the basis for a variety of educational decisions that affect the children' (Division for Early Childhood of the Council for Exceptional Children, 2007, p.10). As with planning, assessment is not a single, once-off event. It is a process that requires educators 'to understand each child's performance based on their knowledge of child development, cultural and linguistic competencies, and age and grade expectations' (Freeman, Decker & Decker, 2013, p.303). It is concerned with what children know, what they do and how they do it, as a basis for educational decisions that inform pedagogical approaches, curriculum development and implementation. Further, assessment leads to accommodations, i.e., alteration of the environment, curriculum or equipment/materials, and instruction to enable a child with a disability to participate in and benefit from the curriculum.

Purpose of assessment

In a busy ECEC setting, it is easy to assume that all children are participating in, benefiting from and, enjoying the learning opportunities and experiences provided through the curriculum. You may not always notice a child who is struggling with social interactions, whose speech and language or gross motor development is delayed. It may be that you are concerned about a particular child that you've noticed being withdrawn, finding it difficult to navigate the environment, listen or communicate in an appropriate manner. Maybe there is a child in your group who is bored, disinterested in activities and displaying behavioural issues, because s/he is exceptionally able and is not being challenged by the curriculum, or is unable to cope because of 'sensory sensitivity to factors such as noise or texture or the number of people in the room (sensory integration issues), or emotional sensitivity to perceptions of unfairness, discrepancy or insincerity' (Probst, 2011). Perhaps a parent has advised that their child has been diagnosed with a special educational need. Systematic assessment, undertaken at regular intervals, is key to addressing these possible scenarios. Assessment enables you to get to know each child, so that you become aware of their learning dispositions, abilities, strengths, interests and needs, and plan accordingly. Essentially, assessment provides you with evidence and data to help you make informed decisions about children's learning and development. It plays a critical role in helping you to:

- relate to curriculum objectives or national learning standards (e.g., the EYFS in England);
- accurately identify children's individual strengths and learning/development needs;
- gain an understanding of what motivates and interests children;
- monitor development of the whole child (e.g., physical, language, cognitive, social, emotional, creative);
- identify children who may be demonstrating signs of learning difficulties or special needs;
- review the curriculum, and match pedagogical approaches, activities, materials and supports with the child's particular needs;
- monitor progress and evaluate the effectiveness of an accommodation for a specific child;
- provide feedback to parents and multidisciplinary professionals;
- reflect upon your own practice, develop knowledge and understanding about how children learn, as well as strategies that work to empower children with special educational needs to meaningfully participate in the general curriculum with their peers.

In short, assessment is central to 'revealing a child's prior knowledge, development of concepts and ways of interacting with and understanding the world so that teachers can choose a pedagogical approach and curricular materials that will support the child's further learning and development' (Bowman et al., 2001, p.259). As noted by the NAEYC (2008) educators' knowledge of each child enables them to plan 'an appropriately challenging curriculum, and to tailor instruction that responds to each child's strengths and needs' (p.13). The ultimate goal 'is to make learning more interesting, enjoyable and successful for children' (French, 2007, p.12), it should benefit children, and not be used for the purposes of ranking or segregating them (Nah, 2014).

Forms of assessment

Assessment can be considered in terms of formative (informal) and summative (formal), both of which are used for different reasons. Summative assessment involves screening, and standardised testing. For example, the Early Years Foundation Stage (DfE, 2017c) requires educators to assess children's achievements at age two in the prime areas: communication and language; physical development; personal, social and emotional development. While these areas are considered the basis for successful learning, the EYFS specifies their role in helping children 'become ready for school' (p.9). In the final term of the year in which the child reaches age five, an EYFS Profile must be completed for each child. The purpose is '[t]o provide a well-rounded picture of a child's knowledge, understanding, and abilities, their progress against expected levels, and their readiness for Year 1' (p.14). As discussed in Chapter 3, an inordinate focus on school readiness does not encompass education in its broadest sense, associating it solely with prescriptive cognitive-based activities, and with standardised testing that does little to foster children's learning dispositions: curiosity, perseverance, resilience; enthusiasm, etc. Because children learn at vastly different rates, tests administered at one point in time alone may not provide an accurate picture of a child's concept knowledge, skills or understanding (Riley-Ayers, Jung & Quinn, 2014). As a result, educators need an effective assessment tool that helps them to understand children's development. This tool should allow them to collect information and, evidence about what children know and can do, to determine their skills and to identify their strengths as well as any areas that require support.

In early childhood, formative assessment is generally acknowledged as the most appropriate mode of assessment for young children. It involves gathering evidence over time, and in the context of the child's interactions with materials, equipment, peers and other adults. The purpose is to build a rich picture of the child's learning. Young children best demonstrate their knowledge, understanding and skills in their natural environment through play, daily activities and routines. Furthermore, educators are well placed 'to notice early signs of potential difficulties and to bring their concerns to parents and relevant professionals' (NCCA, 2009, p.94). Hence, formative assessment is a shared endeavour between educators, families and other professionals working with the child, and involves gathering information and evidence from multiple sources.

Thus information can be gathered from parents, educators and others who have knowledge of the child such as an early intervention team (see Chapter 9). Whereas evidence can be gathered through observations, portfolios of children's work, learning stories, checklists, photographs and video clips, or a combination of all these elements (see Table 8.1 for an overview of assessment tools). As with planning, assessment is not a solitary activity. Rather it involves working collaboratively with other educators, parents and professionals involved with the child. Collaborative working allows for exchange of information about the child, ideas on assessment tools, methods, and interpretation of results (NAEYC, 2008).

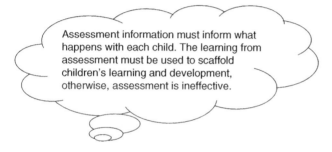

Assessment information must inform what happens with each child. The learning from assessment must be used to scaffold children's learning and development, otherwise, assessment is ineffective.

When utilised effectively,

> Assessment allows all children to receive the individualized instruction they deserve, in particular enabling the high-achieving children to go further, the lower-achieving children to receive the support they need, the quiet children to be heard, and those with challenging behaviours to be understood beyond the behaviours.
>
> *(Riley-Ayers, 2014, p.16)*

The assessment process

ECEC educators become participant-observers and engage in a cyclical process over time which is part and parcel of formative assessment and involves a series of interconnected steps as shown in Figure 8.1. They need a clear understanding of all children's current skills and abilities to ensure access and particpation, and to develop relevant and meaningful learning opportuniies and experiences. Initally, as illustrated in Figure 8.1, information about children's current skills and abilities is provided by parents upon enrolment of their child at the setting.

As shown, assessment involves multiple steps, beginning with gathering information and evidence of children's abilities, skills, learning and interests; reflecting upon, evaluating and analysing the data; and discussions with parents and setting staff.

TABLE 8.1 Overview of assessment tools

Assessment tool	Description	Aspect of development
Target child observation	A focused and detailed observation of a particular child's all round development at a specific time over part of a session.	All domains of development (physical, language, cognitive, social-emotional) Behaviour Interaction Communication Play Concentration
Event sampling	A series of short observations focusing on particular events to build up a pattern of a child's behaviour over a period of time. Event sampling looks at antecedents, behaviour and consequences.	Behaviour Interaction Social skills
Time sampling	Observing children for fixed regular short intervals of time over an extended period.	Behaviour Concentration Interaction
Free description/ narrative observation	A detailed observational account of a child's progress at a particular time, taking into account as much detail as possible about what is happening at the time.	All domains of development (physical, language, cognitive, social-emotional) Behaviour Communication Play Concentration Interaction
Checklist	A list of skills and/or behaviours that the adult ticks off when observed.	All developmental domains (physical, language, cognitive, social-emotional)
Portfolios	A holistic collection of samples of children's work demonstrating growth and development over an extended period of time.	The '100 languages of children' Creativity Imagination Visual arts Music and movement
Conversations	The educator engages the child/ children in conversations about what they are doing and thinking.	Thinking skills Imagination Language Comprehension Communication Social and emotional

TABLE 8.1 (*Cont.*)

Assessment tool	Description	Aspect of development
Self-assessment	Involves children about what they have done, said or made and assessing their won progress. The educator uses prompts to guide the child's thinking and reflections.	Life skills Constructive play Visual arts Language Science
Learning stories	Uses storytelling to describe the learning that takes place in child-initiated play. Learning stories are always positive.	Dispositions Interests Abilities Understandings Knowledge

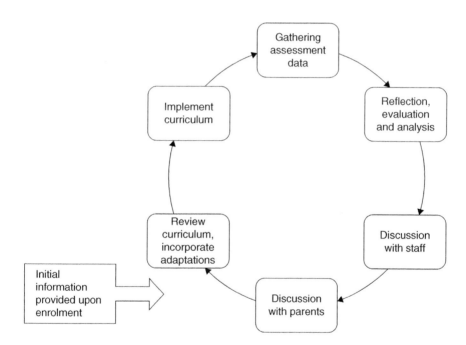

FIGURE 8.1 The assessment process

Following discussions with parents and staff, the assessment data is incorporated into curriculum review, identifying necessary adaptations and, finally, implementing the revised curriculum. The cycle then begins all over again, so that educators can monitor children's progress, identify strengths and, determine ongoing challenges and future learning goals. The quality of children's experiences are underpinned by the interconnectedness of learning, assessing, reviewing and planning.

Authentic assessment

The term authentic assessment is increasingly used in relation to how information about and evidence of children's learning and development is gathered in early childhood. As the following definition from Bagnato and Yeh Ho (2006) indicates, the focus of authentic assessment is upon children as they go about their daily lives in the context of the natural environment, i.e., the early childhood setting: 'Systematic recording of developmental observations over time about the naturally occurring behaviours and competencies of young children in daily routines by familiar and knowledgeable caregivers in the child's life' (p.29). Authentic assessment is designed to provide 'strengths-based, inclusive and individualised care; support child-initiated learning, and promote appreciative understanding' (Zollitsch & Dean, 2010). The critical point here is the emphasis upon strengths-based assessment. Unlike norm-referenced standardised testing practices that focus upon what a child cannot do, authentic assessment is concerned with what children are able to do and what they know, while also identifying areas where they may need additional support. Rather than emphasising deficits in the child's learning and development, authentic assessment begins with a focus on the child's strengths.

Authentic assessment uses a range of data collection strategies including: observations of children, portfolios of their work, learning stories, as well as conversations with team members and parents. Educators regularly collect information about children in the context of play, everyday activities and routines in the early years setting (i.e., their natural environment) where they are comfortable and not under pressure to perform to the test, as happens with formal, standardised testing.

> Evaluating the child within the context of play, social interactions, and care-giving routines requires that the assessment process focus on the demands and expectations of the environments where children live, learn, play, and work rather than merely children's relative standing in a normative group.
>
> *(DEC, 2007, p.14)*

Freeman et al. (2013) suggest that these methods provide educators with opportunities to apply their knowledge of child development and of particular children within the context of a natural or educator-created situation. High-quality authentic assessments of young children share the following characteristics:

1. They are closely aligned to the learning goals identified by the programme/curriculum;
2. They use multiple observation and documentation strategies;
3. They involve multiple stakeholders (i.e., families and other professionals) (Freeman et al., 2013, p.303).

Although authentic assessment occurs within a natural environment and is premised upon a strengths-based approach, it should be guided by state learning goals (where they exist), specific curriculum goals (see Chapter 7), parent goals for their child, and in-depth understanding of child development progression for young children.

Observation

Observational assessments are known as 'authentic' because they capture what the child 'is able to do in real life situations, rather than how the child performs on isolated tasks in artificial situations' (Hearron & Hildebrand, 2011, p. 325).

> The ability to capture a 'true' picture of the child can be thought of occurring along a continuum with the least authentic or most artificial approaches at one end, and the most authentic approaches, most indicative of the child's actual functioning at home as well as the setting, at the other.
>
> *(Hearron & Hildebrand, 2011, p.325)*

Observational assessments focus upon the processes children use to learn, such as problem-solving, experimenting, researching, inquiring, hypothesising and investigating. Educators document each child's individual learning in all domains; physical, social, emotional, cognitive and language development. These observations provide a wealth of rich information that helps the educator to understand a child's behaviour and, make informed judgements about his/her abilities, learning disposition, interests, strengths and needs. They also inform decisions relating to adaptations and supports required to help a child progress in his/her learning.

The excellent teacher uses her observations and other information gathered to inform her planning and teaching, giving careful consideration to the learning experiences needed by the group as a whole and by each individual child. By observing what children explore, what draws their interest, and what they say and do, the teachers determines how to adapt the environment, materials, or daily routines. The teacher can make the activity simpler or more complex according to what individual children are ready for (Copple & Bredekamp, 2009, p.44).

Observations are particularly suited to young children; they are unobtrusive, occur over time, and provide optimal time for educators to get an overall picture of what children can do in all domains.

PRACTICE SCENARIO

Shaun, an educator working with a group of ten four-year-old children is concerned about Erika. He has noticed her tendency to avoid any type of 'messy play' such as gloop, paint, sand or water. Erika also reacts negatively to any change in routine in the setting, often having a complete meltdown that involves her repeatedly banging into the wall. This morning during fire-drill, while the other children were initially startled by the noise of the fire alarm, they accepted the explanation given by the educators and calmly followed instructions to leave the building. Ericka, however, could not be reassured or calmed, and was still screaming, with her hands over her ears, a full hour after the fire alarm was activated.

Consider:

1. Are Shaun's concerns justified? Why?
2. What are the implications of Shaun's concerns for assessment?
3. What steps should Shaun take with regards to assessing Ericka?
4. How could an InCo or a SENCO help?

As this scenario illustrates, it is sometimes easy to determine what type of observation is required. Pritchard and Brodie (2015), for instance, highlight the example of a child who may be stammering and who will therefore need numerous observations on their speech. Equally, parameters may be defined by other professionals that must be observed and recorded, such as how far a child can walk unaided (Pritchard & Brodie, 2015, p.79). The information gathered can then be used to update the curriculum, plan particular accommodations or early interventions.

Observations are used as a tool to document children's learning and development, and in that sense, Basford (2015) suggests they serve as a starting point rather than an end point. This means that observations are the starting point for collaborative dialogue between the educator, the child, and his/her parent/guardian. 'Parents, families, and educators are valued sources of assessment information. They are also the audience for assessment results, and should be actively included in the formative assessment processes' (Riley-Ayers, 2014, p.14). Remember each person brings a piece of the puzzle relating to the child's learning, development and understanding to the table, and the evidence gathered through observations of the child in the setting is a valuable piece of the overall picture.

Assessment data enables the educator to work collaboratively with parents and other professionals involved with the child in determining which skills require particular support, what type of supports are needed to help the child progress in his/her learning and development, and how and when to provide, or indeed access, additional specialised support from other professionals, such as a speech and language or occupational therapist. Equally, when educators share assessment information with parents, it helps the home and setting to work together to support children's learning and development. All child observations and other assessment data must be treated with the utmost confidentiality, and only discussed with the parent/s of the child concerned, then filed in a locked storage cabinet.

Learning stories

Learning stories, which are the mainstay of *Te Whāriki*, were conceptualised and developed by Margaret Carr and Wendy Lee who describe them as a powerful assessment tool for early childhood. A learning story is a record of what an educator or parent/guardian has seen a child or a group of children doing in an ECEC setting. This approach to assessment documents children's learning through stories. Documentation takes many forms ranging from pen and paper to digital formats. It includes written narratives, computer-generated narratives, film-based and digital photography, video footage and examples of children's work. These various forms are assembled together in portfolios, 'not as an end product, but as a work in progress that are fully accessible to children, parents and teachers' (Lee & Carr, n.d., p.6). The documentation includes not only stories but annotated photographs, children's art, recordings or transcripts of oral language, educator's observations and learning stories (MoE NZ, 2017). Critically, portfolios include children's, educators' and parents'/guardians' voices, creating living documentation that forms a powerful framework that gives direction for educators and children in the provision of rich and challenging learning environments (Lee & Carr, n.d.).

> On-going, multi-media documentation is enabling teachers to truly listen to each child and assess what that child's interests and strengths are. This assists them to find the place in which deep involvement in learning can take place… [And it has] also been instrumental in including families on their children's learning.
>
> *(Lee & Carr, n.d., p. 5)*

Moreover, the MoE (2017) highlights the role of learning stories in making use of 'a formative assessment sequence: noticing, recognising, responding, recording and revisiting valued learning' (p.63).

> There are no guidelines for writing a learning story. It may be as short as one paragraph, extend to one page or longer. It is usually focused on a specific incident or episode. It may focus on a group activity, and be a learning story about an activity that the children did together, such as going for a walk, gardening or any other activity in the setting.
>
> When the educator adds his/her interpretation of the child/children's competence and disposition towards learning (e.g., perseverance, curiosity) it becomes a learning story. The learning story highlights what the child can do and is doing, rather than what s/he cannot do.

In keeping with formative assessment, learning stories adopt a strengths-based, rather than a deficit approach to assessment. They make children's learning visible to educators, parents/guardians, children and others.

PRACTICE SCENARIO

This morning, three-year-old Florrie removed all the wooden blocks from the container. She carefully begins to build the blocks into a tower, working quietly and intentionally. She is soon joined by five other children. Florrie continues to build the tower, counting from one to ten. 'What comes next?' she asks Claudia the educator. Together they count from 11 to 15. The other children watch fascinated as the blocks get higher and higher. 'It's getting bigger,' shouts Tom. Florrie laughs as Precious hands her two more blocks and watches as she places these blocks on top of the others, '22'. Florrie tells the children 'move back, I want to see it'. She walks slowly around the stack of blocks examining it from all angles. 'We need to make it bigger,' she says, as she returns to kneeling on the floor and continues to add blocks. She no longer counts. The other children keep handing blocks to her. Florrie stretches upwards, placing another block carefully on top. 'It's very bigger,' Lucy says. 'We need more blocks,' shouts Florrie. She now stands up to reach the top of the tower. Laughing she places another block on the top. 'It's going to fall, it's going to fall,' shrieks Zac. 'No it's not, more blocks, more blocks,' Florrie calls excitedly. She continues to add to the stack of blocks as the other children laugh and clap. Florrie continues to stack the blocks, becoming more and more excited. 'It's very big now,' she says as she stretches towards the top. 'One more, one more, give it to me,' she shouts as Tom hands her another block. Claudia, the educator cautions 'be careful, it's going to topple over'. Florrie pauses, hand in mid-air. She turns towards Claudia, 'I can do this, I can'. She slowly places the block on top of the stack, pauses, and looks at her building. Again she walks around observing her construction from all angles. She then places her right hand at an angle to her forehead measuring where it is in relation to the stack of blocks. As she realises how tall the stack is, she shrieks 'wow, look, it's bigger than me!'

Consider:

1. What skills is Florence demonstrating here?
2. What type of learning disposition is being demonstrated?
3. What conclusions can you draw about Florrie's learning and development?
4. How can her learning and development be extended?

A learning story records only positive information. As mentioned previously, any concerns about aspects of a child's development should be recorded separately and stored confidentially in a locked cabinet.

The use of documentation to make learning visible is also evident in the world-renowned Reggio Emilia approach, which is underpinned by a sense of collective responsibility for children's learning. It is premised on the belief that no one person can verify knowledge about a child's learning; it has to be negotiated between all parties including the family and the child. Moss (2007) argues that in this context, documentation is not a child observation tool that can be used to measure development. Instead it is a tool for 'resisting' the prominent discourses related to universality that seem to be so apparent in English early years childhood policy (Moss, 2007, p.15). The intention of a learning story is to provide a document that situates learning as a process, and that demonstrates how children's involvement with learning in a collaborative context can help to develop their working theories (Hedges, 2011) and demonstrates the complexity of their thinking. Such an approach also acknowledges that learning involves the development of a repertoire of dispositions, rather than just knowledge and skills (Carr, 2001).

Because the educator writing the learning story generally knows little about the child's wellbeing, experiences or behaviour outside the ECEC setting, this mode of assessment must be used in conjunction with other methods, such as observations, to provide an overall picture of the child's learning and development.

Work portfolios

Work portfolios are another form of assessment that can be particularly relevant to young children including those with SEN (Deiner, 2010). They include samples of the child's drawings, artwork and writing. Photographs depicting various projects, skills the child has developed, friendships the child has made and play activities the child has engaged in can also be included. Work portfolios can be personalised for each child, preferably by the child, using drawings, paintings or photos so each child comes to recognise his/her own special book (NCCA, 2015). Start compiling a work portfolio from the very first week that the child attends the setting so that progress can be seen, and monitored over time. The following guidelines for building a work portfolio are adapted from the NCCA (2015):

- Put a date on each item so progress can be seen over time;
- Add a brief note explaining what a photo or item relates to;
- Include captions of what children said to make the entry more meaningful. It also helps the educator to talk about events, items and experiences when looking at the portfolio with the child or when sharing with a parent;
- Include comments to link children's learning and development to the curriculum goals.

Again, only positive information is recorded; concerns about aspects of a child's development should be noted separately and stored confidentially in a locked cabinet.

To maximise the educational value of work portfolios, it is important to involve children in the selection of work samples for inclusion in their portfolio. Children can learn very quickly to put some of their work samples into the portfolio on an ongoing basis. This gives them a sense of pride in and ownership of their learning and development (NCCA, 2015), as well as fostering their growing sense of identity, belonging and wellbeing.

Work portfolios can move with the child as s/he transitions to a new room in the setting, or to another educational establishment (i.e., school), thus providing information for successive educators and ensuring continuity and progression for the child.

Deiner (2010, 63) identifies three different types of work portfolios:

1. **Showcase portfolios**, which include the child's best work;
2. **Working portfolios**, which allow the early years educator to discuss work in progress with the child and to reflect upon their work;
3. **Assessment portfolios**, which are holistic and are scored or graded.

Building a portfolio of work is a valuable tool in empowering children to showcase their achievements through selecting samples of their work that they feel are representative of the progress they have made over time. Educators can encourage a child to celebrate the personal growth s/he has made by comparing what s/he has done earlier with what s/he can do now. The DCYA (2016) identifies the need to encourage children to recognise their individual qualities and the characteristics they share with peers, and to actively engage children in making decisions about their own learning, as core principles of an inclusive culture in ECEC. In relation to assessment portfolios, these particular principles can be enacted by discussing with the children how much they have learned, and providing opportunities for them to share parts of their portfolio with the other children (Moloney & McCarthy, 2010). Naturally, children will love sharing their portfolio with their parents.

Self-assessment

Building upon the principles of an inclusive culture as proposed by the DCYA (2016), self-assessment is appropriate to young children in ECEC settings. Simply put, self-assessment is child-led, and involves children thinking about their own learning. Children often do this naturally as they learn and, they are best placed to assess what they have done or accomplished.

> Over time, they are better able to think about what they did, said or made, and to make decisions about how they might do better next time. Children need time to develop self-assessment skills. The adult plays a key role by spending time with them individually, in pairs or in groups, and revisiting the activities and events they were involved in.
>
> *(NCCA, 2009, p.81)*

The educator plays a key role in helping children to develop self-assessment skills. This can include using the following prompts to guide the child's thinking:

- What did you do when…?
- How did you do that? What did you use?
- What happened next? Why do you think that happened?
- What would you like to do next time?
- Who will you do it with?
- What were you thinking when…?
- What was easy/difficult about this activity?
- Are you happy with…?
- I wonder what would have happened if…
- What would help you to do it better? (NCCA, 2009, p.105).

Blandford and Knowles (2016) stress that questions should challenge and encourage children in their learning, and broader development, provide opportunities for them to start taking responsibility for their learning and open channels for thinking, creativity, problem-solving and decision-making. While self-assessment may be too difficult for some children, for others this approach can work very well, helping them to set personal goals and to work towards achieving them. Moloney and McCarthy (2010) suggest that self-assessment can be particularly helpful for children who are exceptionally able, as it enables them to set a learning pace that is appropriate to their individual learning abilities.

Self-assessment can take many forms. For example, a non-verbal child can be invited to decide which one of his/her efforts deserves a sticker, a stamp or placement on a 'wall of fame' – or indeed which creations will go into his/her portfolio. This decision-making can be modelled for a reluctant child, showing him/her how to affirm him/herself (Moloney and McCarthy, 2010). Be mindful of comparing a child's effort with his/her own previous effort, rather than with the efforts of others. Equally, it is essential to affirm the child's effort more than the quality of the end-product.

Using assessment information to promote children's learning and development

The NAEYC (2008) argues that any attempt to teach children in the absence of assessment information or only to reflect upon the meaning of assessment information is ineffective and does not meet children's needs. The information gathered through assessment must be used in planning for individual children. When examining assessment information, educators must know what they are looking for. Table 8.2 provides an overview of relevant questions, links to curriculum goals and assessment findings.

TABLE 8.2 Overview of relevant questions, links to curriculum goals and assessment findings

Questions	Link to curriculum goals	Findings
How much time did the boys spend in the home corner?	Children will benefit from all interest areas.	Boys are spending more time in the home corner.
How much time did Erika spend playing alone?	Children play cooperatively together.	Erika finds it difficult to play with other children.
How long did Amira cry after her dad left?	Children separate easily from their parents/ caregivers.	Amira is able to separate from her dad without crying.
How many pieces were in the puzzle Cóilín put together?	Children will complete increasingly complex puzzles.	Cóilín put together an eight-piece puzzle.
What did children already know about magnets? What did they learn after our week of using magnets?	Children make connections and associations between new learning and what they already know.	Children demonstrate existing knowledge and understanding, and make connection with new learning.

Adapted from: NAEYC (2008).

Earlier in this chapter, formative assessment was defined as a shared endeavour between educators, families and other professionals. Assessment findings should be shared with parents/guardians so that all parties – educators, parents and children – have an opportunity to share their insights, and interpretation of what is documented. Remember parents can provide unique insight into the child's behaviours and abilities in everyday activities in the home and the wider community or neighbourhood. Basford (2015, p.30) suggests that a child or a parent can provide a different interpretation of the 'documented moment'. Hedges (2011) indicates that these different interpretations are a result of parents sharing funds of knowledge about their child from their unique social and cultural background that an educator may be unfamiliar with. In this way, information from parents, can provide a richer and more authentic insight into the child's life outside the setting.

Bear in mind the need to be steadfast in sharing any evidence gathered through authentic assessments that may indicate a delay in the child's learning and development. Some parents may be sensitive, or even defensive when an educator suggests there may be a problem with their child's development, others may be relieved to have their suspicions validated and will appreciate having specific information from the setting to enable them to advocate for and access support for their child.

A child's special educational needs are often not recognised until s/he attends an ECEC setting, and the educator may be the first person to have concerns. It can therefore be difficult for a parent to hear that their child may have a SEN, and they may resist or react with anger or accusation. The natural instinct is to protect parents from these emotions, and perhaps avoid becoming embroiled in a difficult situation yourself. This should not be used as a reason for withholding information, as it will result in inordinate delays in seeking specialised support for a child who needs it. In this regard, early intervention (see Chapter 9) generally results in positive outcomes across all domains: health, language and communication; physical development; social/emotional development; and cognition. Furthermore, families benefit from early intervention by being better able to meet their child's specific needs from an early age. Delays in seeking specialised support, which is a key element of early intervention, may have a detrimental effect upon the child's learning and development in both the immediate and longer term. Delays in making any necessary special educational provision can give rise to loss of self-esteem, frustration in learning and to behavioural difficulties (DfE, 2014).

When sharing information with parents, it is essential that it is presented in a kind, clear and objective manner.

PRACTICE SCENARIO

Beth and Josh are attending a parent meeting with their child Millie's educator. Millie, their only child, is three years four months old, and as far as her parents are concerned, she is developing normally. However, the educator Alexandra imparts the following information:

Millie is lagging behind her peers in all areas of development. Her speech and language is underdeveloped, she has poor social skills. She does not like playing in large groups and mostly plays with two or three friends. She has scored below average in all subjects, she is not where we would like her to be at this stage in her development.

Consider:

1. What is the image of the child held by the educator?
2. What is the educator's understanding of early childhood education?
3. How was the information delivered to Millie's parents?
4. How do you think Beth and Josh might be feeling?
5. How you would approach this situation?
6. What support could an intentional leader provide in this situation?

Using the assessment data, and in agreement with parents, a range of accommodations can be put in place to support a child's learning and development within the setting. For the majority of children with SEN, the smallest support, accommodation or modification can make a world of difference, and can ensure that children with disabilities can participate along with their peers. Here are some ideas of simple accommodations:

- Provision of **social supports** (e.g., peer-mediated intervention strategies, cooperative learning);
- Using **visual, auditory and kinaesthetic** methods (e.g., use pictures and models when explaining). For example, to help a child transition to a new activity or area, provide him/her with a picture showing where to go or what to do next;
- Using a range of **reinforcers** (e.g., smiles, hugs, praise);
- **Adapting toys/materials.** Simple adaptations such as adding grips to pencils, crayons, markers, paintbrushes and eating utensils make it easier for a child to handle these materials, and also foster independence;
- Providing **specialised equipment** such as alternative and augmentative communication devices, touchscreens and large keyboards make it easier for children to participate;
- **Increasing size** of print/pictures for children with a visual impairment;
- **Altering the environment** (physical, emotional, aesthetic or temporal environment). For example, label containers, baskets, folders and shelves (using pictures and words) so children know where materials go when they are finished with them;
- Dividing an activity into **smaller steps.** For example, help a child to close the zipper on his/her coat by pulling it up half-way, then have the

child complete the task. This generates a feeling of success and fosters independence;

- Providing **more challenging** activities, especially important for an exceptionally able child. For example, engage an exceptionally able reader in a game of alphabet soup where s/he has to find patterns and solve word puzzles;
- Extending or reducing **wait or performance time**. Intentionally plan when children will participate in or transition to an activity. Arrange for an anxious child who has difficulty waiting to take his/her turn first;
- Providing more **individualised or specialised practices** for some children (adapted from DEC, 2007).

Remember that while assessment should lead to the identification of a child's priority learning needs, educators are not doctors or psychologists and must not, therefore, attempt to diagnose a child or guess at a diagnosis. It is also essential to bear in mind that a delay in learning and development in early childhood may or may not indicate that a child has a SEN; that is, 'that they have a learning difficulty or disability that calls for special educational provision. Equally, difficult or withdrawn behaviour does not necessarily mean that a child has SEN' (DfE, 2014, p.14).

Sharing assessment information provides opportunities for families and professionals, including educators, to work as a team to make decisions about how best to support the child to progress in his/her learning and development. In the event that there are significant emerging concerns, or an identified SEN/disability, educators in the UK are required to develop a targeted plan to support the child's future learning and development involving parents and/or educators and other professionals (for example, the provider's SENCO or health professionals) as appropriate (DfE, 2017c).

In the case of Ireland, parents are central to the Access and Inclusion Model and encouraged to work in partnership with the ECEC setting to complete an 'Access and Inclusion Profile' for their child. This profile is based upon observations of the child while in the setting, as well as information provided by the parent/s. The following information is included on the child's profile: physical abilities, communication abilities, social skills, behaviour, health and additional health care needs. Upon completion, the profile is forwarded to the Better Start Access and Inclusion Team. Following this, an Early Years Specialist (Access and Inclusion) visits the setting, meets with educators, observes the child and supports the setting and the parent/s. The overall purpose is to ensure that children with a disability can access and meaningfully participate in the ECEC setting. This may include the development of an Inclusion Plan (IP) to address what is required to enable the child to access and participate in the general curriculum on an equal basis with the other children (Moloney & McCarthy, 2010). The IP outlines the specific education and care targets for the child, along with the additional supports and resources required to enable the child to meet those specific targets. Figure 8.2 provides a sample Inclusion Plan.

Child's Name:	Madu Dweck	
Date of Birth	10th August, 2015	Age: 2 years 8 months
Family	Asu and Amira Dweck	
Educators	Damien & Martha	
Name of ECEC setting	Hybrazil Nursery School	
Present at IP Meeting	Asu and Amira (parents), Damien & Martha (educators), Helena (setting manager)	
Date of IP Meeting	1st November, 2017	
Date of Review	1st May, 2018	

Note: This Inclusion Plan (IP) has been developed to support your child's learning and development. The specific targets that are identified in this IP are focused on the additional support that your child needs and are only a small part of your child's overall programme in the setting.

Nature of concern: Madu has been attending the setting for four months. He is a happy child who loves attending the setting. His main areas of difficulty are in social communication and play. His parents' main goal is that he will make friends and learn to mix with other children.

Priority Learning Needs:

1. Social Communication Skills
2. Play
3. Establishing Friendships

Specific Targets	**Strategies to be used**	**Who**
Social communication. That Madu will greet his educators each morning on arrival to the setting	Use modelling and a puppet to teach greetings Parents to encourage Madu to practice greetings at home with family members	Damien & Martha (educators) Asu & Amira (parents)
That Madu will take turns with other children in his group	Adult/child modelling of turn taking on a one to ne basis Introduce one other child to the activity to reinforce turn-taking. Madu encouraged to wait his turn for the slide Set up activities that prompt reciprocal interactions Parents to encourage Cameron to participate in turn-taking activities at home.	Damien & Martha (educators) Asu & Amira (Parents)
That Madu will comply with transitioning to new activities in his daily schedule with all adults in the setting	Use PECS timetable and schedule board in setting and at home showing all 7 days of the week. Consistent modelling of use of the schedule in the early years setting and reinforcement at home	Damien & Martha, Asu & Amira

FIGURE 8.2 Sample Inclusion Plan
Adapted from: Moloney & McCarthy, 2010.

Reflection

Donald Schön (1983) developed the term 'reflective practice'. He introduced the concepts of 'reflection-in-action' (thinking on your feet) and 'reflection-on-action' (thinking after the event). Education is one of five professional fields he focused on, and he spoke of the inextricable link between the concept of professionalism and the process of reflective practice. Allen and Whalley (2010) describe reflection as the process by which the educator strives to improve and maintain high quality standards in education and care. Indeed, reflection is central to the *Reggio* approach in northern Italy, *Te Whāriki* in New Zealand, *Belonging, Being and Becoming* in Australia, and *Aistear* in Ireland, for instance. Reflective educators who are committed to quality learning experiences for children, who wish to gain a deeper understanding of their practice and bring about positive change continually reflect upon their practice, asking: Am I doing a good job? Are all children participating in all the activities? Can I do a better job? What do I need to enable me to do a better job? Are children with SEN being included in a meaningful way in the all the activities of the setting? Educators who regularly reflect on what they do, why they do it and how this new knowledge can be used to improve their practice achieve the best outcomes for children and families (MacNaughton, 2003; Siraj-Blatchford et al., 2004; Siraj-Blatchford and Manni, 2008).

Through reflective practice, educators can develop a deeper awareness of their attitudes, values and beliefs. When they are aware of their own prejudices, for example, educators are better able to support children from diverse backgrounds because, as noted by MacNaughton (2003), they are more likely to be aware of their own values, personal philosophies and individual belief systems, and thus able to challenge and change ineffective practice and improve outcomes for children.

Like planning and assessment, reflective practice is also a process involving cycles of 'observation, planning, action and evaluation, undertaken on a regular basis' (CECDE, 2006, p.57). The reflective educator should be involved in some or all of the following:

- Keeping up to date with new ideas, theories or ideas about ECEC;
- Developing analytical skills and a critical approach to their work;
- Discussing ideas and theories with colleagues;
- Contributing to discussion and debates through participation at conferences, staff development events or courses of study;
- Joining professional bodies;
- Participating in networking opportunities;
- Observing children and analysing the data gathered;
- Introducing new education and care practices to the setting in agreement with management and colleagues;
- Supporting others to accept and welcome change (adapted from Moloney & McCarthy, 2010).

To paraphrase the NCCA (2009), reflective practice involves keeping up-to-date with current happenings through ongoing professional development and reflecting on existing practices with a view to improving learning from the child's perspective.

Intentional leadership in assessment for inclusion

In this chapter and the previous chapter, planning and assessment are defined as a process. Both require time. Time for planning, time for assessment, time to interpret assessment, time to target children's needs and time for reflection. Educators need time to meet as a team, to work collaboratively to interpret, reflect and plan, and they need time to meet and work with parents. Although planning and assessment should be central to everyday practice, there is no guarantee that they happen on a regular basis. The need for a pedagogical leader was introduced in Chapter 7. Likewise, in relation to assessment, intentional leadership is equally salient and can also be vested in the pedagogical leader. This involves understanding the critical relationship between assessment and children's access to and participation in the setting, and progression in their learning and development.

The intentional pedagogical leader ensures that systematic assessment actually happens. S/he ensures there is a system in place to provide time for educators to observe, compile work portfolios, prepare learning stories, engage children in self-reflection, review data, reflect on the implications for practice, work with parents and professionals when necessary, to plan for children's future learning needs. The intentional pedagogical leader works to provide educators 'with the structural supports necessary to collect and organise assessment information' (Freeman et al., 2013). 'When time, space and collaboration supports are in place, educators are motivated to continually monitor children's development and learning, self-assess and improve their effectiveness and support children's learning and development' (Freeman et al., 2013, p.323). The intentional pedagogical leader knows that allowing educators time to gather information, reflect on their data and make sound assessment decisions makes sense, is worthwhile and benefits children, families and educators. S/he creates a culture of reflection throughout the early years setting, leading to trust, shared responsibility and facilitating reflective dialogue and debate as a normal part of daily practice.

It is imperative that educators focus upon how learning takes place for both the child and for themselves. In this regard, the intentional pedagogical leader ensures that educators have time to reflect on their practice, and to study children and explore multiple perspectives (Coughlin & Baird, 2013). The intentional pedagogical leader asks 'questions that engage educators both intellectually and emotionally and require the consideration of how theory informs practice and practice informs theory' (Coughlin & Baird, 2013, p.2). S/he can use questions to inspire themselves and others to develop intentional practices. The following questions, which have been adapted from Coughlin and Baird (2013), reflect the inclusive culture discussed in Chapter 3, professional values and beliefs in Chapter four, and the establishment of an inclusive learning environment in Chapters 5 and 6.

1. How do we give visibility to the competencies and contributions of young children in a way that challenges us to move beyond traditional checklists?
2. How do we deepen engagement with families as partners in their children's learning and development?
3. How do we value, promote and celebrate respect for diversity, equity and inclusion?
4. How do we engage educators in thinking about learning environments (inside and outdoors), experiences and the daily life of the setting in ways that will challenge and satisfy children's curious minds?
5. How do we study and articulate play and inquiry as learning within the setting to parents and other stakeholders?
6. How do we develop a culture of reflective practice so that professional development happens day after day in the setting as we work with children and each other?

One way of ensuring that educators make connections between their practice and the establishment of an inclusive culture in the setting is for the intentional pedagogical leader to establish a community of practice. The term, 'communities of practice' was first used in 1991 by theorists Jean Lave and Etienne Wenger. According to Wenger (1998), communities of practice are groups of people who share a concern or a passion for something they do, and learn how to do it better as they interact regularly. The key to a community of practice is the extent to which people discuss, formally or informally, their praxis (Nuri-Robins, Lindsey, Lindsey & Terrell, 2011).

Of course, trusting relationships have to be built, along with a desire to contribute ideas and grow as a professional. Through gentle encouragement and modelling, the pedagogical leader initially leads discussion, making educators feel at ease, and over time, establishes trust.

In describing her role with the schools of Reggio Emilia, Tiziana Filippini says: 'The Pedagogista works to promote within each person and between teachers, an attitude of "learning to learn," an openness to change, and a willingness to discuss opposing points of view' (Filippini, 1998, p.130). Through shared discussion, observations and reflection, the intentional pedagogical leader can guide and mentor educators towards self-motivated quality improvement. Ultimately, a learning community can help the members (educators) feel like they are valued for their contributions and opinions, always learning something new, deepening their understanding and growing as professionals.

9

LEADING COLLABORATIVE WORKING

Introduction

The need for mutual information-sharing between parents and ECEC educators was highlighted in Chapter 8. The focus of the present chapter is upon early intervention and collaborative working, which is critical to ensuring that children with SEN receive adequate and appropriate supports and resources in order to maximise their development within the ECEC setting. From its inception, early intervention has involved a multidisciplinary approach to working with a child with SEN, such as speech and language, physical and occupational therapists and a psychologist, all working together to support a child and his/her family. In relation to the child's family, the early intervention team works to support their confidence and competence in promoting the child's development and learning towards any outcomes desired by the family in the child's life at home and in the ECEC setting.

While developing and maintaining collaborative working is not easy, '[a] team around the child, starting with the child, can create a service that is more responsive to the needs of individual children and their parents which should give young children the best possible start in life' (Dame Gillian Pugh in Siraj-Blatchford, Clarke, & Needham, 2007, p.ix). This chapter is underpinned by systems theory, which as previously mentioned, comprises four key components: process, person, context and time, i.e., the PPCT model (Wachs & Evans, 2010). Proximal processes, which involve all types of transactions between the child and his/her immediate surroundings that are responsible for the child's wellbeing and competencies, have been discussed elsewhere in this book (see in particular Chapters 5 and 6). This chapter therefore interrogates the following components:

- Influence of family educators and peers. In this regard, a child with SEN may experience negative social relationships. Moreover, ECEC practices (proximal processes) may differ in accordance with a child's temperament, disability and so on, which in turn, impacts growth and development;

- **Context**, which constitutes four distinct concentric systems: micro, meso, exo and macro, each having a direct or indirect influence on a child's development. The interaction between policy, decisions and resources at a macro-level, and practices within settings at a micro-level are particularly salient here. The role of various agencies and professionals (InCo, SENCO, occupational therapist, speech and language therapist, psychologist, etc.) are discussed as well as the knowledge and understanding that all those working the children can bring to bear on inclusive practice.

As discussed in this chapter, and in keeping with the notion of a unified drive towards maximum participation, it is evident that fostering relationships between educators, parents, and multidisciplinary teams requires ongoing commitment, and intentional leadership.

Systems theory

A child's learning and development is shaped by multiple layers of influence, ranging from the structural, political and ideological; through to individual setting contexts. In this respect, Bronfenbrenner's (1979) ecological systems theory holds that a child's development is shaped by the varied systems of the child's environment, as well as the interrelationships among the systems. Children do not develop in isolation, but within a system of relationships that include family and society. Bronfenbrenner identified a range of systems (macro, exo, meso, micro – Figure 9.1) depicted as a set of concentric circles, within and between which the child develops. Within this construct, the child is located in a 'set of nested structures each inside the next like a set of Russian dolls' (1979, p.3).

Because of its four interrelated components, Bronfenbrenner's ecological systems theory is often referred to as the process-person-context-time, PPCT model.

Process

The first component is the developmental process, which is divided into proximal and distal processes. Proximal processes refer to the multiple transactions between the child and adults in his/her life, and between the child and the environment in which s/he lives, and interacts on a regular basis, i.e., home and ECEC setting. These interactions drive the child's developing competencies and overall well-being. They fuel child development. In the context of the ECEC setting, they are concerned with warm caring relationships (emotionally safe environment, Chapter 6) and a supportive learning environment (physical, aesthetic and temporal, Chapter 5).

Distal processes are directly related to macro structures (see Figure 9.1) and include a family's ability to support their child and to engage with other

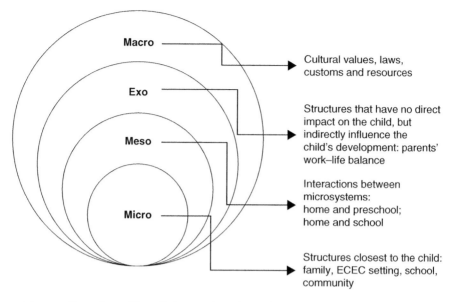

FIGURE 9.1 Overview of Bronfenbrenner's ecological systems theory

environments the child is part of. An unemployed parent, for instance, may struggle to provide materially and emotionally for their child as a result of inadequate welfare payments. A parent whose own experience of education was negative may be unable to interact with the child's ECEC setting. A parent suffering with depression may be unable to provide emotional stability for their child.

Person

The influence of family, educators or peers is largely determined by the characteristics of the child (Wachs & Evans, 2010). A child with a special educational need can be at greater risk of experiencing negative social relationships, as illustrated in the following practice scenario, which describes the challenges for four-year-old Ben, who has a diagnosed expressive language delay.

PRACTICE SCENARIO

Four-year-old Ben's mother notices that he is becoming increasingly withdrawn and demonstrating aggressive behaviour since starting at the local ECEC setting. Ben has a diagnosed expressive language delay. He finds it difficult to pronounce words, has a limited vocabulary by comparison to his peers and therefore he finds social interactions difficult. His mother is concerned that this is causing difficulties for him in the setting.

Following discussions with the pedagogical leader, who has been under-taking systematic observations of Ben engaged in play and everyday routines in the setting, she learns that the other children do not include Ben in their play, and she has noticed that one child regularly teases him about his speech. Together they agree to set up an individualised plan with small achievable speech and language goals to help develop Ben's language skills. They also agree to ask Ben's speech and language therapist to provide information and ideas that can be incorporated into his individualised plan to help him access the general curriculum in the setting.

Child characteristics and temperament also affect relationships between the child and the educator (proximal processes). For example, an educator may find it difficult to foster a positive relationship with a gifted child demonstrating challenging behaviour. While these children need love and support, unless educators understand child development and the context for a particular child's learning and development, they will be unable to provide the supports necessary to help the child progress.

Context

The most important aspect of the ecological systems theory is context, and refers to the multiple 'venues modifying the proximal processes [including] the environments where the child is in constant interaction' (Wachs & Evans, 2010, p.7). With regards to the ECEC setting, Wachs and Evans rightly emphasise the relationship between low adult/child ratios, quality education and care, and positive development.

As illustrated in Figure 9.1, Bronfenbrenner explained context in terms of four distinct concentric systems. The innermost micro-level represents the immediate environment in which the child is involved. This level 'stands as the child's venue for initially learning about the world' (Swick & Williams, 2006, p.372). Surrounding this is the meso-level, consisting of relations between two or more such immediate settings – home, ECEC setting or school, for instance. The meso-level effectively comprises multiple micro-levels. Its power is that it helps to connect two or more systems in which the child, parent and family live, and is evidenced through information-sharing between setting and parent, and parental involvement in their child's early education and care.

Surrounding the meso-level is the exo-level; made up of larger social systems that do not involve the developing child, such as parental workplace. At this level, a child may physically be present in the ECEC setting, while psychologically s/he is present in the parent's place of work. Although experienced vicariously, exo-systems have a direct impact on those involved: child, parent, educator (Swick & Williams, 2006). Enveloping the whole system is a more abstract macro-level, consisting of cultural values, laws, customs and resources, serving as a blueprint for the organisation of the immediate settings (Moloney, 2011).

An ecological perspective recognises that ECEC settings are institutions that are part of but also reflect the larger social system. Accordingly:

> Young children's learning and development occurs within 3 primary social institutions – the family, the early childhood setting and the school. Each institution is located in a city, town, rural area, community or a neighbourhood, and each is influenced by public policy, societal values, beliefs and priorities as well as cultural practices. There are complex interactions between each of these variables that impact considerably on children's experiences within settings. Changes within any system result in changes to the child's experiences and consequent development.
>
> *(Moloney, 2011, 2011, p.23)*

Further, an ecological perspective draws attention to the interpersonal and situational aspects of ECEC, and in keeping with the thrust of Chapter 8, it places a focus on children engaged in authentic tasks, in natural settings, as well as facilitating inquiry into the interconnectedness of each layer that impacts on the child's environment such as policy, practice and supports.

Time

The time component of Bronfenbrenner's model encompasses various aspects, such as ontogenetic time, family time and historical time. Time denotes that environments change; they are not fixed. Different events, such as parental illness or separation, moving home or transitioning from one setting to another can have a profound impact on a young child. Time is a crucial factor also in supporting child development and learning. Children's abilities are not fixed; with support, all children have the capacity to learn and develop over time.

In summary, systems theory recognises that children do not develop in isolation. Rather, they develop within a set of nested structures (home, ECEC setting, school, community) in which they continuously interact. Children's development is not only shaped by the immediate environment, but also by the interaction with the larger environment, which in the context of inclusion, may include interactions with a multidisciplinary team through an early intervention programme.

Working with parents

The European Agency for Development in Special Needs Education (EADSNE, 2012) identifies working with others as a core competence required of educators to support their work in inclusive settings. Working with others, which involves working with parents, families and a range of other professionals, is also a core value of an inclusive culture (DCYA, 2016).

While in the past, a child with SEN was seen as the recipient of services, today collaborative working between the child's parents, family and educators is the norm. Parents are recognised as their child's primary educator, and as mentioned in Chapter 6, in order to develop normally, a child needs someone who is crazy about him/her (Bronfenbrenner, 1991. That person is usually the child's parent/s, and it is only right that they are included in the child's care and education, and in all decisions relating to his/her learning and development.

In Ireland, the preeminent role of parents in supporting their child's wellbeing, learning and development is reflected in the practice frameworks *Síolta* and *Aistear*. This role is further strengthened within the newly introduced Access and Inclusion Model (see Chapters 3 and 8). In the UK, partnership working between educators and parents is a stated goal of the Early Years Foundation Stage, while in the US, the statutory underlying premise of early intervention services for children with disabilities is to 'enhance the capacity of families to meet the special needs of their infants and toddlers with disabilities' (Individuals with Disabilities Education Act Amendments of 2004, Title I, Part C, Sec. 631 (a) (4)), thus strengthening the role of the family as the primary caregiver. Pritchard and Brodie (2015) report that parents appreciate educators who value and demonstrate their understanding of parents as the child's first and most enduring teachers. Partnership working enhances parents' natural abilities to influence their child's learning and development, and as noted by Trivette and Dunst (2004), when they are provided with information, encouragement and an optimistic outlook, they can be good advocates for their child.

Working with and including parents in their child's early education and care is correlated with educator attitudes, values and beliefs (see Chapter 3), and is embedded within the setting's culture (see Chapter 4).

PRACTICE SCENARIO

At a team meeting, Hoda, the pedagogical leader, is discussing child observations with two educators, Antoinette and Mariam. Her suggestion that she and the educators meet with the parents of a child she is concerned about is being met with resistance. The educators feel that it is not their job to meet with the parents. They grumble about the time involved in meeting with them, and one educator asserts that the parents will not be interested in what they have to say.

Consider:

1. What are the issues here?
2. What does this scenario tell you about the educators' attitudes, values and beliefs?
3. How do you would describe the culture in this setting?
4. What does this scenario tell you about partnership working?
5. How would you deal with the educators' resistance to meeting with the parents?
6. What role could an intentional leader play here?

An inclusive culture is predicated upon a belief in a parent's right to be included in their child's development and learning. Each educator has a responsibility to communicate and collaborate with parents and families in supporting their child's development and learning.

Just as children thrive in an emotionally safe environment, collaborative working with parents and families is also dependent upon developing and fostering sensitive, respectful and non-judgemental relationships. As mentioned in the previous chapter, parents may react negatively to a suggestion that their child may have a special educational need. They may be in denial and require time to process the information before they are in a position to discuss support for their child. Educators must be mindful of and, respect both the reaction and the time taken by parents to accept that there may be difficulty with their child's development. In keeping with the PPCT model, learning and development is influenced by interactions between the various environments experienced by a child, as well as the characteristics of the child and the adults (e.g., parents, educators, other professionals) around the child.

Early intervention team

While early intervention is generally associated with the provision of specialised support and services to children with disabilities, Moore (2012) proposes an alternative perspective, suggesting that the aim of early intervention is to provide children with SEN with experiences and opportunities that promote their acquisition and use of competencies that enable them to participate meaningfully with others in the key environments in their lives including home and ECEC setting. Viewed in this way, Moore argues that the focus of intervention will be on ensuring that families and other carers (e.g., educators) are able to provide such experiences and opportunities. In essence, 'the aim will be to ensure that children's everyday learning environments are optimal... hence, the learning environments provided by ECEC settings are major settings for early intervention' (Moore, 2012, p.13).

Sass-Lehrer (2011) describes early intervention in terms of programmes, techniques and strategies that are designed to provide families with the support and information they need to promote their child's growth and development. If, as suggested by Moore, ECEC settings are sites of early intervention, it follows that early childhood educators must also be included in these programmes, techniques and strategies. Ultimately, when early intervention works with and through the ECEC setting and parents, rather than being simply a provider of services, it can enhance parents' and educators' competence and confidence in supporting children with SEN to develop to their maximum potential.

Early intervention teams comprise a range of multidisciplinary professionals, including speech and language therapist, occupational therapist, audiologist, psychologist, social worker and assistive technology specialist. Depending on a child's particular needs, other professionals such as a behavioural specialist, paediatrician or nutritionist may also be included on the team. The composition of the early intervention team is determined by 'clinical' assessment of the child's abilities, strengths and needs, by a family's stated priorities and by individual country policies and procedures (e.g., DCYA/DES, 2016; DfE, 2017c; IDEA, 2004).

The DfE (2014) rightly posit that special educational provision should be matched to the child's identified SEN, and as discussed in Chapter 2, children's SEN are generally thought of in four broad areas of need and support: communication and interaction; cognition and learning; social, emotional and mental health; and sensory and/or physical needs. Individual children, however, may have needs that cut across all these areas, and their needs may change over time. For instance, as mentioned in Chapter 2, speech, language and communication needs can also be a feature of a number of other areas of SEN, and children with an autism spectrum disorder may have needs across all areas.

The special educational provision made for a child should always be based on an understanding of their particular strengths and needs, and should seek to address them all, using evidence based interventions targeted at areas of difficulty and, where necessary, specialist equipment or software (DfE, 2014; Moloney & McCarthy, 2010) to help to overcome barriers to learning and participation.

A multidisciplinary approach plays a key role in supporting a child's individual developmental needs. For example, a physiotherapist can assess a child's gross motor skills and may devise a treatment and home management programme; an occupational therapist can provide treatment and equipment to develop a child's fine motor skills, and also address sensory processing issues; and an assistive technology specialist can identify technological supports to maximise a child's independence.

Section 632 (4) (G) (H) of IDEA indicates that to 'the maximum extent appropriate, [early intervention services] are provided in natural environments, including the home, and community settings in which children without disabilities participate'. This provision does not mean that a child with a special educational need cannot avail of support and services in settings that are specially designed to meet their needs. However, early intervention professionals may wish to collaborate with ECEC settings to work in conjunction with the educators in helping to meet the specific developmental needs of a child with a SEN. Working on fine motor goals within the daily routine in the setting (i.e., the child's natural environment), for example, is usually more motivating and effective than doing so in a clinical setting once every few weeks. Additionally, support given by early intervention professionals for a specific child often helps to inform a setting's overall practice. For example, a speech and language therapist can provide critical information about a child's speech and language difficulties, and details of ongoing speech and language programmes that, if implemented in the setting, can benefit all children.

From the child's perspective, when the early intervention team, parents and educators work together, s/he is enabled to practice and use skills in the natural everyday environments where s/he needs to use those skills (Raver & Childress, 2014). The child actually receives more intervention when the parents and educators 'are able to use intervention strategies throughout the day – more than the child could receive if intervention focused on what could be accomplished by one person during one visit to the home each week' (Raver & Childress, 2014, p.40) or through provision of services in clinical environments. Accordingly, when you reinforce and consolidate speech and language programmes for instance, into daily activities within the setting, it leads to improved outcomes for the child both in the setting and at home. Moreover, when you adapt routines for one child, you usually enrich the learning experience for his/her peers as well.

Effective communication

Positive relationships are founded upon effective communication, which is at the heart of inclusion in ECEC and is a vital skill of the intentional leader (see Chapter 4). The importance of relational pedagogy in establishing and maintaining an emotionally safe environment was emphasised in Chapter 6. It is clear, however, that communication occurs at multiple levels within the setting. Bearing in mind the sensitivities associated with supporting a parent to accept that their child may have a SEN, working with them to make curricular or environmental adaptations, maybe develop an IP and, seeking specialist help from other professionals where necessary, requires effective sustained communication.

The ability to communicate effectively with parents is critical to their role as active participants in their child's education and care, and in the early intervention process. Effective communication bolsters a parent's confidence, and competence in supporting their child. Ultimately, communication is fundamental to developing and maintaining positive relationships with parents. It is also a core aspect in:

- motivating educators to work with parents, engage in ongoing information sharing about a child's progress, and continuous review and planning for a child's ongoing priority learning needs;
- building staff cohesion;
- working with other professionals engaged in providing early intervention services for a child with a special educational need;
- maintaining an inclusive culture within the ECEC setting.

Good communication with and between children, parents, the early intervention team and the setting's staff team affects all aspect of inclusion (see Figure 9.2).

To ensure that communication occurs at all these levels, intentional leadership that comes from within the setting's team is essential. It begins with the manager who establishes an inclusive culture within the setting, based upon his/her attitudes, values and beliefs about inclusion. However, given the complexity of inclusion, there is an inherent risk in vesting leadership for inclusion in one person, who may be spread too thinly across too many areas: culture, environment, planning, assessment, motivating the staff team, working with parents and early intervention teams, and so on. This poses a real threat to inclusion in ECEC settings. Consequently, as discussed in Chapters 7 and 8, other leadership roles such as pedagogical and advocacy leadership may be required. The most important factor is that somebody takes

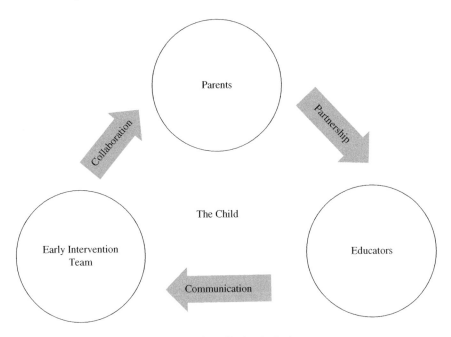

FIGURE 9.2 Communication partners for effective inclusion

responsibility for ensuring that strong child/setting, parent/setting, parent/setting/ early intervention team relationships are established and maintained to best support children and families.

In all discussions with parents/families/early intervention team, it is vital to remember that a child with SEN is first and foremost a child. Person-first language, and using the child's name is vitally important when speaking about him/her. The fact that a child has SEN is secondary to his/her abilities, talents and personality. It is important also to treat parents as equals in the decision-making process. Each of these elements of effective communication can be instigated by and modelled by the intentional leader. For example, the intentional leader can model consultation with parents and members of the early intervention team by asking about their preferred mode of communication, phone, email or text. Whatever their preferred mode, it is essential that it is honoured at all times.

Table 9.1 details a range of strategies to support communication with parents, families and members of the early intervention team.

Other ways of communicating with parents and families includes newsletters, information sheets and home/setting notebooks or diaries. The home/setting note-book in particular is a useful way of sharing uplifting information about a child with his/her parent, letting them know their child jumped in a puddle, played with a friend, joined in a musical activity, completed a puzzle, etc. Likewise parents can share information about the child's behaviour at home in the evenings or at weekends with educators, leading to shared understanding and greater collabor-ation between home and setting.

Consider sending newsletters or information sheets home to parents about the activities that children are engaging in within the setting. For example, let parents know what nursery rhymes or stories are being used during a particular week. This information can provide ideas for reinforcing language development and learning in the home. Parents can also be kept informed about key information about forthcoming activities in the ECEC setting.

Set up a system for communicating regularly with parents. Use communication notebooks/diaries which go back and forth between the home and setting. Alternatively use email, text messaging or the audio file on many new mobile phone devices as a tool or system for sharing communication between the early years setting and the parents. For children who have communication difficulties, record the messages as if the voice of the child is speaking, e.g., *'Today we made...'* *'I helped give out the lunchboxes'.*

Confidentiality

The need for confidentiality was discussed briefly in Chapter 8 with regards to storing observation and assessment data detailing concerns regarding aspects of a child's development. The principle of confidentially is integral to inclusion, extending to communicating with and/or about parents and families. Although this should be a matter of best practice, many countries have rigorous data protection legislation that protects an individual's right to data protection. In the UK, the Data Protection Act, 1998 applies, while in New Zealand, the legal standards for the protection of personal data are primarily set out in the Privacy Act, 1993. Certain privacy laws in the US affect early intervention: Family Educational Rights and Privacy Act (FERPA) of 1974 and Health Insurance Portability and Accountability Act (HIPAA) of 1996. In Ireland, the provisions of the Data Protection Act, 2017 protect an individual's right to data protection when information about them, their child and family is held on a computer, held on paper or other manual form as part

TABLE 9.1 Communication strategies for working effectively with parents and the early intervention team

Strategy	Description
Begin by asking parents/families what they want, what their priorities are, and how to assist them in that regards.	Invite parents/families to share their priorities, concerns and knowledge of their child during all team meetings.
	Once a level of trust has been established, start to use words like 'we' and 'us', which promote the idea of working together.
	Help families feel that they have an active role and their opinion is respected. Ask for input from all members and be sure to consider all points of view when there is a decision to be made.
Ask parents about the child. Find out what the child likes/dislikes and what works well, etc.	Show parents that they are equal partners in the decision-making process.
Maintain a non-judgmental, supportive attitude and manner.	Focus on the child's and parent/family's strengths. Demonstrate a positive attitude about the family and other members of the early intervention team at all times.
Be open honest and transparent.	Address any needs or concerns expressed by the parents/family or other team members in an unbiased manner. When needed, help families consider their options so that they can make informed decisions that are best for them. Avoid imposing professionals' viewpoints on the family.
Use language that all team members can understand.	Avoid technical jargon. Define new terms when used in conversations, or when developing an IP or in other reports, or in communication with parents/families.
Use interpreters when language barriers exist.	Ensure that families of differing cultural and linguistic backgrounds can understand and participate in team collaborations by providing information in the family's preferred language or mode of communication.
Maintain a record or log of all formal and informal communication.	Document all communication and activities with or on behalf of the child and family. Team members can then review the record to maintain supports and services, keep lines of communication open, and follow through on any actions committed to.

Source: Moloney and McCarthy (2010); Raver and Childress, 2014).

of a filing system and made up of photographs or video recordings of a person's image or recordings of his/her voice (www.dataprotection.ie).

Information provided by parents about a child must not be shared with anyone else unless the family has provided written consent for the release of that information. Setting staff including the manager, educators and ancillary staff must not discuss information about any child or family with another family or service provider who is not part of the team (Raver & Childress, 2014). As mentioned, confidentiality applies to written records and reports, which should never be left lying around, nor should a computer screen be left on open view. It is advisable to devise and use a system to code the children's names in order to ensure privacy and confidentiality. Never discuss child observations in front of other children or parents of other children. Always consider what information to share with educators in the setting. Best practice indicates that information should be shared with educators on a 'need to know' basis.

Intentional leadership for collaborative working

The intentional leader plays a crucial role in supporting and empowering staff to communicate effectively and to work collaboratively with parents and other professionals involved with the child. The intentional leader must be fully informed about the child with SEN, be familiar with the curriculum and assessment methods utilised in the setting, and maintain ongoing communication with parents, educators working directly with the child, and the early intervention team.

Some aspects of best practice when working collaboratively with parents involves the intentional leader in building positive relationships and encouraging parents to actively participate in their child's early learning and development. The intentional teacher achieves this through:

- mutual information-sharing;
- inviting parents to attend meetings with the multidisciplinary team;
- incorporating intervention strategies being used with the child at home as part of the curriculum in the setting;
- following up on communication with parents, members of the early intervention team and with educators working directly with the children through informal discussion (e.g., when children are being dropped or collected from the setting, information sheets, home/setting diary), or more formal parent/educator meetings, through text, email, by phone or whatever mode the parent prefers;
- motivating educators to work collaboratively with parents, and to incorporate intervention strategies into the daily routine in the setting.

There is also a role for the intentional leader to advocate on behalf of children. This is especially pertinent with regards to children with SEN, and involves interaction between the intentional leader and various levels within the ecological system.

Advocacy may include: providing information to parents about supports and services available to their child with special educational needs (e.g., leaflets, information booklets, details of workshops); challenging negative attitudes towards inclusion; cultivating relationships with support agencies and services who can be invited to engage in capacity-building with the staff team around inclusion; becoming involved in local/national networks to garner and share information, raise awareness of children's rights and influence decision-making at macro policy level.

10

INTENTIONAL LEADERSHIP FOR INCLUSION: FINAL THOUGHTS

Flowers are red young man
Green leaves are green
There's no need to see flowers any other way
Than the way they always have been seen
But the little boy said
There are so many colours in the rainbow
So many colours in the morning sun
So many colours in the flower and I see every one
(Chapin, 1981)

Introduction

Within any early childhood education and care setting, children are at different stages in their development and learning. They learn at vastly different rates and their developmental and learning patterns can be episodic, uneven and rapid (Ackerman & Coley, 2012). Some children may lag behind in their development, while others are exceptionally talented or able. Children, then, take many different pathways in their learning. Regardless of ability, however, all children have the same need for care, attention and love. They have the same desire to play, and to communicate with their family, peers, educators and others. They need caring, consistent, respectful interactions and relationships, opportunities for play and exploration, choice and meaningful participation. All children, therefore, with and without disabilities, have a right to 'meaningful, high quality educational opportunities in their local community alongside their friends and peers' (European Agency for Special Needs and Inclusive Education, 2015, p.1). Consequently, concepts such as access, participation and supports are fundamental to effective and meaningful inclusion for young children with special educational needs.

The lyrics 'flowers are red young man, green leaves are green' convey a sense of conformity that has nothing to do with inclusion. Neither is inclusion about a one-size-fits-all approach. It is not just about the rights of children with disabilities, it encompasses all children's rights to participate in environments where 'diversity is assumed, welcomed and viewed as a rich resource rather than seen as a problem' (Booth, Nes & Stromstad, 2003, p.2), and where individual differences are seen 'as opportunities for enriching learning' (UNESCO, 2005, p.12). Indeed, as stated by the parent Jennie Fenton in Chapter 2, inclusion is about 'thinking possibility instead of disability'. It is about early childhood educators being open to and seeing 'the many colours in the rainbow, the many colours in the morning sun, and the many colours in the flower', as well as supporting and enabling young children with and without disabilities, to do the same.

The complexity of inclusion

International and national commitments to inclusion indicate the need for educational settings, including early childhood, to create the conditions that will support the full and meaningful participation of children with special educational needs. This alone points to the need for leadership within settings. However, although the concept of inclusion is pervasive at multiple levels within society – for example, political, social; educational and economic arenas – there is no universal definition of what inclusion is or what it involves. In fact, the myriad of available definitions belie the complexity of inclusion, which is about respecting diversity and eliminating discrimination (e.g., UNCRC, 1989; UNCRPD, 2006; UNESCO, 2009); an approach 'for all disadvantaged groups, as well as migrants and minorities and even pupils who are identified as gifted or talented' (Devarakonda, 2013, p.12); directed towards developing children's 'personality, talents and creativity, as well as their mental and physical abilities, to their fullest potential, [and] enabling [them] to participate effectively in a free society' (Article 24, UNCRPD, 2006). Crucially, inclusion is considered 'essential to human dignity and to the enjoyment and exercise of human rights' (UNESCO, 1994, p.11). It is premised upon the principle that all children should learn together, regardless of differences or difficulties within mainstream settings.

Although these positive sentiments are enshrined within national and international legislation and policy initiatives, policy alone is not a guarantor of inclusion. Likewise, while access is one of three core aspects of inclusion (alongside participation and supports), physical access to an ECEC setting does not automatically lead to effective and meaningful inclusion. Instead, access is dependent upon a constellation of factors, including physical and emotional safety; environmental layout that facilitates easy entry, exit, and movement within the physical environment both indoors and outdoors, as well as ease of access to equipment and materials; a flexible, inclusive and responsive curriculum and authentic assessment. More importantly, effective and meaningful inclusion is determined by two interrelated factors; staff who believe in inclusion, and leadership that supports inclusion

Conn-Powers et al. (2006) emphasise the role of universal design in planning ECEC settings to meet 'the needs of all learners within a common setting and begin to move away from specialized programs' (p.1). This extends beyond the physical building, to tasking early childhood educators to plan the environment, learning experiences and opportunities for a diverse population of children with and without disabilities, creating a universally designed setting where all children can actively and fully participate and learn. The extent to which educators engage with inclusion, plan for, develop and sustain inclusive practices is intertwined with attitudes, values and beliefs, which are inextricably linked to their image of the child. As reiterated throughout this book, the image of the child is at the very core of inclusion. Each early childhood curriculum model/framework discussed – spanning Australia, Finland, Ireland, New Zealand, Norway, Sweden and the UK – recognises the intrinsic value of early childhood, as well as the uniqueness and tremendous potential of each child. Each promotes an image of the child as a competent and confident learner. They further stress the need to nurture each child's sense of identity and belonging, which is a core principle of inclusive practice. Notwithstanding the positive principles that underscore these curricular models/ frameworks, educator attitudes are the most important portal to inclusion, they are the 'vehicles for the construction of an inclusive and participatory society' (UNESCO, 2005, p.22). An enthusiastic attitude with regards to creating an inclusive culture, is a prerequisite to planning and maintaining an inclusive learning environment for young children, and it is more important than simply fulfilling a legal obligation to be inclusive.

Access, participation and supports

Access, participation and supports, which are the cornerstone of inclusion, go hand-in-hand and, as noted by Moore (2012), not only is meaningful participation the engine of development, it is the key to attaining a true sense of belonging and a satisfactory quality of life. Thus, as mentioned, participation is more than being present in the setting. Granlund (2013, in Bartolo, Björck-Åkesson, Giné & Kyriazopoulou, 2016, p. 20) conceptualises participation as having two dimensions: being there and being involved/engaged while being there. Therefore, being physically present in an ECEC setting is not enough, and it is not a proxy for inclusion.

Meaningful participation involves children being actively engaged in all activities and routines in the setting, so that their involvement is more than tokenistic. It is inextricably linked to children's agency; their ability to make decisions and choices, to influence events, to act upon their own ideas, to develop knowledge and skills in areas that interest them. This means that the child's role and contribution must be valued by all those involved, including the child him/herself. If we believe in the agentic child, every effort will be made to consult with and incorporate children's ideas and interests into the curriculum. Furthermore, meaningful participation may require environmental and pedagogical adaptations to ensure the setting and the curriculum are accessible and inclusive.

Some children may require minimal support, such as small changes to the curriculum, to help them maximise certain learning opportunities and experiences. Other children, who find it difficult to participate in large-group activities, may need a quiet space where they can relax for a short period of time. For another child, it may be vital to position his/her head during mealtimes to support swallowing. Additionally, augmentative and alternative communication (AAC) may be required. This can include the provision of low-tech (symbols, photos and pictures on printed communication boards or basic voice output devices such as a Big Mack) and high-tech (complex electronic systems or apps that replace speech such as the Tobii Dynavox or Clicker Communicator AAC app). These various adaptations and strategies are essential to promoting children's engagement, fostering a sense of belonging for each child, and ultimately resulting in effective inclusion. Without adaptations and strategies, children with disabilities may be restricted in terms of movement, choice, flexibility and meaningful participation in activities and routines.

Depending on the child's priority learning needs as identified through discussion with parents, and authentic assessment of the child as s/he engages in play and routine activities in the setting, specialist support through an early intervention team may also be necessary. Accordingly, collaborative working involving educators, families and multidisciplinary teams, and others as necessary, is a core aspect of inclusion (DCYA, 2016; EADSNE, 2012) leading to an inclusive participatory ECEC culture.

Ideology versus reality

You may be thinking that the discussion to this point is ideological. It is. The fact of the matter is that inclusion does not just happen. It cannot be left to chance. It cannot be assumed that everybody working with a young child with disabilities in an ECEC setting understands, is committed to or knows how to support effective meaningful inclusion. Neither can it be assumed that even if all staff in the setting understand, are committed to and know how to support effective inclusion, it will happen. As mentioned in Chapter 5, it is all too easy to become complacent as people become comfortable within their surroundings, which can lead to lack of planning, lack of team work, lack of reflection, etc. The thrust of this book, therefore, is upon the need for intentional leadership for effective and meaningful inclusion in early childhood education and care settings. In its simplest form, being intentional is to be deliberate and purposeful in everything you do. It means that somebody, or a number of people within the ECEC setting take responsibility for inclusion, ensuring that participation moves beyond being physically present, to enabling all children with and without disabilities to meaningfully participate in all aspects of daily life.

This is not to suggest that the setting manager cannot be the intentional leader for inclusion. Schein (2004), for example, considers the setting's founder (i.e., manager) the most important factor for cultural beginnings. Hence, it could be argued that establishing an inclusive culture begins with the manager, who not only decides the basic purpose and the environmental context in which the setting operates, but also selects the staff team and invariably imposes his/her assumptions, attitudes, values and beliefs on them (Schein, 2004). However, if the manager is not committed to the principles of inclusion, it is unlikely that a culture of inclusion will be fostered.

In recognition of the complexity of inclusion, and the need for leadership to support inclusion, Ireland has established the role of inclusion coordinator (InCo), through the Access and Inclusion Model (DCYA & DES, 2016), whereas in England, settings are required to identify a member of staff to act as special educational needs coordinator (SENCO) who must have regard to the Special Educational Needs Code of Practice (2015), which provides statutory guidance on duties, policies and procedures. At a minimum, these roles involve:

- ensuring all educators in the setting understand their responsibilities to children with SEN, and the setting's approach to identifying and meeting SEN;
- advising and supporting colleagues;
- ensuring parents are closely involved throughout and that their insights inform action taken by the setting; and
- liaising with professionals or agencies beyond the setting.

However, the leadership role is much more complex and multifaceted. It involves providing vision and leadership, and garnering support for inclusion. It is about being well-versed in child development broadly, special educational needs specifically, early childhood curriculum and, in particular, the role of play in young children's learning and development, as well as pedagogy, assessment, reflection and collaborative working. Drawing upon this knowledge, the leader models positive attitudes and values, challenges stereotypical behaviours, encourages educators to participate in ongoing professional development opportunities, as well as cycles of planning, evaluation and reflection, and works collaboratively with parents and other professionals to enhance children's experiences, leading to effective and meaningful inclusion.

The leader works to empower educators to develop and/or enhance inclusive practice through reflection and cooperative team work. S/he takes responsibility for the development of a culture of inclusion within the setting and the nurturing of critical thinking skills, both of which are essential if inclusion is to become a reality. Critically, as discussed throughout this book, an inclusive culture is dependent upon robust, intentional leadership, so that the ECEC setting can progress from tokenistic to meaningful and effective inclusion.

The various aspects of the leadership role outlined here are not in any way intended as a definitive list of functions. Instead, they serve to highlight the depth and breadth of the intentional leadership for inclusion role. Various broad intentional leadership roles have been identified in the various chapters of this book: leadership as it relates to attitudes, values and beliefs; leading and sustaining an inclusive culture; leading, building and maintaining an inclusive learning environment, and an emotionally safe environment; leadership in planning an inclusive and responsive curriculum; leading assessment for learning to support inclusion; and leading collaborative working. Within each overarching area, the leader is involved in a multiplicity of tasks.

Arising from this is a fundamental question: can the intentional leadership for inclusion role realistically reside solely with one person, such as the setting manager, inclusion coordinator or special educational needs coordinator? Although the identification of an educational leader position through national policy standards is a step in the right direction (Fenech, 2013), given the many aspects, and hence the complexity of inclusion, a single leadership for inclusion role may be spread too thinly across too many areas in the setting. There is a real danger that one person will be unable to accomplish the array of tasks and responsibilities associated with a single leadership for inclusion role, running the risk that inclusion may not occur, and even if it does, it may be ineffective and meaningless for children with special educational needs.

Pathways towards intentional leadership for inclusion

This book signifies the need for shared responsibility for inclusion across the ECEC setting. What is required is a shift away from the traditional view of leadership as being vested in one key individual, to a more collective vision, where the responsibility for leadership rests within formal and informal leaders (Siraj-Blatchford & Manni, 2007). This approach to leadership looks beyond the overall leadership of one person in the setting, and looks instead towards a model of distributed leadership, which is concerned with the practice of leadership. It suggests that there are spheres of influence within the setting with concomitant layers of leadership, and it underpins the need to mobilise leadership expertise at all levels within the setting. Unlike formal leadership roles, which tend to focus upon individual, independent actions, distributed leadership emphasises interdependent interaction and practice.

Distributed leadership is a 'deliberate process' of sharing leadership behaviour, so that team members other than the manager can take an active lead, and accept responsibility for some areas of the work and developing best practice (Lindon & Lindon, 2012, p. 19). It is not about being the overall leader of the setting, but of educators adopting a leadership role within their particular sphere of expertise or influence (Lindon & Lindon, 2012). In relation to inclusion, any such leadership role must be intentional, and directed towards enhancing children's learning opportunities and experiences. Ultimately, intentional leadership is about ensuring effective and meaningful inclusion.

One such intentional leadership role is that of pedagogical leader, somebody in the setting who takes responsibility for curriculum, assessment, reflection and collaborative working. In the words of Nutbrown (2012), 'evidence for the positive impact of good pedagogical leadership in the early years is overwhelming' (p.56). Depending on the size of the ECEC setting, there may be more than one pedagogical leader. For example, if a setting caters for children aged from one to five years, it may make sense to have a pedagogical leader for babies, one for toddlers and one for older pre-school children. Equally, a pedagogical leader for the entire setting, who works collaboratively with the entire staff team may work well. The critical point here revolves around the need for teamwork, information-sharing and reflection. There must, for example, be continuity and progression across the early childhood curriculum, from babies through to the pre-school children.

Critically, distributed leadership can create opportunities to tap into staff funds of knowledge, expertise, interests, skills and talents, serving to sustain an inclusive culture, and achieve the setting's vision through the actions and interactions of many leaders. As discussed in Chapter 4, distributed leadership involves five dimensions:

1. **Context:** Leadership moves from a reliance on power to that of influence, involving collaborative working between people who trust and respect each other's contribution;
2. **Culture:** Leadership moves from a reliance on control to one of autonomy; achieved through an open culture of acceptance and recognition of staff expertise within the setting;
3. **Change:** Leadership is from the bottom-up and encourages greater participation by more staff. This includes encouraging interdependent multi-level involvement by creating processes that provide opportunity for staff to influence policy, rather than policy being simply developed from the top and devolved down for implementation;
4. **Relationship management:** Leadership focuses on collective rather than individual identities. Staff members are encouraged to self-identify as leaders;
5. **Activity:** Leadership assumes a shared purpose through cycles of change. Staff are encouraged to engage in cycles of planning, acting, observing and reflecting (adapted from Jones et al., 2012).

Clearly, the emphasis is upon the relational aspects of leadership which recognises the fundamental change from an emphasis on leaders to leadership. The benefits of relational/distributed leadership can be summarised in terms of:

• **Self-in-relation** – emphasis on interdependence;
• **Social interaction** – ability to create conditions for collective learning by exercising certain strengths, abilities and relational skills;
• **Collective learning** – through learning conversations;
• **Growth-in-connection** – focus on mutuality where the boundary between self and others is more fluid and multi-directional.

Movement occurs from mutual authenticity (bringing self into the interaction) to mutual empathy (hold onto self but also experience other's reality) to mutual empowerment (each is in some way influenced or affected by the other) so that something new is created (Jones et al., 2012, p.12).

Empowering educators

At one level, distributed leadership helps to enhance the capacity of staff in the ECEC setting to improve the quality of children's experiences, and to work towards establishing and maintaining inclusive practices. However, Chapter 3 signifies that even when educators hold positive beliefs about inclusion, they may not feel confident about their ability to work with children with special educational needs and/ or disabilities. Lack of confidence, coupled with an absence of specialised training, is a considerable impediment to inclusion (Moloney & McCarthy, 2010; Kaplan & Lewis, 2013). It is thought that training provided during pre-service programmes 'shapes teachers' attitudes, knowledge and competencies' (Kaplan & Lewis, 2013, p.2) and influences their subsequent work with their own students, leading to better quality care and education (Moloney & McCarthy, 2010). Overall, specific training in special educational needs, results in more positive attitudes toward inclusion, and increased competence regarding how to include a children with a disability (Baker-Ericzén et al., 2009; Moloney & McCarthy, 2010). Working with educators to identify gaps in knowledge and training relating to SEN and inclusion, sourcing and organising training, and motivating staff to undertake it, is integral to intentional leadership. Significantly, if inclusion is to work, the entire staff team in the setting will need to be competent.

While staff development is vital, formal training may not always be warranted. One way of ensuring that educators make connections between their practice and the establishment of an inclusive culture in the setting is for the intentional pedagogical leader to establish a community of practice. This is a group of people who share a concern or a passion for something they do, and learn how to do it better as they interact regularly (Wenger, 1998). The key to a community of practice is the extent to which people discuss, formally or informally, their praxis (Nuri-Robins et al., 2011). Through shared discussion, observations and reflection, the intentional pedagogical leader can guide and mentor educators towards self-motivated quality improvement. Ultimately, a learning community can help the members (educators) feel like they are valued for their contributions and opinions, always learning something new, deepening their understanding, growing as professionals and, ultimately sustaining inclusive practice within the ECEC setting.

Effective communication is central to establishing and sustaining a community of practice. As discussed in Chapter 4, however, this aspect of leadership is largely overlooked and neglected. Yet, a core element of intentional leadership is the leader's interpersonal communication style, which either motivates and encourages educators, or impedes them in their attempt to establish inclusive practices. When it comes to inclusion, leadership is not just about efficiency and effectiveness, it is also about what is good, what is right, what makes sense and what is worth doing (Sergiovanni, 2009). An intentional leader communicates these ideas to the staff team, actively seeks, listens to and incorporates their voice into decision-making processes, motivates, encourages and empowers them to develop, implement and sustain inclusive practice. In addition to supporting early childhood educators to build their professional capacity, the intentional leader for inclusion must also be committed to increasing his/her own professional learning and development, maintaining 'a high level of professional specialism' (Robertson & Messenger, 2010), as well as motivating and encouraging others to embrace and uphold inclusive practices. In effect, this type of purposeful leadership is fundamental to inclusion.

Concluding comments

Inclusion is not about people working alone. Every person in the setting has a role to play. This book demonstrates the critical role of the educator in fostering positive, caring, reciprocal relationships with children to support their emotional wellbeing, identity and belonging in the ECEC setting. This requires significant knowledge, skill and support. It involves systematic planning, assessment, evaluation and reflection. Furthermore, collaborative working with parents, colleagues and other professionals working with the child who has special educational needs is a critical aspect of an inclusive culture within an ECEC setting.

Early childhood is a time of tremendous opportunity for children's learning and development. Missed opportunities in early childhood cannot be made up for later on. Working with young children is an enormous privilege. It is also a tremendous responsibility.

It is for all of these reasons that intentional leadership for inclusion is essential; somebody in the setting who is committed to turning the vision of offering 'every individual a relevant education and optimal opportunities for development' (UNESCO, 2005, p.16) into reality for children, and working tirelessly to achieve this. Intentional leadership for inclusion must be fostered and supported. It is the 'superglue' (Bolman & Deal, 2008) that unites, motivates and empowers all educators to work towards a common goal; that of creating an inclusive culture within the entire setting. In borrowing from Waniganayake and Semann (2011, p.24), we suggest that intentional leadership is 'a journey of joint inquiry, exploration and reflection that can involve everyone who believes in making a difference for children'. Intentional leaders for inclusion must be committed to inclusive values: valuing leaner diversity; supporting all learners; working with others; continuing personal professional development (EADSNE, 2012); and to a leadership style that encourages others within the setting to participate in leadership functions.

In conclusion, effective and meaningful inclusion is dependent upon two interrelated factors; staff who believe in inclusion, and leadership that supports inclusion. In relation to the latter, this book reinforces the notion that intentional leadership for inclusion is paramount. As proposed, distributed leadership can be an effective means of embedding intentional leadership for inclusion practice within ECEC, of ensuring the development of an inclusive culture and of guaranteeing that inclusion becomes the norm, rather than an 'add-on' activity. It is through intentional leadership for inclusion that children, parents and educators will support each other to embrace, and truly see the *many colours in the rainbow; the many colours in the morning sun; and the many colours in the flower.* You must open your eyes, your ears and your mind, to the endless possibilities within every child. You must see *everyone.*

REFERENCES

Abel, M. 2016. *Why Pedagogical Leadership?* Available at http://mccormickcenter.nl.edu/why-pedagogical-leadership

Ackerman, D. & Coley, R. 2012. *State Pre-K Assessment Policies: Issues and Status*. Princeton, NJ: Educational Testing Service.

Ainscow, M., Booth, T., Dyson, A., Farrell, P., Frankham, J., Gallannaugh, F., Howes, A. & Smith. R. 2006. *Improving Schools, Developing Inclusion*. London: Routledge.

Allan, J. 2005. Inclusion as an ethical project. In S. Tremain (ed.), *Foucault and the Government of Disability*. Ann Arbor, MI: University of Michigan Press.

Allen, K. E. & Schwartz, I. S. 2001. *The Exceptional Child: Inclusion in Early Childhood Education*. Albany, NY: Delmar.

Allen, S. & Whalley, M. E. 2010. *Supporting Pedagogy and Practice in Early Years Settings*. Exeter: Learning Matters.

Amanchukwu, R. N., Stanley, G. J. & Ololube, N. P. 2015. A review of leadership theories, principles and styles and their relevance to educational management. *Management*, 5 (1), 6–14.

Australian Children's Education and Care Quality Authority (ACECQA). 2011. *Guide to the National Quality Standard*. Sydney, NSW: ACECQA.

Australian Government Department of Education, Employment and Workplace Relations for the Council of Australian Governments. 2009. *Belonging, Being & Becoming: The Early Years Learning Framework for Australia*. © Commonwealth of Australia.

Bagnato, S. J. & Yeh Ho, H. 2006. High stakes testing with preschool children: Violation of professional standards for evidence-based practice in early childhood intervention. *KEDI Journal of Educational Policy*, 3 (1), 23–43.

Baker-Ericzén, M. J., Mueggenborg, M. G. & Shea, M. M. 2009. Impact of trainings on child care providers' attitudes and perceived competence toward inclusion: What factors are associated with change? *Topics in Early Childhood Special Education*, 28, 196–208.

Ballard, K. 2004. Children and disability: Special or included? *Waikato Journal of Education*, 10, 315–326.

Barr, L. 2016. *Creating and Inclusive Early Childhood Culture*. Available at http://emergingconsulting.com/2016/02/15/creating-an-inclusive-early-childhood-culture-part-two

Bartolo, P., Björck-Åkesson, E., Giné, C. & Kyriazopoulou, M. (eds.) 2016. *Inclusive Early Childhood Education: An Analysis of 32 European Examples. European Agency for Special Needs and Inclusive Education.* Available at www.european-agency.org/sites/default/files/IECE%20%C2%AD%20An%20Analysis%20of%2032%20European%20Examples.pdf

Basford, J. 2015. Documenting and assessing learning: Including the voice of the child. In K. Brodie and K. Savage (eds.), *Inclusion and Early Years Practice.* London: David Fulton.

Bauer, A. M. & Kroeger, S. D. 2004. *Exploring Diversity: A Video Case Approach.* London: Pearson.

Becker, N. & Becker, P. 2008. *Developing Quality Care for Young Children: How to Turn Early Care Settings into Magical Places.* California: Corwin Press.

Bertling, J., Darrah, M., Lyon, D. & Jackson, S. n.d. *Early Childhood Building Blocks: Universal Design for Learning in Early Childhood Inclusive Classrooms.* Available at http://teachingcommons.cdl.edu/tk/modules_teachers/documents/Buildingblocks

Biddle, J. K. 2010. Reciprocal learning in leadership: Redefining leadership. *HighScope.* Available at www.highscope.org/file/NewsandInformation/ReSourceReprints/Spring2010/Reciprocal%20Learning_150.pdf

Blagojevic, B., Twomey, D. & Labas, L. 2002. *Universal Design for Learning: From the Start.* Orono, ME: University of Maine. Available at www.ccids.umaine.edu/facts/facts6/udl.htm

Blandford, S. & Knowles, C. 2016. *Developing Professional Practice 0–7,* 2nd ed. New York: Routledge.

Bluestein, J. 2001. *Creating Emotionally Safe Schools: A Guide for Educators and Parents.* USA: Health Communications Inc.

Bolman, L. G. & Deal, T. E. 2008. *Reframing Organizations: Artistry, Choice, and Leadership.* San Francisco: Jossey-Bass.

Booth, T. & Ainscow, M. (eds). 1998. *From Them to Us: An International Study of Inclusion in Education.* London: Routledge.

Booth, T. & Dyssegaard, B. 2015. *Quality is Not Enough. The Contribution of Inclusive Values to the Development of Education for All.* Available at www.eenet.org.uk/resources/docs/QualityIsNotEnough.pdf

Booth, T., Nes, K., & Stromstad, M. 2003. *Developing Inclusive Teacher Education.* London: Routledge Falmer.

Bowman, B., Donovan, M. & Burns, S. (eds.). 2001. Eager to learn: Educating our pre-schoolers. Report of Committee on Early Childhood Pedagogy. In *Commission on Behavioural and Social SCIENCES AND Education National Research Council.* Washington, DC: National Academy Press.

Brandt, K. 2014. Core concepts in infant family and early childhood mental health. In K. Brandt, B. D. Perry, S. Seligman & E. Tronick (eds.), *Infant and Early Childhood Mental Health: Core Concepts and Clinical Practice.* Washington, DC: American Psychiatric Publishing.

Bray, A. & Gates, S. 2000. Children with disabilities: Equal rights or different rights? In A. Smith, M. Gollop, K. Marshall & K. Nairn (eds.), *Advocating for Children: International Perspectives on Children's Rights* (pp. 32–41). Dunedin, New Zealand: University of Otago Press.

Bridges, D. R., Davidson, R. A., Soule Odegard, P., Maki, I. V. & Tomkowiak, J. 2011. Interprofessional collaboration: Three best practice models of interprofessional education. *Medical Education Online,* 16, 6035.

Brillante, P. 2017. *The Essentials: Supporting Young Children with Disabilities in the Classroom.* Washington, DC: National Association for the Education of Young Children.

Brodie, K. 2015. Challenging the assumptions of multiculturalism and inclusion. In K. Brodie & K. Savage (eds.), *Inclusion and Early Years Practice.* London: Routledge.

Bronfenbrenner, U. 1979. *The Ecology of Human Development*. Cambridge, MA: Harvard University Press.

Bronfenbrenner, U. 1994. Who cares for the children? In H. Nuba, M. Searson & D. L. Sheiman (eds.), *Resources for Early Childhood: A Handbook* (pp. 113–129). New York: Garland.

Bronfenbrenner, U. 1999. Environments in developmental perspective: Theoretical and operational models. In S. L. Friedman & T. D. Wachs (eds.), *Measuring Environments Across the Lifespan: Emerging Methods and Concepts* (pp. 3–28). Washington, DC: American Psychological Association.

Brownlee, J. 2004. An investigation of teacher education students' epistemological beliefs: Developing a relational model of teaching. *Research in Education*, 72, 1–18.

Brownell, M. T., Ross, D. D., Colon, E. P. & McCallum, C. L. 2005. Critical features of special education teacher preparation: A comparison with general teacher education. *The Journal of Special Education*, 38, 242–252.

Bruns, D. A. & Mogharreban, C. C. 2007. The gap between beliefs and practices: early childhood practitioners' perceptions about inclusion. *Journal of Research in Childhood Education*, 21 (3), 229–241.

Bryman, A., Collinson, D., Grint, K., Jackson, B. & Uhl-Bien, M. (eds.). 2011. *The Sage Handbook of Leadership*. Thousand Oaks, CA: Sage.

Buysse, V. & Peisner-Feinberg, E. (eds.). 2013. *Handbook of Response to Intervention in Early Childhood*. Baltimore: Paul H. Brookes.

Carpenter, B., Ashdown, R. & Bovair, K. (eds.). 1996. *Enabling Access: Effective Teaching and Learning for Pupils with Learning Difficulties*, 2nd ed. London: Fulton.

Carr, M. 2001. *Assessment in Early Childhood Settings: Learning Stories*. London: Paul Chapman.

Centers for Disease Control and Prevention (CDC). 2012. *Hearing Loss in Children*. Available at www.cdc.gov/ncbddd/hearingloss/facts.html

Centre for Early Childhood Development and Education (CECDE). 2006. *Síolta: The National Quality Framework for Early Childhood Care and Education*. Ireland: Centre for Early Childhood Development and Education.

Chapin, H. 1981. Flowers are Red. Available at www.youtube.com/watch?v=1y5t-dAa6UA

Cohen, J., Oser, C. & Quigley, K. 2012. Making it happen: Overcoming barriers to providing infant-early childhood mental health. *Zero to Three*. Available at www.zerotothree. org/resources/511-making-it-happen-overcoming-barriers-to-providing-infant-early-childhood-mental-health

Conn-Powers, M., Conn-Powers, A. F., Traub, E. K. & Hutter-Pishgahi, L. 2006. The universal design of early education: Moving forward for all children. *Beyond the Journal: Young Children on the Web*. Available at www.iidc.indiana.edu/styles/iidc/defiles/ECC/ECC_Universal_Design_Early_Education.pdf

Copeland, M. K. 2014. The emerging significance of values based leadership: A literature review. *International Journal of Leadership Studies*, 8 (2), 105–135.

Copple, C. & Bredekamp, S. (eds.). 2009. *Developmentally Appropriate Practice in Early Childhood Programs Serving Children from Birth through Age 8*, 3rd ed. Washington, DC: National Association for the Education of Young Children.

Council for the Curriculum, Examinations and Assessment (CCEA). 2014. *Guidance on Identifying and Supporting Learners with Social, Emotional and Behavioural Difficulties*. Available at http://ccea.org.uk/sites/default/files/docs/curriculum/guidelines_general_strategies/sebd-guidance_identify_and_support.pdf

Coughlin, A. M. & Baird, L. 2013. *Pedagogical Leadership*. Available at http://edu.gov.on.ca/childcare/Baird_Coughlin.pdf

Cross, M. 2011. *Children with Social, Emotional and Behavioural Difficulties and Communication Problems: There is Always a Reason*. London: Jessica Kingsley Publishers.

Darling-Churchill, K. E. & Lippman, L. 2016. Early childhood social and emotional development: Advancing the field of measurement. *Journal of Applied Developmental Psychology*, 45, 1–7.

Deiner, P. 2010. *Inclusive Early Childhood Education: Development, Resources and Practice*, 5th ed. New York: Delmar Publishing.

Department for Education (DfE). 2014. *Special Educational Needs and Disabilities Code of Practice: 0 to 25 Years*. www.gov.uk/government/uploads/system/uploads/attachment_data/file/398815/SEND_Code_of_Practice_January_2015.pdf

Department for Education (DfE). 2017a. *SEN Support: Research Evidence on Effective Approaches and Examples of Current Practice in Good and Outstanding Schools and Colleges: A Resource for Mainstream Leaders, Teaching and Support Staff Working with Pupils and Students with Special Educational Needs and Learning Difficulties and Disabilities*. London: DfE.

Department for Education (DfE). 2017b. *SEN Support: Research Evidence on Effective Approaches and Examples of Current Practice in Good and Outstanding Schools and Colleges: A Guide for Senior Leaders in Education Settings*. London: DfE.

Department for Education (DfE). 2017c. *Statutory Framework for the Early Years Foundation Stage: Setting the Standards for Learning, Development and Care for Children Birth to Five*. London: DfE.

Department for Education (DfE) & Department of Health (DH). 2015. *Special Educational Needs and Disability Code of Practice: 0–25 Years*. Available at www.gov.uk/government/uploads/system/uploads/attachment_data/file/398815/SEND_Code_of_Practice_January_2015.pdf

Department of Children and Youth Affairs (DCYA). 2016. *Diversity, Equality and Inclusion Charter, and Guidelines for Early Childhood Care and Education*. Available at http://aim.gov.ie/wp-content/uploads/2016/06/Diversity-Equality-and-Inclusion-Charter-and-Guidelines-for-Early-Childhood-Care-Education.pdf

Department of Education and Skills. 2016. A Guide to Early-Years Education-Focused Inspection (EYEI) in Early-Years Settings Participating in the Early Childhood Care and Education (ECCE) Programme. www.education.ie/en/Publications/Inspection-Reports-Publications/Evaluation-Reports-Guidelines/A-Guide-to-Early-years-Educationfocused-Inspection-EYEI-in-Early-years-Settings-Participating-ECCE-programme.pdf

Department of Education, Employment and Workplace Relations (DEEWR). 2010. *Belonging, Being and Becoming: The Early Years Learning Framework for Australia*. Canberra: DEEWR.

Department of Health and Children (DHC). 2006. *Childcare (Pre-School Services) Regulations*. Dublin: The Stationery Office.

Devarakonda, C., 2013. *Diversity and Inclusion in Early Childhood: An Introduction*. London: Sage.

Dineen, F. 2009. Does relationship training for caregivers enhance learning and language development in young children? In T. Papatheodorou & J. Moyles (eds.), *Learning Together in the Early Years: Exploring Relational Pedagogy* (pp.169–184). London: Routledge.

Dinnebeil, L. A., Boat, M. & Bae, Y. 2013. Integrating principles of universal design into the early childhood curriculum. *Dimensions of Early Childhood*, 41 (1), 3–13.

Dinnebeil, L. A., Rush, D., Gallagher, P. A. & Rhodes, C. 2003. Design and sequence of professional development activities. In V. D. Stayton, P. S. Miller & L. A. Dinnebeil (eds.), *Personnel Preparation in Early Childhood Special Education: Implementing the DEC Recommended Practices* (pp.159–182). Longmont, CO: Sopris West.

Division for Early Childhood (DEC) (2015). *Position statement. Leadership in early intervention and early childhood special education*. Washington, DC: Division of Early Childhood.

Division for Early Childhood and the National Association for the Education of Young Children (DEC/NAEYC). 2009. *Early Childhood Inclusion*. www.naeyc.org/sites/default/files/globally-shared/downloads/PDFs/resources/position-statements/DEC_NAEYC_EC_updatedKS.pdf

Division for Early Childhood of the Council for Exceptional Children. 2007. *Promoting Positive Outcomes for Children with Disabilities: Recommendations for Curriculum, Assessment and Program Evaluation.* Available at www.dec-sped.org

Epstein, A. S. 2014. *The Intentional Teacher: Choosing the Best Strategies for Young Children's Learning.* Washington, DC: NAEYC.

European Agency for Development in Special Needs Education (EADSNE). 2012. *Teacher Education for Inclusion: Profile of Inclusive Teachers.* Available at www.european-agency.org

European Agency for Special Needs and Inclusive Education. 2015. *Empowering Teachers to Promote Inclusive Education.* Available at www.european-agency.org/sites/default/files/Empowering%20Teachers%20to%20Promote%20Inclusive%20Education.%20Conceptual%20Framework%20and%20Methodology.pdf

Family Educational Rights and Privacy Act (FERPA). 1974. PL 93–380, 20 U.S.C. §§ 1232g et seq.

Fasoli, L., Scrivens, C. & Woodrow, C. 2007. Challenges for leadership in Aotearoa/New Zealand and Australian early childhood contexts. In L. Keesing-Styles & H. Hedges (eds.), *Theorising Early Childhood Practice: Emerging Dialogues* (pp. 231–253). Castle Hill: Pademelon Press.

Fenech, S. 2013. Leadership development during times of reform. *Australasian Journal of Early Childhood,* 38 (1), 89–94.

Fenton, J. 2013. *Inclusion, Belonging and the Disability Revolution.* TED Talk, Bellingen, Australia. Available at www.youtube.com/watch?v=VAM9nh8WC-8

Filosa, S. 2012. *A Nurse Agency Model Effect on Registered Nurse Retention and Patient Satisfaction.* ProQuest, Umi Dissertation Publishing.

Filippini, T. 1998. The role of the pedagogista. In C. Edwards, L. Gandini & G. Forman (eds.), *The Hundred Languages of Children.* New York: Ablex Publishing.

Finnish National Board of Education. 2016. *National Core Curriculum for Early Childhood Education and Care.* Helsinki: Finnish National Board of Education.

Fisher, J. 2010. *Moving on to Key Stage 1: Improving Transition from the Early Years Foundation Stage.* Milton Keynes: Open University Press.

Freeman, N. Decker. C. & Decker, J. 2013. *Planning and Administering Early Childhood Programs.* New Jersey: Pearson.

French, G. 2007. *Children's Early Learning and Development: The Framework for Early Learning.* Research paper. Dublin: NCCA.

Fullan, M. 2002. Principals as leaders in a culture of change. *Educational Leadership.* Available at http://michaelfullan.ca/wp-content/uploads/2016/06/13396053050.pdf

Goodfellow, J. 2009. *The Early Years Learning Framework: Getting Started.* Available at www.earlychildhoodaustralia.org.au/nqsplp/wp-content/uploads/2012/05/RIP0904_EYLFsample.pdf

Graham, I. 2017. *Realising Potential: Equality, Diversity and Inclusion Practices in Early Years.* Dublin: Barnardo's.

Harris, A. 2013. *Distributed Leadership Matters: Perspectives, Practicalities, and Potential.* London: Sage.

Harris, A. & Spillane, J. 2008. Distributed leadership through the looking glass. *Management in Education,* 22 (1), 31–34.

Harvard Centre on the Developing Child. n.d. *Serve and Return.* Available at https://developingchild.harvard.edu/science/key-concepts/serve-and-return

Hearron, P. & Hildebrand, V. 2011. *Management of Child Development Centers.* New York: Pearson.

Hedges, H. 2011. Connecting snippets of knowledge: teacher's understandings of the concept of working theories. *Early Years: An International Journal of Research and Development,* 31 (3), 271.

Hersey, P. & Blanchard, K. H. 1982. *Management of Organization Behaviour: Utilizing Human Resources*, 4th ed. Englewood Cliffs. NJ: Prentice-Hall.

Hughes, B. 2002. *A Playworker's Taxonomy of Play Types*, 2nd ed. London: PlayLink.

Individuals with Disabilities Education Improvement Act (IDEA). 2004. PL 108–446, 20 U.S.C. §§ 1400 et seq.

Isbell, R. 2008. *The Complete Learning Centre Book*, 2nd ed. Beltsville, MD: Gryphon House.

Isbell, C. & Isbell, R. 2005. *The Inclusive Learning Center Book: For Pre-school Children with Special Needs*. Beltsville, MD: Gryphon House.

Isles-Buck, E. & Newstead, S. 2003. *Essential Skills for Managers of Child-Centred Settings*. London: David Fulton.

Johansson, C. D. 2015. *Empowering Employees Through Communicative Leadership*. Available at http://lasics.uminho.pt/ojs/index.php/cecs_ebooks/article/view/2081

Johansson, C. D., Miller, V. & Hamrin, S. 2014. Conceptualising communicative leadership: A framework for analysing and developing leaders' communication competence. *Corporate Communications: An International Journal*, 19 (2), 147–165.

Jones, C. 2004. *Supporting Inclusion in the Early Years*. Milton Keynes: Open University Press.

Jones, S., Lefoe, G., Harvey, M. & Ryland, K. 2012. Distributed leadership: A collaborative framework for academics, executives and professionals in higher education. *Journal of Higher Education Policy and Management*, 34 (1), 67–78.

Jones, C. & Pound, L. 2008. *Leadership and Management in the Early Years: From Principles to Practice*. Milton Keynes: Open University Press.

Kaplan, I. & Lewis, I. 2013. *Promoting Inclusive Teacher Education Curriculum*. Paris: UNESCO.

Kagan, S. L. 2015. *Leadership for Young Children*. Presentation at the Early Childhood Personnel Center Leadership Institute, Hartford, CT. Available at www.ecpcta.org/pdfs/Leadership_FINAL_12-9-13.pdf

Kelley, D. 2014. Extemporaneous idea formulation: Innovating beyond vision. *Emerging Leadership Journeys*, 1 (7), 21–26.

King, G., Tucker, M., Baldwin, P., Lowry, K., LaPorta, J. & Martens, L. 2002. A Life Needs Model of paediatric service delivery: Services to support community participation and quality of life for children and youth with disabilities. *Physical and Occupational Therapy in Paediatrics*, 22 (2), 53–77.

Klein, M.D., Cook, R.E. & Richardson-Gibbs, A.M. 2001. *Strategies for Including Children with Special Needs in Early Childhood Settings*. Albany, NY: Delmar Publications.

Knutton, S. & Ireson, G. 1995. Leading the team: Managing staff development in primary school. In J. Bell & B. T. Harrison (eds.), *Vision and Values in Managing Education*. London: David Fulton.

Kolzow, D. 2014. *Leading from Within: Building Organisational Leadership Capacity*. Available at www.iedconline.org/clientuploads/Downloads/edrp/Leading_from_Within.pdf

Kostelnik, M., Soderman, A., Whiren, A. 2007. *Developmentally Appropriate Curriculum: Best Practices in Early Childhood Education*. N.J: Pearson/Merrill Prentice Hall.

Lave, J & Wenger, E. 1991. *Situated Learning: Legitimate Peripheral Participation*. Cambridge: Cambridge University Press.

Lee, W & Carr, M. n.d. *Documentation of Learning Stories: A Powerful Assessment Tool for Early Childhood*. Paper presented at the Dialogue of Documentation: Sharing our Understanding of Children's Learning and Developing a Rich Early Years Provision. Pen Green, Corby: United Kingdom. Available at http://newzealand.anniewhite.cikeys.com/wp-content/uploads/2016/04/Documentation-of-Learning-Stories-Wendy-Lee-Margaret-Carr.pdf

Levins, T., Bornholt, L & Lennon, B. 2005. Teachers experience, attitudes, feelings and behavioural intentions towards children with special educational needs. *Social Psychology of Education*, 8, 329–343.

Lewis, I. & Bagree, S. 2013. *Teachers for All: Inclusive Teaching for Children with Disabilities.* Available at www.eenet.org.uk/resources/docs/IDDC_Paper_Teachers_for_all.pdf

Lewis, J. & Hill, J. 2012. What does leadership look like in early childhood settings? *Every Child*, 18 (4).

Lindon, J. & Lindon, L. 2012. *Leadership and Early Years Professionalism.* London: Hodder Education.

Lindsay, G. & Dockrell, J. 2002. Meeting the needs of children with speech language and communication needs: a critical perspective on inclusion and collaboration. *Child Language Teaching and Therapy*, 18, 91–101.

MacNaughton, G. 2003. *Shaping Early Childhood: Learners, Curriculum and Contexts.* UK: McGraw-Hill Education.

MacNaughton, G. & Willaims, G. 2008. *Teaching Young Children: Choices in Theory and Practice.* Milton Keynes: Open University Press.

McMonagle, A. 2012. *Professional Pedagogy Project.* Ireland: Donegal County Childcare Committee.

Maggi, S., Irwin, L. J., Siddiqi, A & Hertzman, C. 2010. The social determinants of early child development: An overview. *Journal of Paediatric Child Health*, 46 (1), 627–635.

Malaguzzi, L. 1993. For an education based on relationships. *Young Children*, November, 9–13.

Meijer, C. & Watkins, A. 2016. Changing conceptions of inclusion underpinning education policy. In A. Watkins & C. Meiger (eds.), *Implementing Inclusive Education: Issues in Bridging the Policy–Practice Gap* (pp. 1–16). Bingley: Emerald Group Publishing Limited.

Miller, L. & Cable, C. (Eds.). 2011. *Professionalization, leadership and management in the early years.* London: Sage.

Ministry of Education, New Zealand. 2017. *Te Whāriki: Early Childhood Curriculum.* Available at https://education.govt.nz/assets/Documents/Early-Childhood/ELS-Te-Whariki-Early-Childhood-Curriculum-ENG-Web.pdf

Ministry for Education and Research, Norway. 2011. *Framework Plan for the Content and Tasks of Kindergartens.* Norway: Ministry for Education and Research.

Moloney, M. 2011. *Locating Quality in Early Childhood Care and Education Discourse: Pre-school and Infant Classrooms as a Crucible for Learning and Development.* Unpublished PhD thesis. University of Limerick, Ireland.

Moloney, M. 2017. *PLÉ response to the Organisation for Economic Cooperation and Development (OECD) International Early Learning Study.*

Moloney, M. & McCarthy, E. 2010. *Framework for Action for the Inclusion of Children with Special Educational Needs in Early Childhood Education Settings.* Ireland: Mary Immaculate College & Department of Children and Youth Affairs.

Moloney, M. & Pettersen, J. 2017. *Early Childhood Education Management: Insights into Business Practice and Leadership.* London: Routledge.

Moss, P. 2007. Bringing politics into the nursery. Early childhood education as a democratic practice. Available at www.bibalex.org/Search4Dev/files/282610/114945.pdf

Moore, T. 2012. *Rethinking Early Childhood Intervention Services: Implications for Policy and Practice.* Melbourne: Murdoch Children's Research Institute.

Moss, P., Dahlberg, G., Grieshaber, S., Mantovani, S., May, H., Pence, A., Rayna, S., Swadener, B., and Vandenbroeck, M. 2017. The Organisation for Co-operation and Development's International Early Learning Study: Opening for Debate and Contestation. *Contemporary Issues in Early Childhood*. Vol. 17 (3) 343–351.

Moyles, J. 2006. *Effective Leadership and Management in the Early Years.* Milton Keynes: Open University Press.

Muijs D., Ainscow M., Chapman C. & West M. 2011. *Introduction: Networking in Schools. In: Collaboration and Networking in Education.* Dordrecht: Springer.

Mulvihill, B., Cotton, J. N., & Gyaben, S. L. 2004. Best practices for inclusive child and adolescent out-of-school care: A review of the literature. *Family & Community Health,* 27(1), 52–64.

Mulvihill, B. A., Shearer, D. L., & Van Horn, M. L. 2002. The effects of training and experience on child care providers' perceptions of inclusion. *Early Childhood Research Quarterly,* 17, 197–215.

Myers, J. & Bagree, S. 2011. *Making Inclusive Education a Reality.* Haywards Heath: Sightsavers.

Nah, K.-O. 2014. Comparative study of child assessment practices in English and Korean preschools. *European Early Childhood Education Research Journal,* 22(5), 660–678.

National Association for the Education of Young Children. 2008. *Assessment of Child Progress: A Guide to the NAEYC Early Childhood Program Standard.* Washington, DC: National Association for the Education of Young Children.

National Council for Curriculum and Assessment (NCCA). 2004. *Towards a Framework for Early Learning.* Ireland: National Council for Curriculum and Assessment.

National Council for Curriculum and Assessment (NCCA). 2009. *Aistear: The Early Childhood Curriculum Framework.* Ireland: National Council for Curriculum and Assessment.

National Council for Curriculum and Assessment (NCCA). 2015. *Síolta/Aistear practice guide.* Ireland: National Council for Curriculum and Assessment.

National Quality Standard Professional Learning Programme (NQS/PLP). 2012. *Sustained, Shared Thinking.* Australia: National Quality Standard Professional Learning Programme.

National Dissemination Center for Children with Disabilities (NICHCY). 2017. *Visual Impairment, Including Blindness.* Available at www.parentcenterhub.org/visualimpairment/ #kids

National Education Psychological Service (NEPS). 2010. *Behavioural, Emotional and Social Difficulties – A Continuum of Support – Guidelines for Teachers, National Educational Psychological Service.* Available at www.education.ie/en/Schools-Colleges/Services/National-Educational-Psychological-Service-NEPS-/neps_besd_continuum_teacher_guide.pdf

Norwegian Directorate for Education and Training. 2017. *Framework Plan for Kindergartens.* Available at www.udir.no/globalassets/filler/…framework-plan-for-kindergartens2-2017.pdf

Nuri-Robins, K. J., Lindsey, R. B., Lindsey, D. B. & Terrell, R. D. 2011 *Culturally Proficient Instruction,* 3rd ed. Thousand Oaks, CA: Corwin.

Nutbrown, C. 2011. *Threads of Thinking: Schemas and Young Children Learning,* 4th ed. London: Sage.

Nutbrown, C. 2012. *Foundations for Quality: The Independent Review of Early Education and Childcare Qualifications. Final Report.* Available at www.gov.uk/government/uploads/ system/uploads/attachment_data/file/175463/Nutbrown-Review.pdf

Nutbrown, C., Clough, P. with Atherton, F. 2013. *Inclusion in the Early Years,* 2nd ed. London: Sage.

Odom, S. L., Buysse, V. & Soukakou, E. 2011. Inclusion for young children with disabilities: A quarter century of research perspectives. *Journal of Early Intervention,* 33 (4), 344–356.

Odom, S. L., Vitztum, J., Wolery, R., Lieber, J., Sandall, S., Hanson, M. J., et al., 2004. Preschool inclusion in the United States: A review of research from an ecological systems perspective. *Journal of Research in Special Educational Needs,* 4 (1), 17–49.

O'Leary, S. 2011. *Supporting Behaviour Management in School for Students with Behavioural, Emotional and/or Social Difficulties (BESD): Practical Data-Based Approaches to Selecting, Implementing, Monitoring and Evaluating Interventions at Multiple Levels of Behaviour Support.* Available at www.sess.ie/sites/default/files/Categories/Emotional_Disturbance/BESD_ SESS_2011.pdf

Organisation for Economic Co-operation and Development (OECD). 2016. *Call for Tenders: International Early Learning Study*. Available at www.oecd.org/callsfortenders/CfT%20100001420%20

Ostrosky, M. M., Laumann, B. M. & Hsieh, W. 2006. Early childhood teachers: Beliefs and attitudes about inclusion: What does the research tell us? In B. Spodek & O. N. Saracho (eds.), *Handbook of Research on the Education of Young Children* (pp. 411–422). Mahwah, NJ: Lawrence Erlbaum Associates Publishers.

Papatheodorou, T. 2009. Exploring relational pedagogy. In T. Papatheodorou & J. Moyles (eds.), *Learning Together in the Early Years: Exploring Relational Pedagogy*. London: Routledge.

Pearce, C., Wassenaar, C. & Manz, C. 2014. Is shared leadership the key to responsible leadership? *Academy Of Management Perspectives*, 28 (3), 275–288.

Pritchard, G. & Brodie, K. 2015. A family's perspective on special educational needs and inclusion. In K. Brodie and K. Savage (eds.), *Inclusion and Early Years Practice*. London: David Fulton.

Probst, B. 2011. *Managing Life with a Challenging Child: What To Do When Your Gifted But Difficult Child is Driving You Crazy*. Available at http://sengifted.org/managing-life-with-a-challenging-child-what-to-do-when-your-gifted-but-difficult-child-is-driving-you-crazy

Purdue, K. 2009. Barriers to and facilitators of inclusion for children with disabilities in early childhood education. *Contemporary Issues in Early Childhood*, 10 (2), 134–145.

Rafferty, Y. & Griffin, K. W. 2005. Benefits and risks of reverse inclusion for pre-schoolers with and without disabilities: *Perspectives of Parents and Providers. Journal of Early Intervention*, 27 (3), 173–192.

Raver, S. A. & Childress, D. C. 2014. *Family-Centered Early Intervention*. Available at http://archive.brookespublishing.com/documents/collaboration-and-teamwork-with-families.pdf

Read, M. & Rees, M. 2010. Working in teams in the early years. In C. Cable, L. Miller & G. Goodliff (eds.), *Working with Others in the Early Years*, 2nd ed. Milton Keynes: Open University Press.

Report of the Interdepartmental Group. 2015. *Supporting Access to the Early Childhood Care and Education (ECCE) Programme for Children with a Disability*. Available at http://nda.ie/nda-files/Supporting-Access-to-the-Early-Childhood-Care-and-Education-for-Children-with-a-Disability.pdf

Riley-Ayers, S. 2014. *Formative Assessment: Guidance for Early Childhood Policymakers (CEELO Policy Report)*. New Brunswick, NJ: Centre on Enhancing Early Learning Outcomes.

Riley-Ayers, S., Jung, K. & Quinn, J. 2014. *Technical Report: Kindergarten Early Learning Scale*. National Institute for Early Education Research. Available at http://nieer.org/wp-content/uploads/2016/08/KELS_Concurrent20_Validity_Technical_Report.pdf

Robertson, C. & Messenger, W. 2010. *Evaluating and Enhancing the Quality of Provision in Early Childhood Intervention: Exploring some European Perspectives*. Available at www.exedrajournal.com/docs/s-internacionalizacao/11-159-174.pdf

Rose, D. H., Harbour, W. S., Johnston, C. S., Daley, S. G. & Abarbanell, L. 2006. Universal design for learning in post-secondary education: Reflections on principles and their application. *Journal of Post-Secondary and Disability*, 19, 2–17.

Sass-Lehrer, M. 2011. Birth to three: Early intervention. In M. Marschark & P. Spencer (eds.), *Handbook of Deaf Studies, Language and Education*, 2nd ed. New York: Oxford University Press.

Schein, E. H. 2004. *Organisational Culture and Leadership*, 3rd ed. San Francisco: Jossey-Bass.

Schön, D. A. 1983. *The Structure of Reflection-In-Action: The Reflective Practitioner*. New York: Basic Books.

Schubart, B. 2007. *Educational Culture*. Available at http://schubart.com/2007/08/educational-culture

Scottish Network for Able Pupils (SNAP). 2011. *Highly Able Children in the Early Years: A Report of Practice in Nurseries in Scotland*. Available at www.pef.uni-lj.si/fileadmin/Datoteke/CRSN/branje/SNAP_2011_Highly_able_children_in_the_early_years_report.pdf

Sergiovanni, T. J. 2009. *The Principalship: A Reflective Practice Perspective*, 6th ed. Boston: Allyn & Bacon.

Siraj-Blatchford, I. 2005. *Quality Interaction in the Early Years*. Available at www.tactyc.org.uk/pdfs/2005conf_siraj.pdf

Siraj-Blatchford, I., Clarke, K., & Needham, M. 2007. *The Team Around the Child: Multi-Agency Working in the Early Years*. Stoke on Trent: Trentham Books.

Siraj-Blatchford, I. & Manni, L. 2004. *Good Question*. Available at www.nurseryworld.co.uk/nursery-world/news/1100998/good-question

Siraj-Blatchford, I. & Manni, L. 2007. *Effective Leadership in the Early Years Sector: The ELEYS Study*. London: Institute of Education: University of London.

Siraj-Blatchford, I. & Manni, L. 2008. Would you like to tidy up now? An analysis of adult questioning in the English Foundation Stage. *Early Years: An International Journal of Research and Development*, 28 (1), 5–22.

Siraj-Blatchford, I., Sammonds, P., Taggart, B., Sylva, K., Melhuish, E., Manni, l., et al. 2004. *Effective Provision of Pre-School Education*. London: DfES.

Skolverket. 2010. *Curriculum for the Preschool Lpfö 98*. Stockholm: Skolverket.

Smith, A. 2013. *Understanding Children and Childhood*, 5th ed. Wellington, New Zealand: Bridget Williams Books Ltd.

Spillane, J. T., Halverson, R. & Diamond, J. B. 2001. Investigating school leadership practice: A distributed perspective. *Educational Researcher*, 30 (3), 23–28.

Spreitzer, G. M., Sutcliffe, K., Dutton, J. E., Sonenshein, S. and Grant, A. M. 2005. A socially embedded model of thriving at work. *Organization Science*, 16 (5), 537–550.

Stayton, V. D., Miller, P. S. & Dinnebeil, L. S. (eds.). 2003. *Personnel Preparation in Early Childhood Special Education: Implementing the DEC Recommended Practices*. Longmont, CO: Sopris West.

Swick, K. J. and Williams, R. D. 2006. An analysis of Bronfenbrenner's bio-ecological perspective for early childhood educators: Implications for working with families experiencing stress. *Early Childhood Education Journal*, 33 (5), 371–378.

Sylva, K., Melhuish, E. C., Sammons, P., Siraj-Blatchford, I. & Taggart, B. 2004. *The Effective Provision of Pre-School Education (EPPE) Project: Technical Paper 12 – The Final Report: Effective Pre-School Education*. London: DfES/Institute of Education, University of London.

Technical and Assistance Training System (TATS). 2009. Available at www.tats.ucf.edu

Trivette, C. & Dunst, C. 2004. Evaluating family focused practices: Parenting experiences scale. *Young Exceptional Children*, 7 (3), 12–19.

UNCRPD. 2006. UN Convention on the Rights of Persons with Disabilities.

Underwood, K. 2013. *Everyone is Welcome: Inclusive Early Childhood Education and Care*. Available at www.edu.gov.on.ca/childcare/Underwood.pdf

Underwood, K. & Frankel, E. B. 2012. The developmental systems approach to early intervention in Canada. *Infants & Young Children*, 25, 286–296.

UNESCO. 1994. *The Salamanca Declaration and Framework for Action*. Paris: UNESCO.

UNESCO. 2005. *Guidelines for Inclusion: Ensuring Access to Education for All*. Paris: UNESCO.

UNESCO. 2009. *Policy Guidelines on Inclusion in Education*. Paris: UNESCO.

UNESCO. 2017. *A Guide for Ensuring Inclusion and Equity in Education*. Paris: UNESCO.

United States Department of Labor. 1990. *Americans with Disability Act.* Washington, DC: US Department of Labor.

Urban, M., Robson, S. & Scacchi, V. 2017. *Review of Occupational Role Profiles in Ireland in Early Childhood Education and Care.* Available at www.education.ie/en/Publications/Education-Reports/Final-Review-of-Occupational-Role-Profiles-in-Early-Childhood-Education-and-Care.pdf

Urban, M. & Swadener, B. 2017. Democratic accountability and contextualised systemic evaluation: A comment on the OECD initiative to launch an International Early Learning Study (IELS). *International Critical Childhood Policy Studies Journal,* 5 (1), 6–18.

Vera, D. & Crossan, M. 2004. Strategic leadership and organizational learning. *Academy of Management Review,* 29, 222–240.

Wachs, T. D. & Evans, G. W. 2010. Chaos in context. In T. D. Wachs & G. W. Evans (eds.), *Chaos and its Influence on Children's Development: An Ecological Perspective* (pp. 3–13). Washington, DC: American Psychological Association.

Waniganayake, M. & Semann, A. 2011. *Being and Becoming Leaders.* Available at http://citeseerx.ist.psu.edu/viewdoc/download?doi=10.1.1.931.8718&rep=rep1&type=pdf

Weisner, T. 2008. The Urie Bronfenbrenner top 19: Looking back at his bioecological perspective. *Mind, Culture and Activity,* 15 (3), 258–262.

Wenger, E. 1998. *Communities of Practice: Learning, Meaning and Identity.* Cambridge: Cambridge University Press.

White, J. 2016. *Introducing Dialogic Pedagogy: Provocations for the Early Years.* London: Routledge.

White, E. J., Peter, M. & Redder, B. 2015. Infant and teacher dialogue in education and care: A pedagogical imperative. *Early Childhood Research Quarterly,* 30, 160–173.

Willis, C. 2009. *Creating Inclusive Learning Environments for Young Children.* California: Corwin Press.

Yukl, G. 2013. *Leadership in Organizations,* 8th ed. Harlow: Pearson.

Zollitsch, B. & Dean, A. 2010. *Authentic Assessment in Infant and Toddler Care Settings: Review of Recent Research.* Portland: Muskie School of Public Services, University of Southern Maine.

INDEX

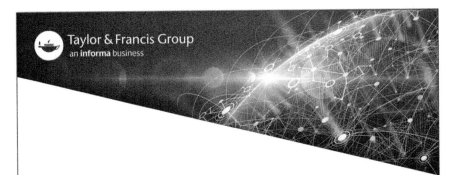